SEX, DEATH AND OTHER INSPIRING STORIES

THE ADVANTAGES OF AGE HANDBOOK TO GROWING OLDER FUNKILY

Edited by Rose Rouse

For more information contact:
Riverdale Avenue Books
5676 Riverdale Avenue
Riverdale, NY 10471

www.riverdaleavebooks.com

Design by www.formatting4U.com
Cover by Scott Carpenter

Digital ISBN: 9781626016682
Print ISBN: 9781626016699

First edition published by November 2023

I considered what it meant to be 66. The same number as the original American highway, the celebrated Mother Road that George Maharis, as Buz Murdock, took as he tooled across the country in his Corvette, working on oil rigs and trawlers, breaking hearts and freeing junkies. Sixty-six, I thought, what the hell. I could feel my chronology mounting, snow approaching. I could feel the moon, but not see it. The sky was veiled with a heavy mist illuminated by the perpetual city lights. When I was a girl the night sky was a great map of constellations, a cornucopia spilling the crystalline dust of the Milky Way across its ebony expanse, layers of stars that I would deftly unfold in my mind... I'm still the same person, I thought, with all my flaws intact, same old bony knees, thanks be to God.

Patti Smith—*M Train*

Acknowledgements

A huge slice of gratitude to all the contributors who have penned pieces for the illustrious Advantages of Age website—advantagesofage.com—and also to those AofA members of the FB group—Advantages of Age—Baby Boomers and Beyond who have replied, postulated ideas, discussed thoughtfully and appreciated each other on those threads. This book could not exist without you. We are a community. A community that does age differently.

Thanks in oodles are also due to Suzanne Noble who writes, sings, presents and also significantly drives the business side of Advantages of Age alongside business coach, Mark Elliott. They run the AofA offshoot Start Up for Seniors together which supports older people with ideas that they want to make into businesses.

And a special mention to writer and actress, Hanja Kochansky who contributed a fair few tales from her extraordinary life to AofA and her lockdown story is included. Hanja died in 2022 at 84. All hail to her.

Another special mention to performer and singer, Topaz Chanteuse who died earlier this year at 89. She was our poster woman in NYC, she pimped her walker with tinsel and she didn't stop being out there. Suzanne and I met her on the AofA Flamboyant Subway Tour in NYC 2017.

And to Lori Perkins, the publisher at Riverdale Avenue Books, for picking up this project.

TABLE OF CONTENTS

Foreword

As a former glossy magazine editor and the founder of a therapist-matching platform, I have an insatiable professional interest in the zeitgeist. My readers are no longer teens or fashionistas, and I care more now about how they feel than how they look, but still I want to know what is hot and new!

My personal focus though is fixed on my own cohort, people who are past 55, or 60, and looking towards a vivid, purposeful, future. I want to know how to get older, bolder

Advantages of Age is a resource that amuses, entertains and impresses me. People write about their experience or opinion not to earn a living, or tot up likes, but because they believe it may also appeal to others. Old age, as Bette Davis said 'ain't no place for sissies' so community and camaraderie are not platitudes, but valuable qualities.

Age is covered in the media, but lots of people bridle at the limited conventions. Not so long ago those were grannies with floral dresses and weekly sets, their partners (always male) trudging across the golf course. These days the imagery is grounded in anti-ageing, so contemporary talk is of the absolute necessity of HRT, or the best foods or exercise regimes for looking and feeling younger than you are. In my opinion, there are many, many more interesting ways of getting older.

AofA-ers tend to toss such cliches out the window too. The stereotypes don't suit their more radical mindset, plus they just don't care what others think. Surely, this is one of the great insights of having lived three or four decades as an adult? You finally, really, understand yourself, and are resistant to the opinions of others, and the trends that sweep younger, more impressionable people along with them.

I won't pretend that self-knowledge will necessarily keep you safely happy. Loneliness, loss, ill health, money problems, family strains—

1

getting older has got to be hard, sometimes. But I know, from the number of post-55 year olds coming to my platform Welldoing to find a therapist or counsellor to help them untangle challenges in relationships, or negotiating the last stages of life, that finding others to share your thoughts and worries with does help.

So, community is found at AofA, but so too is inspiration. Out of the adventures and opinions of strangers, you find you too want to join in, trying something different. It might be an old interest revived, it might be something completely new to you, it might be to do with sex, or relationships, or alternative ways of living, nothing is ruled out. Ideas aren't sold as solutions, and the spirit of those who visit is generous and kind, rather than proselytizing. Finally, I rate this space for older women and men for its creativity. Prose or poetry, photography, artwork, gardens, those who have created can stand back proudly while the rest of us admire, or critique (though not nastily). Compared with 24-hour news platforms and social media madhouses, it's a quiet place, but if you fancy sharing time with an open-minded, age-appropriate tribe, I recommend you take a look.

Louise Chunn is the founder of Welldoing, UK's leading therapist-matching platform. She was editor of *In Style, Good Housekeeping* and *Psychologies*.

Introduction

What is Advantages of Age? Co-founded by myself, a journalist, editor and poet, and Suzanne Noble, a serial entrepreneur and jazz singer, in 2016, it is a social enterprise that challenges the media narrative around ageing. We had the idea in a hot tub in London with a group of women aged from 46 to 64 who felt misrepresented by the saggy, tired, sad, granny stories in the media. We want to re-frame, re-imagine and re-vision **old in a much sexier, more rock 'n'roll, more helpful, more positive, more creative way.**

What have we been up to? Suzanne has found a partner in Mark Elliott who is a business coach and they have set up **Start Up for Seniors** which supports people over 50 who may have been made redundant, can't find the right employment, may be retired, who have an idea and want to create a thriving business out of it. It is much-needed and a roaring success being commissioned by different councils in the UK.

Meanwhile I have been commissioning and writing articles for the website/magazine—advantagesofage.com—that tell the powerful personal stories of **people doing ageing differently. With wildness, vulnerability and panache. With difficult health conditions that they are embracing in all sorts of ways. With relationships that may not be all the 'normal' ones. With flexibility and the capacity to consider that we are always learning rather than we actually know it all. We are proud to be unwise elders at times. We are old and curious, old and spirited, old and able to be consciously vulnerable, we are old and willing to learn, we are old and joyful, we are old and able to talk about our pain. We are multi-layered and that's the point.**

We have a lively, well-informed, willing-to-engage-in-discussion, considerate and often funny FB group—**Advantages of Age—Baby Boomers and Beyond**. There are threads about different aspects of getting older—what do we want to be called for a start, from Olders and

Elders to Oldsters to Hags and Crones—to relationships and what they can be, for instance, some of us are single and older and living rich lives, some of us choose not to live with our partners, some of us are grandparents, some of us are not. Our comments reflect our eclecticism in who we are and who we would like to be allowed to be by society.

I often commission pieces based on comments and threads in the FB group. That gives me great pleasure. I pick up on something someone has experienced and invite them to write about it. I love to foster community. And everyone who contributes on the threads or in articles is an important part of the AofA Community. We are a creative bunch and some of us are professional writers and journalists, while some of us are writers who enjoy expressing themselves in words and want to do more. I have discovered how much I relish supporting AofA members in their writing voyage. There are well-known, prize-winning writers in our midst. And that makes us even richer.

Sex, Death and Other Inspiring Stories—Advantages of Age, the handbook to getting older funkily is a dynamic collection of articles and essays. **Articles and Essays that tell stories that don't get told.** On taboo subjects like having sex in your 70s as a man or imagining your own death and how it might be. On travels by her wild lone self by an older woman who takes off to remote places, sleeps there in her estate car and feels into the magic of the landscape. I write about my Living Apart Together relationship—we've been together 10 years, he's 80, I'm 70 and we live five hours drive apart. How can that work? Yet, it does. There are the health tales where writers tell us about their inspiring experiences with challenging medical conditions. And death. And sexuality. And voyages. And lockdown.

This is an evolving tale. How are we travelling into the unknown, how are we travelling towards the end of our lives? Can we still be rock 'n'roll? Can we still be flamboyant? We can, we can.

Rose Rouse, Sept 2023

SECTION ONE
OUT AGEOUS

I'm Okay with Being Called Old—
Finding ways to re-imagine that word

By Rose Rouse

Not long ago, I was discussing my 70th birthday celebrations with a male friend and I declared that I was old as part of the conversation. I didn't mean it in that British understating-slightly-funny-because-I'm-embarrassed way, I meant it in a quietly proud way. He didn't get it. He thought I was being self-effacing.

No, you're mature—he replied thinking that he was giving me a compliment.

No, I'm old—I answered and explained why.

It's still so very prevalent—this idea of old that is negative and has to be rejected immediately and replaced with *oh but you look so much younger, you are so youthful, age is just a number, Seventy is the new 40. And more and more.* Every day, even in the Advantages of Age FB group—we hope is the bastion of age acceptance—I read members claiming that they may be 50, 60, 70 or 80 but they feel so much younger.

WE KEEP ON RE-ANIMATING THE IDEA THAT OLD IS WRONG AND THAT YOUNG IS RIGHT. THAT YOUNG IS WHAT WE ASPIRE TO ALWAYS AND OLD IS WHAT WE'RE WANTING TO AVOID. Like the plague that won't go away.

I realise that culturally and societally, this perspective is the common one here in the West. We are bombarded daily with adverts of lithe young things—when it's not stair lifts or incontinence pads—selling stuff, being in that position of desired and therefore desirable. Younger people are now—opinion formers, influencers (okay there's the occasional older person on Tik Tok) and movers—in the positions that we might have occupied earlier in our lives. Rishi Sunak, the UK Prime Minister, is 43. Clare Farrell, co-founder of XR, is 40.

7

The marketing/advertising fixation with youth is also partly to do with death and rebirth. And neo-liberalism. Ha ha. Older people are nearer to death so there's only so a finite amount of time that they have left to buy stuff. Plus young people are beautiful and older people are repulsive. Who wants to be near someone who is wrinkled and reeking of old age—anyone marketing the Death perfume, they probably are, not just to Goths—not even literally, but beneath the surface? Through rejecting our near-deathness, the marketeers reject their own not-so-near-death. Society turns away from the inevitable end of life by drinking at the fountain of youth perpetually.

And we on-the-ball oldsters, we Advantages of Agers, have to be the movers and shakers in changing this pervasive societal attitude. If we detest our own 'oldness' and simply want to be younger, how is anyone else going to change their way of seeing the world?

There is a change afoot but it is barely perceptible. Vivienne Westwood in her 70s and 80s was defiant and funky even when she was not well. She was a role model in many ways. Her style. Her attitude. Her activism. And in terms of not having cosmetic surgery. However much we repeat—which we do often at AofA—that cosmetic surgery is a choice; it is inevitably part of a huge movement to supposedly stem the tide of time and her effects on our bodies. It is a huge part of pro-youth ageing.

The Centre for Ageing Better—with The Bias Cut and Ageism is Not in Style—is running a campaign in the UK that has gone viral called I Look My Age. Well-known women like presenter, author and entrepreneur, Pru Leith declares—*I am 83 and I look my age*—and that is a very good thing. There are lots of other videos by women Over 50 doing the same. As a way of re-enforcing that we don't automatically look younger if we look good—we look our age and that is expansive in what it means.

I am proud to say that *I am 70 and I look my age.* Hence there's absolutely no need to tell me that I look good for my age or that 70 is the new 40, etc.

Actress Frances Dormand when she turned 66 said—*My position has always been that the way people age and the signs that we show of aging is nature's way of tattooing. It's natural scarification, and the life you lead gives you the symbols and emblems of your life, the road map you followed.*

There are glimmers—artist David Hockney at 86, fashion designer Zandra Rhodes at 83, the UK Relate campaign with older people in sexy, intimate situations, the Elders Company of dancers at Sadlers Wells, actress Sheila Hancock at 90 and her book Age Rage, Start Up for Seniors, the initiative set up by AofA's Suzanne Noble and Mark Elliott to support older people who have ideas and want to become successful entrepreneurs. Older artists finally getting exhibitions like 92 year-old Faith Ringgold and 89 year-old Rose Wylie. 76 year old Marina Abramovic getting the first female retrospective at the Royal Academy in London. Helen Mirren and her everything. Punk musician, Gina Birch from the Raincoats still being on the road. Discos specially for Older People. The Punk Gardeners. Academic and TV presenter, Mary Beard has been brilliant around this very subject. Grand Gesture who are an older physical theatre group. The Centre for Ageing Better.

However, in order for society to change its mind. WE ALL HAVE TO AGREE TO STOP USING YOUNG AS A PERPETUAL ASPIRATION FOR US AS OLDSTERS AND AS PEOPLE WHO WANT THIS TRANSFORMATION OF SOCIETY. And remember that how we frame ourselves linguistically shapes how we are regarded in society.

Imagine if **old** evoked beautiful, spirited, creative, energetic, loving, wild, free, sensual, compassionate, fascinating, real, all-embracing and was therefore something we looked forward to. We are old. I am old. I look older. But there Is a choice there. I can look interesting and old. Or creative and old. Or sexy (yes, I know we don't want the pressure but hey, it's still possible) and old. Or working in a fabulous job or for ourselves and old. And dancing and old. And a brilliant grandmother and old. Or a spirited leader and old. The possibilities are endless if we let them be.

Yes to re-envisioning old. Will you?

Older Women Rock
By Leah Thorn

Leah Thorn, a poet and artist, explains who Older Women Rock are. They are based in the UK. She started this inspiring group when she was 65. She's now in her 70s.

blood memory

I am an old age, all age woman,
no way past my use-by date.
Walking in ancestral sisters' footsteps,
I am an archive on legs,
a time traveller, alive to life,
I embody time, provide testimony,
a radical, lyrical, womanist legacy

Women's blood memory speaks in me

**A found poem by Leah Thorn,
created after reading
'Out of Time' by Lynne Segal
and 'How to Age' by Anne Karpf**

Using poetry, personal stories, 'fashion' and film, 'Older Women Rock!' creates pop-up art spaces in which to raise awareness and explore issues facing early-old-age women in our 60s and 70s. It challenges our invisibility by placing us centre stage on our own terms; strengthens our resilience and our networks as we move into older age; and importantly, subverts society's assumptions and prejudices about us.

 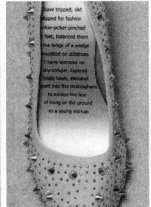 

How it started

I started 'Older Women Rock!' when I was 65. My generation of women made decisive change. I hope we never give up our vision of the world we want and our intention to have it.

In my 70s now, I am inundated daily with messages that as an older woman I am inconsequential and my thinking outmoded and no longer needed. This attempt to invalidate us builds on decades of oppression, where our existence has been diminished and erased.

I wanted to 'hang out' with older women to stop my growing sense of isolation and struggle. I was keen to see what their experiences were and to find a creative way to share what I was learning.

I set up opportunities for conversation with different kinds of women in their late 50s to mid 70s. I led workshops for women in a Zumba Gold class; women in prison; a deaf women's group; women at a MIND Day Centre; lesbians in an Age UK Older LGBTQ project; daughters of Holocaust survivors; Women's Institute members; unpaid carers; women who identify as feminist and those who definitely do not.

We addressed issues such as—

- the lack of older women in the media or the misrepresentation of us as a stereotype or a joke
- the fortune the beauty industry makes from the insecurity we feel that is manufactured by sexism and intensified by old age oppression
- poverty and the fact that many women have small state pensions

because of low-paid work and/or breaks in employment to raise children or to care for ageing parents

- body image and the need to conceal or be 'discreet' about physical changes, like greying hair, facial hair or incontinence
- sexuality
- being a carer

Poetic clothing

Based on our conversations, I created poetry and then collaborated with older women artists to embroider, burn, print, bead, engrave and spray-paint words and images onto retro clothes sourced from local charity shops. Here are a few examples—

1
You speak of me in metaphors
of catastrophe. Soon I will be
an agequake, a grey tsunami.
My age is your nightmare.
A numerical fanfare
to fan your fear

Sculptor Nicholette Goff interpreted this poem by customising a 1940s jacket with skeins of grey hair and a beautifully constructed bar of 'medals',

2

Only men grow old on screen.
Women disappear from film and TV by 50,
hit dread and disgust in early middle age
and suddenly we're no longer fit for public display,
unless we're flogging stair lifts, baths or wills
or we have a frozen face
or we're de-aged by digital alteration.
It's a kind of symbolic annihilation

Fashion designer and stylist Claire Angel burnt words from this poem onto a leather jacket.

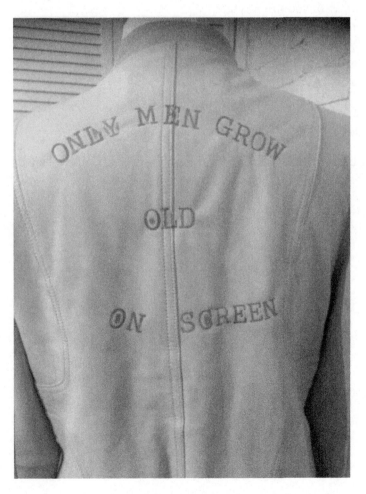

3

The beauty counter screams 'Buy This Cream'.
Got taut, tight skin? You're in.
Got ticking clocks? Botox. Detox.
Resist signs of ageing at all cost.
Stop. Reverse. Hide. Slo mo.
Smooth your skin ego.
Feel the urge for a youth surge?
Want a victory of science over time?
Want to reignite your youthful light?
Deny age. Defy age.
You're in control with phenoxyethanol.
Replump with sodium phytate.
No. Retaliate. Fight age hate.
It's a diabolical conspiracy
for women to age agelessly,
line-, scar-, crease-free

I refuse to let the forever-young drug erase
the handwriting of life across my face

Allie Lee of the Profanity Embroidery Group embroidered an image onto
a 1980s jumpsuit in response to my poem—

4

Vulva lost its youthful lustre?
Want a quick fix?
Try My New Pink Button,
rouge for labial lips

Annie Taylor of the Profanity Embroidery Group interpreted this poem onto a vintage negligee

5
I'll never have
a designer vagina
that vajazzle dazzles
and permanently dilates

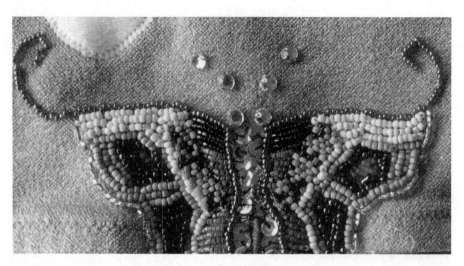

Allie Lee of the Profanity Embroidery Group embroidered and beaded this poem onto a 1970s swimsuit.

6
In my day, stockings came in black, bronze and American Tan,
opening a bank account needed the signature of a man,
girdles held in sexual urges, touching below the waist was no-go
and Dusty passed as hetero
There was no such thing as pubic hair wax and you daren't use Tampax
or have a sexual climax for fear of being thought nymphomaniacs

A collaboration between members of the Profanity Embroidery Group, sculptor Nicholette Goff and myself, an extract of this poem was emblazoned onto a vintage wedding dress.

Pop up shops, a flashmob and films

There have been—

- three pop-up exhibitions of the poetry clothing in shops in Folkestone, Stoke-on-Trent and Newcastle-under Lyme and one extended exhibition in the art gallery of Keele University
- several 'Older Women Rock!' programmes of talks, performance, film screenings and workshops creatively celebrating 'early old age' women

- Subversive Catwalks of older women 'modelling' the clothing while I read the poems
- a wild Zumba Gold flashmob in Folkestone Shopping Centre

And three films have been made during the project—

- 'Older Women Rock!: The Documentary' by filmmaker Clare Unsworth, a creative record of the pilot project in Folkestone showing poetry-emblazoned retro clothes, nineteen older models strutting a subversive catwalk and the Zumba Gold flashmob
- 'Love Your Lines', a Public Service Announcement film shown on performance artist Tammy WhyNot's YouTube channel 'watch', about the impact of dementia on my relationship with my father http://www.leahthorn.com/film/watch-2/

What next?

Fashion designer and stylist Claire Angel and I are responding to requests to buy 'Older Women Rock!' jackets by creating pieces for sale.

There will be 'Older Women Rock!' workshops including 'Customise Your Clothes With Pearls' and 'Try Out Skateboarding' and an intergenerational workshop, 'Tattoo Stories'.

For more information follow us on Instagram @loveolderwomenrock or contact us at loveolderwomenrock@gmail.com

On Turning 60

By Suzanne Noble

I had a big 60th party planned six months before as we were in lockdown, and I wanted to allow guests to fix a date in their diary. Friends commented on my forward planning and enjoying having an event to look forward to.

I envisaged singing, dancing, a gorgeous vanilla sponge cake, delicious cocktails surrounded by all the people I know and love. I didn't want to hide my light under a bushel or pretend I was anything other than my age. When you co-run an organisation about the positives of growing older, it's essential to walk the walk and talk the talk. Turning 60 is a milestone birthday, and I wanted a big, f*** off party in which to celebrate it.

It didn't happen because of more lockdown. Instead, I took my newly acquired Oyster 60+ card, entered the underground and spent a rainy Monday visiting a handful of friends across London with a keto-friendly chocolate cake cut into slices. I arrived home at 7.30 p.m. to finish the celebrations with my then partner Bob. We ordered a takeaway pizza and burrata, joining a dozen friends from across the world via Zoom, who stopped in to wish me a Happy Birthday. I felt cheated and underwhelmed, the previous two decades celebration held in clubs complete with drinking, dancing and lively conversation.

On reflection, turning 60 hasn't felt nearly as dramatic as turning 40 or even 50. At 40, I had recently gotten divorced and spent the next 10 years perpetually in heat, exploring sexual avenues that were extreme by most people's standards. At 50, menopause arrived and with it, hot flashes, sleepless nights and my libido going off a cliff which took about three years to accept. I sold my house, moved my career into technology and, with it, encountered ageism for the first time.

Setting up Advantages of Age with Rose, more by accident than design, was a turning point that opened up opportunities and a whole new friendship group. At 60, I am comfortable in my skin which may not be as dramatic as turning 40 or 50 but is a boon.

I'm in a better place mentally, moving forwards financially after some rocky starts. I'm settled in a good way. I've rediscovered my voice and taken up jazz singing again after a 35-year lapse, and it feels good to be engaging with that side of my creative life again. I like the attention and the occasional praise. Occasionally I consider all the mad escapades and the frankly dangerous circumstances in which I would often find myself, especially in my 40s, and wonder whether there's any of that younger me still left. While the desire for that outrageous behaviour no longer holds the same attraction for me, I'm not quite ready to let go of the thrill that comes when stepping into the unknown.

The ongoing battle to be in better shape continues. This week a pair of jeans I have struggled to get anywhere close to buttoning slipped on without a hint of fat spilling over the sides. It has taken 10 months of changing my eating habits, exercise and daily listens of a 'Thinking Slimmer' audio download to achieve this personal goal. I have lived in tent-shaped dresses the past year when I have a wardrobe full of figure-hugging clothes.

Last week I decided to take frumpy ole me in hand, not in an attempt to turn back the clock but instead to reflect the older-but-still-glamorous me and to become more visible. I hired a former stylist I met while working as an entertainment publicist in the 90s; I wanted a 'look' for performing jazz & blues. Standing in my bedroom, watching her dig into my wardrobe to find suitable clothes, retrieving dresses and high-heeled shoes from my younger days was a form of therapy. 'I've never seen you look like this,' she said as I paraded around in 4″ heels, a tight red ruched dress, flower in my hair. I almost didn't recognise myself.

She issued me with set of instructions.

Cut my hair shorter into a graduated bob.

Trim and tint my eyebrows.

Buy a new colour of blush—something with a pink tint.

Obtain new shoes, with a wedge heel but comfortable.

'I want glamour,' she said. 'Older woman glamour. Sexy, a bit louche. I want to see you perched on a high stool, leaning back but with attitude.' I looked in the mirror and saw a different me. Yes, I thought.

20

I've still got 'it.' Issuing me a shopping list and a recommendation to turn three dresses into pencil skirts has led to a new feeling. I am developing a persona who is me with all the lived experience, the awareness and the self-confidence that has taken me all of 60 years to acquire. I'm well aware it's an ongoing process.

Although 60 and I had a crap start, I'm aiming to make up for it now, starting with these shoes. Wowza!

Age is No Barrier to Getting Published

By Judy Piatkus

It was 2019. I had no plans to write a book as I travelled to a café in Islington, North London, for a women's networking lunch organised by a friend of mine. Yet one of the women I was to meet there was to set my life on a new and unexpected trajectory during the next three years.

Helen Elizabeth Evans offers a process called Scientific Hand Analysis which helps you understand yourself better. I was fascinated when she looked at the palm of my friend's hand and revealed information about her that she could not have previously known as they had only just met. I booked my own session with Helen and discovered that I had ideas I wanted to communicate to the world, stories I wanted to share. Writing some of them down seemed an obvious route to go and so it began.

My background is book publishing and I had founded my company, Piatkus Books in 1979 and sold it successfully in 2007 to one of the largest publishing conglomerates. I had made a first attempt at writing a book after that but the three eminent literary agents I offered it to were not impressed and so I abandoned it.

At the start of 2019, I determined that writing my book would be my project for that year and that I would approach it in a more professional way. I joined a writing class run by a previous colleague from my publishing days. It soon became clear that memoir would be the form of writing that came most naturally to me and so I began. Interestingly, I didn't write about my life in a linear way. I wrote the easiest chapters first and then amalgamated them with later chapters which were harder to write and didn't flow so effortlessly.

After I had written 40,000 words, I sent them to an experienced freelance editor who a publisher friend recommended. It was an anxious time waiting for her response. However, she was very encouraging and suggested guidelines that I could follow. I persevered and finally, the book was completed. It was a great feeling to finally write those two immortal words 'the end.'

I sent the completed typescript which was by then about 80,000 words to the freelance editor and asked if she would copyedit it so that I could look for a literary agent to represent me. She got to work, subtly improving what I had written. Nevertheless, it was still a shock when the early pages were returned to me as she had cut 20,000 words from my text. As an ex-publisher though, I knew that whatever she had chosen to leave out would improve my book immeasurably and after a couple of days of adjustment, I was able to send it out on a quest to find a literary agent who would represent me.

Although a former publisher myself, I hadn't given much thought to which company might publish it. Over the next eight months a literary agent took it on and she sold it to Watkins Books, a perfect fit, as it turned out because Watkins publish books in the genres I was writing about.

My memoir is entitled *Ahead of Her Time: How a One Woman Startup Became a Global Publishing Brand*. It's the story of how I started the business in my bedroom at home in the 1980s when I was pregnant with my second child and how my colleagues and I gradually built it into one of the UK's most successful independent publishing companies. We became known for publishing popular fiction and for being pioneers in the area of alternative health and personal growth publishing. In the 1980s we published classic bestsellers such as *Colour Me Beautiful* and cookbooks by Mary Berry whose first book for Piatkus, *Fast Cakes*, is probably on many of your shelves. We also published the earliest works by Jon Kabat Zinn, who brought the concept of mindfulness to the West and a range of health and mind, body and spirit titles including the first UK books on detoxing and decluttering.

Finally, my book was published. And so, after all these years of enabling other authors' voices to be heard, I too found myself holding my own book with my name on the front and not on the spine this time. By now the UK publishing trade has of course changed considerably. Amazon controls over 50% of the marketplace and my book is available as a hardback, as a kindle download and as an audiobook. I already had a platform on social media (essential for all aspiring authors) but it was nevertheless quite an adjustment to find myself personally connecting with readers via Twitter. There was also a lot of new terminology to learn.

The advantage of being able to look back on a richly-lived life at this time of my life has been immeasurable. I feel very grateful that, at the age of 71, I am still capable of taking on a fascinating new project and of being able to see it through to completion. My memoir also won the Business Journey Award in the 2022 UK Business Book Awards. Age truly is no barrier when you have the right mindset.

A Breath Before 60

By Caroline Bobby

My hair is grey.

I return from my hairdresser having had the last bits of colour chopped out. I'm now sporting a choppy, silver and pepper pot, topknot, not entirely dissimilar from my beloved dog.

I don't fully understand the impulse to grow out the colour, which had me ditch the hair dye in April. I knew it was related to my 60th birthday, which is now a mere two weeks away. I wanted to see my hair. I had been using colour for 15 years, ever since my hairline started to grey.

It wasn't anything clichéd about aging and grey hair, that drove this. It hasn't been comfortable at some points during the process, seeing the half in, half out thing going on, on a daily basis. Now I'm here. My hair is grey and I'm surprised by the strength of my feeling. Oh. I say to myself in the bathroom mirror. Hello.

I limp and lurch towards my 'big birthday' not only as a metaphor, but literally, as I'm long overdue for back surgery. Limping and lurching is what I do—though, my bulging discs notwithstanding—it is a blessed relief to understand that stumbling, staggering and lurching, is the human condition of our little lives. My own little life has become much sweeter, since giving up on getting life right.

Sixty.

The shoreline. The beginning of being old: to my way of seeing it, anyway. No, I am not the new 40. I am not still middle-aged. I am averse to ageing euphemisms.

My mother died, just days after her 60th birthday. She was bitterness and sorrow as an art form, and I never really understood how that came to pass. I was on the other side of the world, caught up in my own version of sorrow and bewilderment. We were estranged for years. Her death coincided—although I wasn't to know it for quite some time—with the death rattle of my addiction. No coincidence. I was so nearly dead myself, on my knees in the shadows of Sydney's yellowest sun. My mother died and I stayed alive.

Thirty years ago: half my little life ago. And, here I am with my grey hair, having somehow descended into tenderness. I wish my mother and I had had more time together, an opportunity to see if there was any other way to dance our dance. It was a brutal dance and I needed kindness like a desert landscape needs water. I nearly died of thirst. I believe that is exactly what she died of—she was latched on to the breast of death, and didn't ever get to know there was another place to drink from.

Twenty years ago, when I was in therapy and starting to interpret past events, I went to the graveyard on the edge of Dartmoor where she's buried and lay down on her grave. It was a pilgrimage of sorts, though I was making it up as I went along. I didn't know what I was doing or why, but I managed to trust the imperative. If it were physically easier (those discs again), I'd go back there now to lie on the ground that holds her body. A mother and daughter, with 120 years between them: 30 of them in this world at the same time.

This turning a new decade, it has some juice. As an exquisitely understated friend of mine would say—'it's not nothing'.

I don't have any recollection of reaching 10 except for a tiny, waft of unease. Neither do I remember a 21st birthday, which was undoubtedly due to drugs and alcohol. Turning 30 was the milestone of my life. I don't remember anything at all with my conscious mind, but almost dead from self-hatred and drugs, I finally turned my face towards this human world.

Ten years later, I celebrated becoming 40 around a table with friends. I had a profession: psychotherapy, and a partner. I was trying to force myself into an idea of myself and it was only a partial success.

By 50, I had escaped the partial partnership and some internalised constraint. I had found and then lost again, the love of my life and the daughter we called in. I had a proper party with catering and dancing and wore a sea green dress. It seems so long ago.

Sixty.

With a light, yet serious touch, I've dedicated a few ritual acts of love and kindness towards this birthday. In May, I went on a pilgrimage to Hydra, the Greek island where Leonard Cohen lived, wrote and loved. More recently, I commissioned a photo shoot. At home with Leonard The Dog and Bebe The Cat. Family life. Love.

And, it was not nothing—to see the sweetness and comedy I live inside, from the outside.

These last 10 years I have been winding myself home. Many things I'd thought I needed, turned out not to matter much. I found the Fields of Kindness and Simplicity. I discovered they had been here all the time. I had been here all the time.

I wonder what the next decade of me, and of this wailing world will be. I'm viewing my personal next decade through the lens of no real appetite for more than that. My sense of having the capacity for another ten years, but not much more, is clear as a mountain stream. No drama. Nothing complicated or ambivalent. Just its ring of truth. And, of course I know ideas, beliefs and passions change, so I'm not gripping on too tightly.

I am trusting my own precious heart. If this is my last decade, I'll do the very best I can with it.

If you are wondering about why a person might 'only have another decade to give or to live,' I can only say I'm very tired. I've been tired all my life. Living with depression is tiring. I've been dragging myself through the days of my life, and while I finally fell from the self-violence that came down through my mother's line, into something like Grace, it will always be heavy. Dragging the heavy is wearing and I am worn.

The thing is, all of this is gentle. I did, eventually get home to that precious heart I mentioned. The fact that it took a long time, and that in many ways I'm ready to go now, just makes me smile. Maybe I'll make it to 70. Maybe I won't. If I do, and still feel like this, I'll be writing about ending my life. If I get to seventy and don't feel like this, I'll be writing about that instead.

Depression and weary aside, I know I don't want to be old, old. Seventy feels doable. More than that feels dangerous. We don't hold old age with compassion and respect in these broken systems of our government. I am crystal clear I don't want to spend my last years in that system. Unequivocally not.

So, here I am, stumbling sweetly towards my 60th birthday, which incidentally I'm celebrating by going on a Death Retreat. I tell people, and they mostly grin at the perfect pitch of it. So very me, and so very lovely to be seen and understood in my deepest longings.

As Leonard (Cohen) would say:
And here is your love
For all things.
And here is your love
For all of this
May everyone live,
And may everyone die.
Hello, my love,
And my love, Goodbye.

Note—Caroline had the back surgery and it was successful and that's another story.

Starting an MA in Creative Writing at 62

By Elizabeth Shanley

As a child I loved to read and write but where did that come from?

Our story is a familiar one. Dad came over from Ireland in the 1950s as the farm could not support him. He met and married mum and as Irish Catholics, children kept arriving. Dad worked away from home supporting us and sending money back to his mother on the farm. When he was away, in the evenings to settle us mum would sit in the armchair by the fire, we would be in our pajamas, huddled at her feet, the latest baby in the cot by her side. It is not a romantic memory. This was a council house and the coal fire in the living room was the only heating.

But I loved these evenings. She would read to us—Dickens' *Oliver Twist*, one of my earliest memories, then Louise May Alcott's *Little Women*. I was entranced by the stories she read aloud so when I was old enough to read, we shared the duties. It was a natural step therefore to put pencil first, then pen, to paper. I wrote stories, letters, poems, plays and stored them in a box under my bed.

I was good at English and my journey through school was a joy enhanced by that one teacher that everyone has; Don Whitby was mine. He took us from *To Kill a Mockingbird,* to more Dickens, Hardy and poetry that was not on the syllabus—sometimes song lyrics. He was a romantic figure who had been a dancer in a popular dance group in the early 60s and we adored him. He taught us drama and we put on fabulous productions. It was another easy step for me to apply to read English, Drama and Theatre studies and there followed the best three years of my life at Royal Holloway College, University of London. Graduating and needing a job I could not see how pursuing the Arts was ever going to earn me a living so I took a different path, signing up as a commissioned officer in The Royal Air Force—and that's another story! But I continued to write, stuffing notebooks with my words and dreams.

Seven years ago, it was becoming clear that Mum wasn't going to be around much longer. She was 83, in good health but frail and so I sat with her one evening grilling her on her childhood—stories she had told us from our early years but I was now thinking like a writer—I wanted detail, information, I was doing research before I lost her and her amazing mind. When she died, I vowed to myself that I was going to write something based on some of her stories and created a character plotline that I have been developing ever since.

In December 2019 I found a creative writing course in Ireland. This was it for me. It was in a farmhouse on an island off the west coast. I had visions of days sat around a large wooden table with other writers, swapping our daily output, reading aloud, challenging, feeding each other words and ideas. And at night musicians, the flames of a dancing fire, a bit of whiskey; I would be wrapped in a gorgeous cashmere shawl and wearing fingerless gloves. And then lockdown. I was offered an online version of the course and for six glorious weeks spent two hours every Sunday evening with the tutor and another writer who lived in Geneva. It was a lifeline in an isolated time. I live alone so it was me and the dogs and Zoom but those Sundays were wonderful.

As lockdown eased, I started to think about how I might build more formal writing processes into my life and then in November 2021, my 17 year-old niece, Maeve, was telling me about her A level English course work and I offered to read it. The subject was 'Compare and contrast Ibsen's *A Doll's House* and Louisa May Alcott's *Little Women* and their depiction of ideological power.' Reading her work was revelatory. I had forgotten how much I enjoyed deep analysis of text and then committing to research. Thanks to Maeve I started looking for academic courses. I vowed years ago, on completion of my MBA, that I would never return to academia and yet here I was, aged 62, researching MAs in creative writing. I wanted a fully online programme as I was still fearful of COVID, I have a compromised immune system and had stayed safe for the best part of two years so I wanted to stay well. I looked at many programmes at various universities and then found one. It is a fully online programme and its biggest appeal was the international nature of the participants on the course. I applied, was offered a place and started in January 2022.

I went into the course clear about my objectives: to write my novel. I find myself half way through the taught modules and each time I sit down to write the strangest thing happens. I read the task assignment, weekly activity and then start to write. Stories appear, some based on events that are familiar to me, but mainly they are tales that spring out of my fingers onto the keyboard. When the task was to write using sensory detail I found myself back in the Belizean rain forest, a young female military officer in a beautiful, lush and challenging environment. Leaf cutting ants with their smell of formic acid crossed my path as I hacked through with my machete—humming birds hovered in the open mouths of scarlet hibiscus flowers. Where did it all come from?

The greatest joy of the course work is the writers' workshop where each week we are set a task and assigned a small group. We submit our work to each other for critique and comment so that we develop our own critical thinking skills as well as our editing ability as we write. But that's not the best bit.

At the end of the first week our tutor suggested that we might want to set up a private group to chat outside of the formal taught elements and one of the women set up a Zoom call. Since that first week, in and out of term we have met every Saturday when able, on an informal basis, for our water cooler natter. This is where the real work is taking place as we develop relationships, support each other, challenge and laugh a lot. With more easing of restrictions, a summer school was proposed by the university and those of us who were able to, eagerly signed up.

It was with great joy that I headed up to the north of England to the campus for the residential in August. I booked an Airbnb and two of the women joined me. We had only ever met virtually but it was a breeze. We went to school each day together and met up with the rest of the gang—there was a group of 10 of us. They came from Singapore, France, Majorca, Northern Ireland and various parts of England. During the day we were students, we did real time writing workshops and activities, attended some terrific lectures—my favourite being—writing the taboo. And in the evenings, meals out and more—suffice to say what goes to summer school stays at summer school!

Our last day was a Saturday so the water cooler natter was held in a room at the library and we Zoomed in Macao, England and France to share our connectedness. Without a doubt, the most valuable and life affirming part of doing this MA in creative writing is meeting my fellow writers, making deep friendships, and working collaboratively to ensure that we all fulfil our potential and stretch ourselves beyond anything I certainly could possibly have imagined.

We have just received another marked assignment and the results have been mixed with some bitterly disappointed people, some mildly disgruntled (me for one) and others joyous. But in all of it there has been tremendous support, love and practical offers of help. This weekend's water cooler natter will be an interesting one as we move forward into our next module—writing from life. Non-fiction!

My novel is put to one side as I explore another facet of writing that isn't my natural medium and so far I have surprised myself and I look forward to seeing what this one brings.

Beyond The Dross of Invisibility

By Lindsay Hamilton

Let's start by asking what we mean by 'invisibility?' Not feeling like the head-turner we were at 28? No one homing in to chat us up at a party? Not having a voice? Being ignored? Being unable to find anything to wear suitable for our age, shape, and physical needs? Having no sense of role relevant to us? Finding adverts, films, series, radio programmes largely aimed at those far younger than us?

Or those meaningful and very earnest, utterly tedious films that deal with 'a loving older couple facing serious illness' or 'a loving older couple dealing with infidelity,' or the 'comedy' of love and sex in the golden years.

I suspect all of the above for some; some of the above for others; and none of the above for the rest. What does 'feeling invisible' mean to you? Whilst I was thinking about what to write here, it occurred to me that I was both very wrong and very right to be focusing on this subject. I'm 62, usually mistaken for being in my 40s (lucky me, hey?).

But it's not always fun and games, when I'm having difficulty clambering off the bus or some (to my eyes) young buck, makes a half-hearted pass at me—sometimes nice—mostly just eye-rollingly irritating. I've spent all my teen and adult life being relatively invisible because I bypassed the adolescent growth spurt, recalcitrantly staying put at the 4'10" of the 11-year-old that I was.

This puts me within the upper height range for people of restricted height, formerly referred to as dwarves, but without the cachet of some of them. We had a fellow student at my alma mater called Tom Shakespeare who sported punk Dalmatian spotted bleached hair and a lively wit. He was of restricted height and frequently seen being carried around good-humouredly on the shoulders of our peers. He was feted, enjoyed, and celebrated while I—not exactly overlooked with my orange Mohican and the standard ripped fishnets of the mid-'80s—but never in the same league as Tom. You see, even shorties envy other, more sleb shorties. I was always invisible in a crowd, always at the front or far side of any photos, and always asked my age in pubs.

Anyway, I digress. We both are and are not invisible. In terms of the market, we barely exist. 'Anti-ageing' creams don't celebrate age, social media is based around glossy youthful images and in-words, in-people, in-places to go, the culture of usually youthful, or youth-obsessed celebrity, fashion, music… Nothing new here.

But—isn't invisibility restful? We can either coast along, letting waistlines grow and fashion sense fade away, or we can find the stuff we like, fight the flab (or not), polish up our style, continue to develop our minds and cherish our feelings. Either way, who's really going to care? We are not adolescents with crippling peer pressure; we are not young or older parents hoping to fit in at the school gates. We are not even, any longer, middle-aged, somehow hoping for a handsome or pretty stranger to catch our eye as we whirl across the dance floor of our existence.

We are beyond the lower foothills of the ageing process and into the mid or even advanced slopes of age. We are the elders. While we may chafe against the limited style options, feel irritated when a younger person demonstrates limited interest in soliciting our opinion, wonder whether sex with a hot man or woman is really worth the effort, or if it might be more pleasant to retire to bed with a hot chocolate, grind our teeth when yet another series features 30 or even 20-somethings, and know that we are no longer eligible for another mortgage—there is gold amongst the dross.

Have you actually met anyone of 50 plus, 60 plus, 70 plus or older who does actually NOT have a voice? In my experience the most vocal, articulate, passionate, and, let's face it, pushy, people are those over 50. In my youth, because I was small, if in a queue, I'd always stand tightly to the person in front of me. Why? Because there would inevitably be an older person who wielded their shopping bag on wheels—love those things, I have a turquoise one with four racer wheels—like a weapon of mass destruction to force their way into the queue in front of me. Some Neanderthal instinct shouted in their ears: 'Choose the small one! Easy meat!'.

'Old' equals savvy and feisty. 'Ageing' equals taking no prisoners. 'Over the hill' means don't mess with this fecker. And this,

babes, means us. We have lived through, depending on your country and age—fascism, rationing, the horrors of Thatcherism, radical feminism, sceptical feminism, post-feminism (whatever that twaddle means—how can there be 'post' feminism without equality?), the fall of the Berlin Wall, the end of State Socialism and the emergence of State Gangsterism in the former Eastern Bloc, various and varied governments, emerging climate change scary enough to make your hair turn white overnight if it wasn't already, and then the worst, the very worst of the pandemic and its multiple lockdowns.

We are the aunts, uncles, grandparents, great aunts, great uncles, and honorary all of these. We are the ones with ears to listen, the wisdom of the years, the time to play, the rocks of the family and community. The marketplace may be wheeling itself around much too slowly to the fact that many of us have the spare funds that the younger do not, but this may be to our advantage.

In the meantime, who can really say that we are invisible when we have honed our style, developed our voices, celebrated so many steps along the road less travelled that we have almost worn it to the bare rock? We are only failing to be seen by those largely irrelevant to us in our maturity and without our gravitas. We are a grand club of the ageing and aged and it behoves us to hold this in mind when we set up yet another astonishingly rich poetry gathering, go together to an exciting club night, try out an excellent restaurant, help out our local political group, volunteer for a worthy establishment (not talking Cynthia Payne style here, unless this floats your boat).

Here's to not going quietly into that good night!

SECTION TWO
BEYOND
THE BOX

Travels with My Wild Lone Self

By Ruth Fox

This is what I call them. These trips, when I go away in my car alone and I do this thing where I choose to 'go where I will'. No fixed plan.

My plans form in a kind of organic way. Some of them have notions beforehand that develop into options, then only sometimes into actions. Others are completely spontaneous and others are somewhere in between the two. Decisions made on my inklings and urges, fantasies and on weather forecasts. Or on something someone said. Or a sudden yearning for something like driving eight miles to a shop for one of the best pies I had ever had—to get one again. Then an onward journey beyond the pie shop that took me somewhere else. To ancient stones and to a lighthouse where the land ends and the wind has free reign.

Or just to stop in a layby and crawl into the back and sleep for two hours in the middle of the afternoon. Or pause by a river and stay all night there, all cosy inside as the rains drenched the land and swelled the river to a dramatic wild torrent below me, suddenly it was no longer a place to bathe!

Or to drive off in the predawn light, finding a high spot from which to watch the dawn over Snowdonia and walk up a grass slope scattered with a million rainbow diamond dewdrops glittering at me as I pass and then find the perfect spot, from which to glory in the sweep of the dawn and the mist lying like a soft sea in the lowland fields and marshes below.

Freedom.

The qualities and experiences of these journeys include, spontaneity, freedom, peace, solitude, the unknown, joy and what I can probably best describe as magic.

When we were children many of us believed life was full of magic, or at least that magic was possible. Later we learned that it wasn't so. But guess what?

39

We were lied to.

The world is *full* of magic.

One of the reasons I often prefer to encounter the world alone is because most people, when they go together, for a walk or a journey, unconsciously collude with each other to maintain the ordinary, the usual. Which, while it can be enjoyable, companiable and delightful in many ways, is sometimes good to get a break from, as it can distract us from the beauty and the magic all around us. My aloneness seems to transform the journey into something very different.

I become my Wild Lone Self. Answerable to no one. No one to observe me but my own self. No one to evaluate or influence my decisions, unless I choose it. No one to interrupt my reveries, my joy, my peace, my love affair with the beauty all around me, my own unknown and extraordinary adventure.

I am going to attempt to tell the story of how I do it, on both inner and outer levels, to share the practicalities of how I physically do this, and possibly an inkling of the magic too. Who knows? Keep your ears eyes and noses open for it!!

Then maybe later I will take you on a trip into the story of one of my adventures.

Perhaps I should begin with why, or should I say an attempt to explain why. Why I do this thing of going away by my Wild Lone Self.

Bear with me, I am figuring this out as I write. I will see if I can list the reasons as I think of them.

I have a love of freedom.

I have a love of the land, of the natural world, of this beautiful extraordinary trillion billion faceted jewel of a planet I am living on.

I love Unknown Adventures.

I love Journeys.

I love walking barefoot on the land and swimming in the wild waters, naked if there's no one around.

I love the sun on my skin and in my eyes.

I love gazing at it all, photographing it, sinking my hands into soft mosses and feeling the movement of the trees in the wind, listening to the sounds that travel through them. Feeling the air on my bare legs. Lying on ancient rocks, standing in the still water in a deserted cove at the lowest of the low spring tide for 20 minutes, relishing the drama of how very, very low the tide is and seeing if I can experience the movement of the water down or up my shins while a small hermit crab tickles my toes.

I didn't know I was going to do that until I did.

Cooking outside. I love cooking my meal on a rock, a riverbank, a wall, a concrete block by the beach put there years ago to stop the Germans landing, my tummy leaned up against the warm concrete and a pleasant breeze on my bare back.

I love sitting in the back of my car—tailgate up wide open with a glorious view along the beach to the mountains beyond, brewing up my coffee, open aired yet sheltered from the wind, after a delicious early morning dip in the wild western UK breakers.

What else do I love about going away by my Wild Lone Self?

Mmm let me think...

I am not always alone. There is something I call Chance Meetings and Encounters... though I really do not believe anything in life is chance, but more the incidence of co-creation, the multi-connected matrix of everything that intersects constantly in every experience, every nuance of life... but perhaps I digress. Or maybe not.

Chance Meetings and Encounters. I like the poetry of that phrase. And I savour them. These moments. I meet people. Sometimes it is the minimal, a smile and hello or a casual remark about the weather, the day, their little dog, how the water was. Anything. Sometimes more. A conversation, maybe laughter. Or they tell me something of their life and I tell something of mine. Sometimes snippets, sometimes more than that. In each one of these encounters something is given, something received. There is an exchange. Then we go on our way.

They are like precious jewels on a thread.

One day I told a man from eastern Europe about how big steam trains used to pass along this path running right by the old hotel he was staying in, right where we were standing, three or four yards from the windows, and how as a child I was once a passenger on the train as it passed, like a great iron dragon taking me and my granny to the coast... to a place I loved. Enjoying his surprise as I evoked the power of those sudden moments as the great engines thundered past between the inn and the wate

Another day and another place a beautiful vibrant woman served me tea and cake. I was the only customer in the café and she told me about her life. She was strong, and tired. Our hearts met. I felt a quiet awe in

41

the face of human survival, endurance and the power of love, as we laughed together and swapped stories.

I once met a woman who had just come out of the sea as I was going towards it—on a vast empty windy beach. In our shouted conversation as the wind buffeted our words, she invited me to stay in her home anytime. 'If you go to my village just ask for me, they all know me,' she said. Perhaps one day I will. Maybe we will meet again. Maybe not. It matters not. But the warmth of her impulsive invitation matters and it stays with me, warms the cockles of my heart whenever I remember it, and that wild wind, her little dog running madly around the creamy expanse of wet sand and barking. And the cold clear refreshing waters I entered, naked, after she left. Then the wide sweep of the land, the silver sand reflecting the light and the deep turquoise sea was empty again. Only my wild lone self and the seabirds remained.

These memories are all part of the gathered treasures of my adventures, my meanderings, my travels with my Wild Lone Self.

Precious extraordinary encounters.

There is a quality to taking a journey in solitude. I am somehow more sensitised to everything that happens, to my own self as well as to the world around me. There is a greater intensity to my experiences. Greater joy. A more intense perception of beauty. A far greater connection to nature and the elements—the presences of the places, of the life in the life I encounter, and also the rock, stone, air, water, light, the elements as well as the elementals. And of the sun, moon, stars and the cosmos.

My physical senses are also enhanced by solitude. The feeling of walking into cold clear Northern waters and feeling the bite of the wind as I emerge, the sun's warmth as the clouds move aside and the body's response of standing tall and wanting to stretch out my arms and join with all of it. And later the snuggled warmth as I drink hot chocolate in my own 'nest' out of the wind and relaxing with the beautiful cold turquoise sea view outside, enjoying my retreat into warmth and relaxation.

In this highly sensitised state the interactions with the personality and the ego that accompany myself can also be highly intensified. The process of making decisions can get interesting when the personality starts to offer some of its less helpful input. Procrastination. Unfriendly or unhelpful self-evaluations (criticisms) can elbow their way into the adventure, attempting to sow doubt or even anxiety.

But over the years I have gotten better at withstanding and letting go of those moments. Reclaiming my innocence and understanding the perfection of my meandering, sometimes stumbling, curiously wondering wanderings. Though recently my self-feedback system did suggest, usefully, I believe, that it may be good to get better at not driving further, at night, when tired! Amongst the dreaming and wandering, it is also very good to be practical!

The practical. The arrangement that enables me to wander off without a plan, taking what I need with me.

The Practical and the care of the Physical.

What is my setup?

What comprises my vehicle, my shelter, my home from home on my travels?

The current vehicle is a 15 year-old moderate-sized estate car. I like the old Ford Focus because everything goes down to completely flat in the back with just enough length for me to sleep stretched out full length. I am five foot ten. Plus there's no raised lip at the back door so it's comfortable to sit on the rear edge. A smallish car such as this doesn't have space to pack chairs or tables and suchlike. I prefer more space and less things wherever possible. So a back end that also works as a sitting spot is nice to have.

I have very seldom in my life paid more than three figures for a vehicle. When one breaks irrevocably or is no longer economic to repair, I go, usually these days onto FB marketplace and find another one. They last me one to three years.

My current car cost me £750 just over a year ago. An 07 plate with a genuine low mileage. A few minimal scuffs on the bodywork and dog hairs in the back (it had been on a farm apparently) kept the price down. Good sound mechanics. Cleaned up great. My previous one was £600 and ran beautifully for three years. That was the one that took me on my wunnerful midsummer adventure to the Western Isles for the first time in my life!! But that is another story I will begin soon. Or later.

Back to the car. I have a very comfortable bed. An old three-inch deep foam 'base camp' Thermorest that no longer seals, so is a little firm and a little soft, topped with a three-inch deep memory foam, which is very soft and very warm. They fold up into thirds during the day and are comfy for sitting, lying or leaning on. A pillow and a quilt and other 'warmies' go into a furry cushion cover for the daytime. I have no patience for unentangling myself from a sleeping bag to get out of bed in the night and a trip made for pleasure should never cause bad sleeps or aching bones! Minimal kit and maximum comfort is the intent!

Having the 'right kit' can really make a difference to the comfort, safety and convenience of all those things we humans need to keep us warm, cool, safe, fed, cleaned and serviced. So can the quality of the space. I can get quite obsessive and fascinated about kit, systems, finding good ways to do stuff and so on. I have what I call an 'engineering mind.' By which I mean I have practical, spatially aware abilities and I love discovering better ways for systems to work and space to be optimised for maximum space, comfort and convenience. It's a kind of fascinating game to see how good I can get it all.

So, what do I have? I have my very comfy bed and coffee pot but have no need for a plate or bowl as I happily eat out of the pot. My kitchen is in a bag that can be easily carried outside onto the riverside, beach etc. to cook.

My system is that almost everything lives in several bags that I lined with boxes. The ultimately flexible system as everything can be easily moved around to change how I am using my space according to wind direction, comfort, what I am doing and where is the best view!

The Kit

Kitchen bag—contains a tiny stove and windshield, tray and everything for cooking and making drinks.

Water bag—contains several water containers. Smaller and easy to handle.

Clothes bag

Miscellaneous kit bag—my bag of useful things.

Chill box—The chill box is a recent acquisition and still on trial. Seems good though after its first week away with me. I can plug it in when driving, I have a Tupperware box in there that contains the ice cubes I buy on my way to keep things cool when not plugged in. The top is flat and is a useful desk table space I have so far used to place my tablet for an away from home Zoom training. That was in Dungeness recently. It worked well. I had a nice view from the car and was connected to a world-wide group for 90 minutes while away in my car. How brilliant! I love finding out what's possible!

Food bag—contains any food not in the cool box

Facilities bag—contains whatever I need to use when a toilet is not available.

Rucksack

Bag of warm and outdoor clothing.

Shoes/boots, stashed in footwell

Large umbrella—storm-proof and sunproof, very useful as an awning or a shelter under which I have cooked and eaten outside in the rain, sheltered completely.

Squashy bucket to put wet things in etc.

Blinds & curtain for the windows.

I think that's about it.

Organisation is vital or chaos ensues, then the space feels smaller and things cannot be found when needed!

For instance. I sleep with a small head torch around my neck and also the car key on a lanyard. It's just easier and safer. I am not a nervous type and not given to fear and anxiety but my common sense decrees when sleeping in strange places to lock the doors, cover the windows thoroughly and to keep the key and the light around my neck on retiring to bed and my flip-flops handy for stepping out in the night.

Always knowing where the key is, is important, both day and night!! Always knowing where the light is, is vital at night so I keep it in my purse bag in the daytime too so when night falls, I know exactly where it is. These kind of structural details keep me safe and comfortable so I can relax and enjoy my time away by my Wild Lone Self and not waste time looking for things or fretting about losing them!

I have chosen the box-in-a-bag system I formulated because it gives me total flexibility. I can put everything at the back, front or side of my space. The boxes line the various cloth **bagforlife**s I use and make them stable and easy to pack and find things in. Also if I want to park up inconspicuously and leave the car in the daytime I can put everything behind the back seats under a black cloth 'backshelf' I made so that it looks like there is nothing in the car.

Sex in my 70s, the Pressure is Off

By Asanga Anand

Much of my life, despite discovering meditation in my 30s, has been about achieving goals—either physical ones in different sporting activities or intellectual ones in my medical career. Although often denying it, I was very competitive. I competed in sports at school and university and later on became obsessed with achieving improvement in performance as a rock climber and mountaineer. Even during meditation competitiveness could creep in, in the form of achieving good results.

And as a man, this applied in the field of sex as much as anywhere else. The goal of course was to achieve that desirable yet elusive ever-more earth-shattering orgasmic ejaculation; and not only that, but to make sure the woman had the same, simultaneously. It was even my responsibility that she did, or so I thought—what misguided arrogance to think that I should be in charge of her body. No matter how hard I tried this scenario was doomed to fail and end in frustration and worse: projection and unspoken recriminations towards the other—familiar picture anyone? And putting oneself under pressure can inevitably lead to the issue of performance anxiety with burn out and even physiological failure, i.e. erectile dysfunction.

I would like to think that now in my 70s, life is more laid back but am not sure this is so. What I can say is that I am less obsessed with achieving goals and happier to enjoy the landscape along whatever way I travel. Of course, there are still goals but they are simple, practical, everyday ones: when cooking a meal I want the result to be pleasing—both on the eye and palette. Also I am less concerned with impressing others and happier to be me: eccentric, opinionated, flamboyant, insecure. Of course, I still catch myself slipping back into old habits around wanting to be the best but I am not perfect and have come to realise that to pursue perfection is pointless!

And along the pathways of getting older—my mountaineering

accident, the death of my wife—I have chosen to face the nooks and crannies within myself. I have attended personal development workshops in which I have had to face and own my shadows in public. I have taken risks exposing sexual and emotional issues around shame and weakness to strangers. I have dared to ask for what I want from another person while showing them who I am and seeing who they are—without masks. And as a result, I have re-discovered a zest for life, my big heart and how much fun I can have. It has definitely been life-changing.

I am blessed by finding a strong-willed, like-minded woman to share in this. When I asked her to be my 'tantric sex goddess,' after some hesitation she said it was an offer she could not refuse, but then spent months backtracking every time I came forward. I had to learn patience, to respect another's boundaries and compassion. She had to learn how to show her vulnerability. In any case, I had no idea what I had meant by such a request, which although I thought was what I wanted, was also a fantasy. I was soon to find out the nitty gritty of real relating. And it has not been a particularly smooth ride but a real and honest one. We choose people to relate to intimately because they mirror ourselves and press our buttons. Accepting this, however difficult, can be a springboard to deeper intimacy.

We first came to know of each other's existence four years ago in a seven-day group process known as the Path of Love which is about getting in touch with our potential to be in our hearts. It is not about sex as such but sexual energy is our life force and this process is also about taking risks and living life to the full. Participating in such groups together can be scary but also bring a deeper intimacy and tenderness between couples. Partly in order for our relationship to survive, we have taken part in several residential events including Path of Love as staff, and as participants in a Shadow Work weekend and a seven-day Making Love Retreat where the emphasis was on Slow Sex, a flowing, organic, playful immersion into consciously sharing body, mind and spirit. Basically, it includes spending sweet loving time together. Another discovery was how it is possible to do soft penetration: the penis entering the vagina while only semi-erect! I believe relating to another has to be worked at and this applies to sexual relating. I prefer the word 'relating' to 'relationship' as I think it gives the impression of something dynamic rather than static.

Gradually, over the last four years, my partner and I have found a way to become slower and less expectant in our sexual life. And I have been able to—after quite a few red-hot battles—allow myself something more organic. Somehow it now no longer matters whether she has an orgasm, or I do, or no one does, we're on a continuum of sexual pleasure which in traditional terms might be considered foreplay. With penetration added. But no pressure.

Something we use as a resource when there is friction between us is to sit facing each other, holding hands, starting with eyes closed focusing on breathing into the belly, and then when ready opening the eyes and gazing softly at the other's face with no judgment, being passively receptive, not actively looking. Then taking it in turns to share what we appreciate about each other. This avoids the mind's tendency to dwell on negative thoughts and projections and inevitably dissolves the friction. And it is always nice to feel appreciated and not taken for granted.

So, whenever we can, we bring little rituals into our love making as part of setting the desired scene: giving a sense of erotic sacredness. Like slowly undressing each other to a backdrop of lyrical, meditative music and then having a bubble bath together and washing at least each other's feet and legs—slowly and lovingly, while lying facing each other. In the past I would resort to candles and incense but that was it. Now there is no rush or goal to be achieved and everyday actions become part of making love—even going for a walk or drinking a cup of tea together.

This period of intensive self-exploration has happened over the last five years of my life probably as a result of having more time on my hands to reflect on my real priorities and want I want out of life. This includes making a commitment to make it work between me and my woman.

But the pressure to achieve unrealistic goals is off, which means we can enjoy the adventure.

Is it said that life begins at 50? Well, I know that life begins whenever you choose a new beginning. It's never too late.

A Paean to Raving at 53

By Lili Free

Seven years ago I acquired a pair of Caterpillar biker boots, not my usual form of footwear, being more your-trainers-(or in various muddy fields over the years, wellingtons)-kind-of-girl. These stylish and oh-so-comfortable, magic boots have been the caretakers of my dancing feet at every club, festival and rave I've attended since. I think I shall cry when they wear out.

I'm one of the world's oldest ravers and I'm still raving. I consider it a radical act of defiance against the fear machine that promotes hard work until retirement, after which you're expected to tip-toe quietly towards death. Dancing, especially the kind of trance-dance that sends you into an ecstatic state of Oneness, is an activity that keeps me looking, feeling and most importantly *thinking* creatively. I'm happy to reveal my age when asked. In fact, every time a spring chicken bounces over to me at a ridiculously late hour and shouts over the pounding sub; "How old ARE you?!" and I scream back, '53' I feel a frisson of pride.

The only difference between me and the youngsters that I find myself clubbing with—is that I'm wearing earplugs and they're generally not. Okay, to be fair, there are a couple of other differences; in order to prepare for a night of jumping up and down in mad abandon, I make sure I've had a nap and eaten a solid meal. I don't remember making sensible plans ahead of time when I was in my youth. One of the luxuries of raving in your early 20s is the permission to be in the Now, think Fuck It, Pop another Pill and not worry too much about recovery time. At that age most people are still relatively free of roles and responsibilities. After years of forging a career out in the 'real' world, becoming mortgage-laden, raising kids, it's easy to fall into the trap of designing your days around TO DO lists rather than letting life spontaneously *happen*.

This week I'm actually retiring from my career of the last 15 years, and am determined to get back *there*—to the intoxicating freedom of dancing all night with no anxiety around potentially being tired the following day and thus not able to cope with the schedule.

Fuck the schedule.

My kids have both left home. I consider it a job well done. I've conscientiously worked for a living since I was in my teens. I've filed my tax returns and been through the menopause. The only major project I have going right now is cutting myself free from the ties that bind, abandoning those 'roles,' and setting off to find a place to be in the world where I can dance to my heart's content.

When it comes to dancing, it appears I've tapped into a source of boundless energy. If you see me out there, water bottle in hand, looking like all the ecstasy-fuelled revellers swirling around me with dilated pupils, it's more than likely I'm going all night on a chai latte. And when they start to flag, I begin to surf my second or third wave of energy and dance till dawn.

I'm not a fan of alcohol for two reasons: a) it brings out the worst in people and b) it renders one incapable of dancing all night. Being a responsible adult living in a country where any drug that makes people happy, in love, or free-thinking, is made illegal, I'm not about to condone the use of class A drugs, am I? Having said that, I completely understand the desire to get out of your head. In my humble opinion, most human beings I meet could well do with some form of radical, mind-altering experience, but these days I do just as well getting high on everybody else's high. Mainly, it's the music and the tribal experience that sends me into an altered state of cosmic expansion.

I started raving in 1983 when I joined about 50,000 other people at Glastonbury festival. I adore the thrill of the large party, everyone in love and loving it. The invention of Ecstasy did wonders for the raising of human consciousness. It is an intelligent substance. Ecstasy opened people's hearts and brought them together. Furthermore, it got blokes dancing! This is a radical difference between my generation and my kids' one. They seem to be *born* with rhythm. They speak the language of complex cadence. Rhythm courses through them, the guys as cool on the dance floor as the girls.

My sons got their love of music through me. I'm eclectic in my taste and my stereo was played at full volume through both pregnancies. The oldest went to Leeds University, the youngest followed four years later. Both left in their second year to become professional DJs and I was actively proud. These days DJing is a true art form and my sons are highly skilled. I've danced to many of their sets in clubs and at festivals and nothing gives me more joy than seeing my boys doing what they love: working a crowd.

There are close to a thousand music festivals in England every summer. Not bad for a country that sees more rain than most. The one festival I make sure I attend every season without fail is called Give and it's a classy knees-up for ravers of my age group. We get together once a year, leave our smartphones in the car, unplug for a weekend, and go mental. Sadly I'm going to miss it this year as I'm heading off to Denmark on a silent retreat.

I had one chance to get to a festival before leaving, and last week I was lucky enough to be welcomed as a guest of honour at Virgo in Devon, a thank you for producing two of their acts. My oldest son Liam's band, Desert Sound Colony, was playing live and Reuben, his brother, was booked for a disco set in the rose garden during the afternoon. Eight hundred kids in their 20s, and I (the only 'mature' person apart from the owners of the house) met in the grounds of a stately home and rocked the valley through the May bank holiday weekend. The sun shone, the music was perfect and much dancing was done by all. Some of the folk in the drum 'n' bass room might have been a tad surprised at 4:00 a.m. to find a decidedly middle-aged woman, throwing herself about like a maniac in front of the mammoth speakers, but hey, in for a penny, in for a pound…

On Sunday afternoon, while the sun was setting, and I chilled on the banks of the lake with a yogic, spiritually-aware guy who resembled Jesus, I looked around and realised that a bunch of young DJs and their mates, most of them not long out of university, had put this extraordinary event together themselves. They hadn't sat around talking about how great it would be to create a boutique festival of their very own—inspired by the music they're passionate about—they'd actually made it happen! People who know how to throw a good party are my kind of people.

I have actually pictured my own death. It's more like an ascension really. It happens on a dance floor, my last breath exhaled at the point of a particularly good drop in the middle of a brilliant set played back-to-back by the boys. And as I breathe out, throwing my best shapes ever, I vanish in a puff of stage smoke, never to be seen again.

The Ages Project—Not about age and all about age

By Philip Pool

I'm a 56 year-old parent of two near adult sons. I've had operations on many of my joints, I have been diagnosed as well having ADHD and bipolar; I work in the civil service and I make photo art/protest projects when I am not working. I have a strong interest in how we are as individuals and how societal rules and expectations affect us. I'm also fascinated by how we can break free from those expectations if they don't suit us. I also believe that it is good to stop, to question and to make changes in our lives if we are not yet satisfied.

Ages is a photo/protest/body positivity project. And, it is about the social construction of age, not about how many years we happen to have been alive. What do I mean by a social construction? I mean nearly all of the things that we think, believe and 'know' about age that aren't to do with how many years we have been alive.

The vast majority of that awareness isn't based on an objective truth, it's based on what we as members of this society have been stewing in since we were tiny. That awareness is built on foundations that we repeatedly add to, over time. We construct what we know about age just as we construct most of what we 'know' about people from their gender or the colour of their skin.

I think age is largely a harmful construction. It messes with how we think about ourselves and about other people. It's deeply ingrained and most of it is bullshit. I think we need to pause, stare at its puffed up and bloated form, stick a large pin in it and watch it parp off into the distance.

Ages invites people to offer a snapshot of their lives through writing, through images of how they are dressed and in their skins, naked. I'm gradually adding more people and hope, eventually, to have participants from all ages of life from 20 upwards. Each person has a story to tell—me too.

I am a naturist in the broadest sense—I am a human animal and I feel comfortable naked in the environment. I enjoy the sense of freedom from being naked and from not feeling a need to hide myself away although I respect the fact that not everyone wants to see nudity. For me though, being naked in the sea and under the sky is deeply joyful.

Very often, when people pause and reflect on their lives in the middle or older years of our lives, we find that we would like to be living in a different way. Some of us make a change, we step or leap in a different direction All my life I've really not wanted the 'man' label that has been attached to me—I have no interest in conforming to what is expected of me as either a man, or as a woman. Has that been a hard thing? Absolutely! But what's the value of life if it's not the life we want?

I'm trying to reject what I'm expected to be like at the age I am too—it's not easy either. And I am inviting the participants in the Ages project to tell me and to show me who they are, whatever age they are. If they are wanting to be different, or to be better able to accept their bodies, they tell me that too.

I'm not denying that age has an impact. It's obvious that as we get older our bodies change and we pick up the marks of the lives we have lived.

The Ages project isn't just about older people, it's about all ages. I've been researching age as a subject for a year or so and it's clear that we mainly think about it in terms of negatives. Most of the connotations are negative and most of them are linked to older ages, but there also negative stereotypes attached to younger ages too. **It's as if there is nothing more positive to offer than hollow compliments such as 'well you look good for your age' or to offer some rather ridiculous phrase such as 'I'm 75 years *young.*' It doesn't matter what age you are— talk about who you are.**

Those in their teens and 20s are subject to endless absurd expectations of what they should look like and what they should do to fit impossible ideals. The 'perfect' body type is shown constantly in the media and social media. But that ideal body type is rare—most of us have never looked much like that ideal—and nor should we. Most younger people are fatter, thinner, taller, or shorter than whatever they are being told they should be like. With all the pressure there is on younger people to fit in, to develop and show their worth, it's extremely hard on many of them. When I hear older people denigrating these aspects of contemporary, I think of it as a failure to put ourselves in other people's shoes. Empathy is a life skill that one hopes older people have developed.

We often talk about the problems with the young—the millennials. There can be the stereotyping of young men as aggressive youths or 'snowflake' younger people who are portrayed as being overly offended by all manner of issues. And yet, as we did, they are trying to negotiate a very complex world and they are doing their best.

We set up youth as an ideal and, somehow, we are expected to try to retain the youthful look of that ideal—one that most of us have never attained. Or we cease to bother, we 'let ourselves go.' Well, some of us do let ourselves go.

Some of us reject the whole lot of it. We choose to try to live our lives as we wish to live them irrespective of how we are supposed to be, at a 'certain age.'

When we read or speak about people in middle age, the tone is often jokey or patronising. We joke about body parts no longer working so well, about middle-aged men trying to comb-over their thinning hair, or middle-aged women as 'mutton dressed up as lamb.' Our middle-aged crises are seen to lead us to stray from marriages and from 'good taste.'

And yet, we could consider it to be a wise thing in one's middle years (or at any point in our lives) to pause, to consider the direction we are going in and to check it's where we want to go. I suspect that any yearning to own a sports car or get a boob job has more to do with just continuing with that urge to show off the signs of youth that most of us have never actually had.

Most of the information that you'll find about ageing is about the older ages. Most of it is to do with the problems of older age and the language is largely (not entirely) negative. The focus is on poor health, disability, frailty, dementia, the loss of vitality, on becoming stuck in our ways, or becoming the rather bigoted, 'miserable old sods.'

Yes, we need far better support and care for older people but we, you, are not 'past it' and speaking to us as if we are children is unacceptable—it's not even a good way to speak to children! I spent a good deal of my time in the last 10 years witnessing my parents and their lives in care homes, observing how other people and the staff spoke to them as if they were childish idiots rather than simply more and more confused and lost in their own minds.

With a lack of information about age that isn't more rehashed stereotypes, I decided to create a photo and story collection of intimate snapshots of people's lives. They are, at once, ordinary, and, of course, exceptional and unique. They are united by being people who have gradually come to hear about my Ages project and have felt that it's right for them.

The majority, so far, are in their 40s and 50s, there are some 70 year-olds and some in their 30s and 20s. It's an organic project and I'm in no rush to fill gaps in the spread of years—that will happen gradually as people come to the project. If you read the stories they tell and look at their photographs, you will see that they have some things in common—such as being absolutely wonderful people. Some are fatter, some skinnier, some older, some younger, some fitter, some disabled—and I really hope to have more people with all sorts of body types and skin colours.

It really concerns me that we have so many images and stories about the really small number of people who happen to fit the ideal type. They are a rarity and yet theirs are the body types we see the most. I don't think that is healthy.

So far, I've attracted many more women participants than men. And it's interesting to note then when people are surveyed, women are far more likely to say that they have negative views about their own bodies. There clearly are expectations about how men should look, most of which are unobtainable, but generally the pressures are less extreme than they are on women. Perhaps because of that, I think that many women come to reject the expectations and rebel. We can choose to reject the expectations of having to look like a 'fit' 20 year-old but it's not easy, and that applies to 20 year-olds too.

Many of the women in the Ages project have mentioned how they have sought to cast off what is expected and to stick two fingers up at how they are supposed to be and to start again. They are growing into their bodies, being their bodies, being their scars, their arms, legs, fat, skin and bones.

Having people join the project, taking their photographs and reading their stories, is a huge privilege for me. I have met wonderful people and I feel deeply humbled and grateful for the time and thought they have put into it. It's not been an easy process for most of the participants, and that includes me. It is very exposing to write about oneself and to pose dressed and even more so naked. And, it is yet another challenge to have that information made public. However, one thing that is obvious to me is that facing challenges, such as accepting how we look, and overcoming them, is deeply satisfying. Without exception, the participants have said that they feel really positive about the experience—it's been good fun as well as challenging.

Clearly to be able to take part, the participants all have to have reached a point in their lives where they are ready to accept who they are. Or, they are ready to move further along on that journey of self-acceptance. It was harder to be among the first few people in the project as we were just one of two, then three, then four. Now we are one among 19, and soon we'll be one of 30 or more. Our individuality, our uniqueness, will be retained. And our normality as examples of what people just happen to be like, whatever age they happen to be, will be increasingly apparent.

And, it's not for everyone—although I would encourage everyone to find a way to stand naked under the sun from time to time. There is something deeply liberating about being naked, especially outside. Quite apart from the wonderful feel of the air and sun on one's skin, simply being naked, being seen and saying 'this is me—I am not that different from you.'

SECTION THREE
GLORIOUS COMPLICATIONS

Choosing to Live Apart—
How does that shimmy down as we get older?

By Rose Rouse

We were old when we met. Asanga—Pete, Albert variously—was almost 70 and I was almost 60. And we lived five hours apart by car. Holy non-matrimony, that's quite a trip. From West London to North Wales. And now I'm 70 and he's 80—we're still doing it. And relishing the difference.

Honestly, it was a nightmare to step into this relationship. At least for me. I can't speak for Asanga but I'd been on my own for 17 years (apart from various mad, bad and dangerous carry-ons with unavailable men—from the drunken difficult psychotherapist to the charismatic alcoholic /would-be property developer, more likely to be found eating the carpet, let's call them the classics) whereas he'd been married for 30 years. He was more used to a solid relationship.

Asanga found it difficult to comprehend my anxiety levels. Oh— they were so there. Especially when my family were around. For a woman who never wanted to be married (and still doesn't) and lived her life amid squats, hippies and punks plus has never really been employed; I became incredibly conformist when it came to this relationship. I was constantly anticipating disaster of an erotic or embarrassing kind. And to give him his disaster credentials, Asanga did live up to my expectations. I won't go into all the details. But there was the time that he managed to use the bidet—no one actually used it, it was a throwback from 1970s new housing aspirations—and break it in my mother's Yorkshire abode. I was beyond mortified.

And I absolutely hated that he didn't know, understand or seem particularly interested in my vivid personal history or vast web of friends—my lumbering baggage. And equally, I abhorred having to get to know him. There was so much of it—on both sides. I'd always wanted to connect to someone who understood my roots and all their little rootlings. That was a part of that woodland, my particular wood.

However—thank heavens—I did love being transported to heavenly North Wales. I'd drive (and still do) my mother's golden Fabia down his track and wonder at this little piece of earthly paradise full of oak and ash nestled behind Pentrefelin. I still do. Something happens to me as I arrive—a dropping down. Well—it does now. In previous years, we'd have a fight as soon as I got there. To bridge the gap and then we'd have to find a route through. We practised a lot of vulnerability-revealing in those days. It was hard work but good practice, ultimately. We discovered alleys through conflict.

There is so much to negotiate when you live together and yet apart. And there is so much richness too. I love being alone and with someone. It suits my psyche especially now that I'm 70. I don't want to be with another person all the time. But I relish the web that holds me in the relationship. There is such freedom here for me. And for Asanga. We can have the best of both worlds. Well, we can now that we've been doing it for so long.

Phew, we are now familiar with the long bags that we drag behind us. Although we are still learning new aspects of each other through misunderstanding and trying to find understanding. Take not long ago. Here is a small example. Asanga is called Asanga because it's Sanskrit for aloneness and the spiritual healer, Osho or Bhagwan gave it to him. Sannyasins are not big on boundaries because they are so great at being without boundaries which can be wildly exciting and it can make life feel very unsafe for people like me who are insecure. This is a minuscule example. A FB friend of his, an older woman, also an older sannyasin, responded to Asanga's climbing post by commenting 'Great Shape.' It was a comment about his body, his physical shape, she liked it. To me, that was going over a boundary. She knows he's in a relationship and she decided to not care. I wasn't majorly upset, just a little put out. |And of course, that's my stuff.

Asanga and I have had a lot of toing and froing about this kind of issue. Examples more serious than this one but all along a similar line-crossing. Either by him or other women. I've often felt that because he's not insecure in this way, I am being too much. This time—and we have done a lot of personal work on it—I messaged Asanga and wondered if he would act on it. In the past, he would have been defensive and then claim it was absolutely fine. This time, he understood. He messaged her privately in a good way, then she took down the comment. O, the simplicity and calm that I yearn for.

For me, that was a hugely giving action even though it wasn't. That action made me feel so seen. My love for him instantly deepened.

And we're still driving 240 miles to see each other. There is no regularity about it. Sometimes it's every two weeks, often we meet in other places—I love being on neutral terrain with him so that we can relinquish our territorial attachments, especially me. I'm forever clearing his belongings away into the study, mind you, I do live in a small flat—like Ilkley in Yorkshire, Bristol—although next, I am going up to North Wales for a month.

I enjoy the feeling of organic endeavour between us and that it's not regular but is dependable. We trust each other. We're in contact every day, mainly messages on WhatsApp and photos of what we're up to. That's the safety of the web that I feel holding me/us. We don't talk much, maybe once a week. But since our energy wanes in the evening, one of us might cancel. Often me. I just don't feel like talking on the phone when I'm at home alone. Or anywhere else for that matter. And I love that it's okay. Although I appreciate that he'd like to chat more and I will try to do that in the future. There's always an ebbing and flowing.

I appreciate that he's having a good time in North Wales as I am in London. We're interdependent rather than dependent. It's taken me a long time to get to this place. And of course, we're lucky that we've both got homes that we own, and are financially stable independently. Neither of us spends much money. Asanga is frugal, my mother was frugal. And—as long we have occasional splurges on travel and a delicious meal out—I'm content to be careful in this way. Money and how we as humans spend it, and what we feel comfortable about spending is such a hugely fascinating topic. And can be equally troublesome.

And we are both getting older. We're aware of it—we're talking about death and dying. The question came up not so long ago—what will we do if one of us can't drive anymore? The answer is that we'll adapt. If Asanga became unable to drive, I'd be the one who did all the driving, or perhaps I'd move up there for longer periods.

It's good to be prepared and talk but you can't be prepared for everything. Going with the flow is one of those hippie things that we can both do. As a family, we the Rouses, learnt when my mother first got Alzheimer's—she died in 2018—that it's important to be organic in terms of finding solutions. My mum moved in and out of different stages—at first, she could be at home with a little extra help and occasional companions to take her out, Then it came the time for her to have more care and she moved into a residential home where there was a day care centre. The day care centre was so good—mum was ready there and waiting every day, she loved playing games and being sociable. It reminded her of her cruising days. We kept on the paid companions to take her out and about when we weren't there. Neither I nor my sister lived near Ilkley. Eventually, she moved to a nursing home nearer to us. It was an ever-changing scenario where we tried as hard as we could to fulfil her needs as well as see her as much as we could.

Although I hope our experience in our older years is different to that of my mother's (in terms of getting Alzheimer's plus she didn't have many friends), I know one aspect will be the same. We will be organic around what happens to each other. Fortunately, Asanga has a daughter who lives with him—her boyfriend comes to stay—and that is also a boon for me, because I know he has company and support in maintaining his large four-bedroom farmhouse and 14 acres of land. There have been times in the past when I've thought that he's crazy to keep it on, but he's 80 and he's still doing it! And it's gorgeous, so why not? He's happy in his wild land. I'm also very happy about his wild land when I'm there.

I also have a son—who's 37—and he lives in London with his partner. We're very close. I have just become a grandmother, and I'm happy to be nearby. Another reason that Living Apart Together suits me.

I also have to confess that I'm a sucker for anticipation and the ritual of preparation. I'm already thinking about what to take to Wales when I go very soon. I'll be working there this time—I did that in lockdown too—and Asanga has cleared out his office (formerly a dumping ground for every discarded item) for me. I am touched.

What will the future bring? We've really no idea. But I have confidence that we'll roll with it. And that there'll be complications and we'll roll with those too.

Lotus, Nun, Mysterious—
some brief notes, at 51, of a *Hetaera* woman

By Monique Roffey

Years ago, while in psychoanalysis, and, luckily, fairly early on in this five year period of my life, my shrink suggested, quite casually, that I might be what he termed a 'hetaera' woman. I blinked at him. I'd never heard the word before. He directed me to a little known, but seminal paper written in 1951 by Toni Wolff, Carl Jung's lover, long-term collaborator, his 'mystical sister,' ex-analysand and fellow analyst. Wolff was a great analyst too, in her own right, and she analysed Jung during his famous creative breakdown/breakthrough and the production of his most famous piece of work, the Red Book.

Hetaera was a type, or archetype Wolff herself identified with. It is the word for 'companion' in Greek and refers to a kind of educated courtesan found in ancient Greek society, an archetype directly opposite to mother in Wolff's reckoning. In Greek antiquity, women who were mothers remained indoors, with little freedom to go about in public life, let alone the world of politics. The hetaerae, by contrast, mostly slave girls given an education, were allowed to attend the symposium and be part of things; some, such as Aspasia, the companion of Pericles, were even influential. The hetaera was free, and yet, yes, she was expected to offer sexual favours; she was a kind of man-made female companion, friend/sexual partner who enjoyed some freedom, who had been given it by men, and who, depending on luck and how she played her cards, could even fare well.

Soon after this comment from my shrink, I found as much information as I could about Wolff's little known paper, *Structural Forms of the Feminine Psyche*, which identified four basic female archetypes: mother, hetaera, amazon and medial woman (a woman who

63

can commune with the spirits). I found an examination of the paper in a book called *Four Eternal Women*, by Mary Dian Molton and Lucy Anne Sikes, a book I highly recommend. To begin with, I didn't even bother reading about the other three types because they were so well known to me; all I wanted and needed was to read about this hetaera woman, who was she? And was she me? If so, was the news bad? If not bad news, what was the low down, what *was* the news? I read on. Looking back, it was probably the first time I had a sure feeling of being known and 'got,' sync-ed in, understood, by another person, another woman too. High Five. Thank you Toni Wolff.

Her overall definition of hetaera sounded like a definition of me and many of my friends, of herself too, a woman who had a deep conviction about her own creative needs and ambitions, her life's work, her own sacred space, her growth, personal development, her time to think, make work and to be in the world and, to in some way, to contribute. Wolff's examination of the hetaera was written in between the first two major waves of Western feminism. Mostly, it was this: the hetaera was a woman for whom marriage meant certain death. I understood this, implicitly. For many years I had a recurring dream of being walked up the aisle of some stain glass-windowed old church, only, once reaching the altar, to faint or scream or bolt away, veil trailing.

Death. The death of me and my dreams of being the thing I most wanted to be. To write, and to read, and to be left alone to do as I pleased. I like men, but none of that *other thing*, the marriage thing. None of that; not for me. Even now, age 51, I can feel breathless and suffocated by the idea of a lifetime of monogamous sex. *Dear God*, what a hellish idea, what a huge price to pay for one's very dear life. In the Greek myth of Eros and Psyche, Psyche is also to be married to Death, a great joke, and this part of the myth also echoes my life long fears. Except in that myth Eros pricks himself with his own arrow, falls in love with Psyche and later, Psyche falls in love with him, though she is not allowed to 'look at' i.e., know him, she is set impossible tasks, which she completes, and they have a huge and happy wedding. The moral learning of the Eros and Psyche story is that Psyche, learns to commit to erotic love and to mature within marriage; in short, she learns the great art of compromise, she softens in motherhood and she succumbs to Eros, who plays the role of master in her life.

Fuck that.

Dear men reading this, this story of Eros and Psyche is embedded in your collective unconscious too. Many of you yearn to meet Psyche and to have her commit and surrender and soften to you as master. Eros and Psyche is THE great heterosexual love story handed down to us from antiquity. It's a sexy story too, however, the myth has no 'after the wedding' part, the part where poor Psyche, once wed, gets to spend the rest of her life indoors, minding babies, while Eros, the lover, is out all day and night, being a hero and a God and having a God's good life. Poor Psyche, there simply isn't an 'after the wedding' part of the myth. Death, you could say, finally, wins.

So, fast forward a few thousand years; along comes 20th century feminism. Equal rights, and all that; women get to go to The University, and well, Psyche gets an education, Psyche now wants to do a PhD in neuroscience, write poetry, fly to the moon, drive cars, and God forbid, take part in the life outside the home.

Actually, yes, the Gods did forbid it.

Married women were for the home and the home alone, that is except for those called hetaera, the ones given an education, by men. It took 20th Century feminism to liberate the modern hetaera type, and many of these hetaera also married, is my thinking, and had children; some fared well within marriage, some struggled. The 'have it all' woman: job, babies and marriage are stories that are rare but do exist, I know a handful of these women. Good for them. Marriage? For me, the idea of *hieros gamos*, the sacred marriage written about in many myths, or, the notion Plato wrote about, that we are creatures split in half, forever doomed to search for our other half, is questionable. Life isn't about finding an outer soulmate; rather, it is about loving and nurturing the sacred marriage of the masculine and feminine principal within.

You see, for me, being hetaera has been a primary ego choice, my truthful motivation of how to live and be. It is the direct opposite ego choice of mother; in fact, mother and hetaera is a dynamic pair of opposites. They are both strong ego preferences and there is a strong tension between us, as I have experienced, many times, and still do, when I walk into a room full of women who are mothers. I set them off, sometimes, and they can make me feel awkward, too. I like children, and find them original, but caring for one, for what—15 years—would have been disastrous. I am a woman who has killed a cactus. I have given away much-loved hand-reared cats. I have abandoned men in one country, to follow my work in another, only to fall for a man in that country and then leave him behind too, to follow more work. My work has always come first.

While I am capable of loyalty, compassion and good friendship, marriage would have stifled me and my children might have ended up applying for someone else, another mother. I wouldn't have been 'the right sort'. My children might have liked me but needed more help.

A modern day, 21st Century hetaera woman, such as myself, has evolved from the ancient lineage, from these hetaerae of old, who were then, given an education by men, and for men alone, however, we are women who flourished in modern times, thanks to feminism. We are women who prefer our freedom over the bond of marriage, women for whom having children is not a priority.

When Toni Wolff died in 1953, Jung was distraught; his life-long partner, creative collaborator and mystical sister had gone. In a garden, he left a small stone memorial for her with the words 'Toni Wolff, Lotus, Nun, Mysterious' written vertically in Chinese letters; these were his words for her. They are good words, too. Since my archetypal discovery and self-naming, I have thought about Wolff a lot, and Jung's names for her. I would love to write more about Wolff because there is surprisingly little written about her even though she was such an important figure in the history of psychoanalysis, and in such an important man's life. My guess is her family has guarded her estate and her letters very closely. To date, there is no biography of Toni Wolff, and there should be. Suspicious, no?

When I received this valuable tip from my shrink, I had been 'releasing' information about the ups and downs of my affairs of the heart. I had been dating a well-known sex worker, and he was a queer, polyamorous man, an anarchist, a Scorpio, and a professional lover man. It had been tough going, (it was my first experience of trying polyamory) and yet it had been a love bond and a friendship too and I had known, unconsciously, that I had picked this man to help me grow. I had wanted to be like him, you see, somewhere, dimly, a lover and a person who could love openly more than one person. I wanted a role model and a mate. I hadn't picked and pursued this man for babies and marriage, that was for sure. This is a common trait of hetaera women, picking partners (male and female) to help them fulfil their potential. Finding out about this hetaera archetype helped me to understand my own past patterns when it came to relationships and what motivations lay behind my significant relationships. At 46, (then), I'd remained happily unmarried; free to be myself in the world. I had avoided the dicey subject of children, and, I had chosen men who had helped me, in Jungian terms, individuate.

My six-year relationship, in my 30s, with a fellow writer was a passionate love affair and also a creative collaboration. We were both writers and ran a writing centre together and our time was full of books, learning and helping each other write. It was much more, but, hey, there's a memoir out there with all those details, so I won't elaborate. My four-year on/off, lover/friend/lover relationship with a sex worker in my 40s, was similar in that it brought two enquiring seekers together. Both these relationships had been about thinking and living and being in a creative, ongoing dialogue about work and not about kids, and when/if we were going to get married.

The hetaera woman makes a good long-term creative collaborator with a man and or another woman, or even a good short-term dynamic relationship. The hetaera is a good lover and co-creator; she is an intellectual and she is creative and she seeks dynamic relationships in which Eros, the lover, is also an intellectual friend, not a master of any kind, a relationship in which she and Eros are equals.

So, when my shrink made this comment about me and my type, I nodded, I did some research and never really looked back. An actual *bone fide* type for the woman that I feel I am, had always been; there is even a lineage, a long one, in the creative arts and sciences, too, for women like me, stretching back to antiquity.

Here are a few examples of other hetaera women: Mary Magdalene (Christ's companion, of course, but not wife), Aphrodite (as opposed to the virginal ingénue Psyche), Calypso, Cleopatra, Sappho, Circe, Delilah, Innana, Lilith (the insubordinate who refused to lay down under Adam and was banished to the desert) and more recently, of course, women like Madame Curie, Georgia O' Keefe, Yoko Ono, Anaïs Nin, Freda Kahlo and Simone de Beauvoir and many, many more… all hetaera women.

In a rapidly changing, modern world where people are trying (rightly) to self-identify and explain themselves, I had already found a list I was happy with: tantrika, sex positive, kinkster, bi-curious, hetero-flexible, etc. But this new name hetaera felt like the one that landed best. I even had a chain of women to look back at, and yes they all checked in as friendly towards my past and current way of life; all of them felt like sisters-in-arms. Most of these women were single; they hadn't been mothers or felt drawn to mothering. For them, mothering wasn't a priority. So, with one casual suggestion from a man, (and yes, I get it, a man?), I came to look on as a guide and a person of immense compassion and wisdom, one word, and *clunk-click*, I'd found my status amongst my fellow womankind, my true archetypal identity in this crazy, busy, over-informed and under-educated contemporary world we live in.

However, there are shadow associations, too, for the hetaera woman, of course there would be. Of course, we also get a bad rap.

1. Selfishness/narcissism. Oh yes, I've had this levelled at me many times, mostly by my own mother, 'You never had children, you're selfish.' Ah, well, there's as essay here in this alone. As I mentioned, it has been a strong silent motivation, for me, to *live the life I have lived*, sans the bonds of marriage. I never declared anything outright; it was more like an instinctive dodge. Do we call men who pursue their vocational dreams selfish or narcissistic? No. But for men marriage is a bonus; they gain something, lose nothing; it is a status symbol to have a wife, a family. For women, we lose the freedom we once had; we go under, for years, into motherhood. Is it a selfish thing to protect the self? If so, then yes, I am selfish. And as for narcissism, well, all creative people have that element to their core *modus operandi*, that's how we make our books, art, music; it comes from a strong need to make a mark. Often it is narcissistic rage, sometimes it is just a strong need to create. Yes, we creatives tend to be the narcs; we are the ones who say 'me no fuck give' and drive empaths mad with despair at our lack of concern for them; and yet all empaths want to sleep with us, make us better, heal us. It's a bittersweet this thing called erotic attraction, but hey, that's another essay too.

So, to my mother, who has never been able to understand me, I say, 'Okay, yes, I am selfish and narcissistic.' AND, I have never once hurt or offended women who are mothers. I respect mothers, deeply, and ask only to find my place amongst them.

2. The hetaera is man-obsessed. We live life for our relationships with men. Toni Wolff was Jung's helpmate, collaborator and colleague; more than anything, she wanted to make work together with him. This meeting of minds that they shared also ignited Eros; it was a deep love they had, a clear and honest respect charged with sexual attraction. I'm wondering if this describes the love I have always yearned for too and even enjoyed more than once. Is this, then, man-obsessed? To want to cultivate this kind of bond? Respect + Eros, to me, feels like a very healthy and dynamic combination.

3. The hetaera is bad with other women, mostly women who are mothers. I reject this. This is a patriarchal critique. Men like to think we women are cat-like creatures and spend our loves plotting each other's downfall and competing over men. But leave all us women alone and we find our own way towards each other. Yes, that is key: red tents, women's groups, even Suzanne Noble's hot tub evenings, these are powerful places of female love, bonding and cross-connecting and they have existed since the dawn of time and, yeah, leave us alone together and there is nothing more powerful than a bunch of women hanging out, without men. It is a vibrant space and any woman who has enjoyed this space understands what I mean. A hetaera woman, such as myself, - an unmarried, childfree, creative, a hopeless narc and a lone wolf? I have often felt so very happy to be amongst my sisters in these times, married women and mothers. There, I have felt accepted too, for all I have achieved and for all that I never have achieved, which is fine re children.

And here, a note. I have never slept with another woman's man or a married man, a high point of principal. This feels like a serious moral crime; I have a deep allegiance to the sisterhood and consider it the lowest of the low to steal another woman's man, no matter how unhappy he is or they are together. And besides, like Khalo, many hetaera women are bi-sexual and have a love of women, so 'no' to this third shadow area.

4.   The hetaera doesn't have her own career; instead she dedicates her life to supporting a man's career, often a famous man. This could well have been true prior to the 20th Century feminist movement, when it would have been hard, if not impossible for women to find their way into education. This is an old critique, pre the women's movement. End of.

5.   The hetaera woman is a prostitute. Ah, women of the light! Sex workers, yes, I am of their lineage, make no mistake about that; I am of their type, I am their offspring, come down from Adam's first wife, Lilith, banished to the desert for being insubordinate, yes, that's me. I'm of that line of womanhood. Mind you, Eve, Adam's second wife, (taken from Adam's rib, urgh) didn't make much of a good wife either, did she? What with causing the actual 'fall of mankind' with that apple and eating from the tree of life. So Lilith and Eve, no matter which type a woman identifies with, the wife or the banished harlot, eventually we are all aligned with man's downfall; we are sisters of sorts. One type is just a lot worse than the other. Lilith, the first model had waaay too much sexual agency, and Eve, well, she also had a mind of her own. Bad us. Few woman, mother or hetaera, get through life without being reprimanded for our sexuality, or called a slut.

6.   The hetaera is a spinster. Being unmarried, we have a lack of status in the mainstream world. We have, in some way, been left on the shelf, not been picked. We have gone unfulfilled, i.e. we have not been filled, (oh the receptive vessels that we are), by a man's sperm/bank account/status etc. One of the happiest results of my hetaera lifestyle has been that, over time, I have created and shaped my own status: writer. It has taken a long time, and often I walk into a room alone, without a man on whose arm I hang; it's just me. I go with my own life/world/ways and I do not feel in any way a less significant woman to my married female friends. I am not, in any way at a 'loose end'; rather I go home when I like and with whom I like.

So here I am, age 51, gently ageing and living a life full of good friends and good work. My future plans include more writing and more books, and also more mentoring of emerging writers, probably and especially women. I will hang with the Buddhists and the yogis, and hopefully get to northern India and Nepal some time soon. My feeling is that 20th Century feminism, amongst many other benefits, has made it easy for the hetaera to flourish in the world and gain acceptance, carve out our lives. I am not at all alone in this hetaera thing either; I have met a lot of others and spy them everywhere, especially in my creative writing classes, for all women who want to write have the same drive towards freedom.

In the near future I will also see my own mother die, come to terms with her death and also the end of the chain, for I have no daughter. The great actual lineage of women I am born from, Yvette, my mother, Maman, Laure Garrana, my grandmother, Irma Mifsud, or Nona, my great grandmother, are awesome women. They all married and they all had daughters and I am the end of the line, a hetaera. And my books will outlive me; they have been my creative progeny. And, maybe, in the future, I will make a trip to Vienna and find the garden in which the great Carl Jung erected the memorial to my other mother, my creative mother and mentor, role model, Toni Wolff, the woman who showed me who I am. And maybe, just maybe, I will find a way to talk to the Wolff family, persuade them I'm the right person to write her biography. And I will call it Lotus, Nun, Mysterious.

How to Live a Rich Life Alone

By Becca Leathlen

I've been pondering this question lately, prompted by a number of posts about single life on the Advantages of Age group.

I was particularly struck by the post on Bella DePaulo's book, *Singled Out—How Singles are Stereotyped, Stigmatised and Ignored, and Still Live Happily Ever After.* Also, the topic was already on my mind because last year I started writing a memoir. It's about a life lived alone, almost entirely without a family or a partner.

Growing up, my father lived on the other side of the world and my lovely mother (5 ft-nothing, bright and resourceful) was often absent, by virtue of being severely mentally ill. Running wild at 10 years old, I was sent to boarding school. When I was 15, my mother began an unprecedented 22 years in care. But that's another story.

At boarding school, friends' parents generously invited me to spend the school holidays with them. When I left school after my 'A' Levels, I spent the summer living with my gang in a Ladbroke Grove squat, then took myself off to a new life at Goldsmiths' College on the 36 bus.

I did manage a couple of relationships at university—weirdly opting for guys who turned out to have mental health problems. I had a number of short relationships throughout my 20s and early 30s. I had my heart broken twice (usual pattern was to fall head over heels for someone who didn't feel the same way about me and grieve over the break-up for years after). Then, apart from what a friend memorably called my long term 'non-relationship,' I just called it a day.

My father died when I was 24, my mum when I was 37. I don't have any siblings. I don't have children of my own, and I've never lived with a partner. I'm rarely in touch with my cousins. I guess in family terms, I'm about as alone as they come.

One good consequence of going to boarding school is that I made a handful of friends for life. I've known my best friend since I was 12—and I'm fortunate to have other close friends (from that era and later) who feel like family.

I've never really missed having a family of my own, but I've always felt the need to connect. I started out as a journalist—I loved interviewing people and telling their stories. I moved into documentary filmmaking—always focusing on those who are usually ignored. In 2000, at the age of 38, I toured the Southern States of America with an advance to write a book about the death penalty. At 39, I did an MSc in Criminology & Criminal Justice at Oxford University. I stayed in Oxford and worked in Restorative Justice until 2005. Then, after failing to get work when I returned to London, I opened a shop selling Spanish arts, crafts and eventually tiles, which I distributed worldwide. In 2018, I closed the business, rented out my house and came to live in Spain, where I've owned an old 'cortijo' (cottage) since 1997.

Where others have had structure, I guess I've had freedom.

I did feel lonely while I was running the business. Working alone and living alone was a double-whammy, especially with the pressures of the company. I made friends through it but was often too tired to socialise.

Life as an older single woman in rural Spain can be a bit challenging too. The majority of English-speakers are retired couples—'Barbara and Brian,' 'Martin and Jane,' 'Judith and Bob.' You rarely hear a woman's name spoken on its own. If you do, she'll be a divorcee or a widow—I don't know any older woman here without children and grandchildren. Spanish society is even more family-focused. And to the Moroccans, you are not even a woman unless you're a mother!

I've never felt overt prejudice, indeed I have friends and acquaintances in each of these groups—I just get left out of things. With some honourable exceptions, it does seem that couples socialise exclusively with other couples, plus the occasional single man or woman who was married once.

You could get very lonely—and I certainly hated the feeling of being left out, to the extent of being relieved when the first lockdown started, so I couldn't be. But I've never felt that not having a family (or job) means I have less value as a human being. And, as single people form a surprisingly large proportion of most Western societies, it's surely time for us to be taken seriously, and for the discrimination to stop!

So, in the absence of a family, what does give my life meaning?

Firstly, connecting with diverse groups. I've always made friends with all sorts of people. I've travelled on my own since I was in my 30s and I cherish the connections I've been able to make with people all over the world. It works on a small scale, too. Recently, my day was completely rescued when I managed a friendly chat in Spanish with the local chemist followed by another with my Moroccan neighbours on the way home. Recently, in the absence of workmates, I've been connecting online. I take part in online 'Cave Days'—joining other freelancers (mostly in the USA) to work together on Zoom. And luckily, I do have some good friends locally—mainly older single guys, younger single women (English, German and Spanish) and the above-mentioned honourable couples with whom I share mutual interests. Phew!

Secondly, music. I've always been passionate about roots reggae. During the first lockdown I made a Spotify reggae compilation for my UK friends. It went down well, so I developed it into an on-going series of YouTube 'world reggae' compilations—the Lubrin Dub Club. I love researching new music to put on the playlists, and dream of finding a way to take this further.

Thirdly, nature. I go on fantastic walks, often by myself. A few weeks ago, I noticed a little path behind the mountain spring where I get my water and decided to follow it. It led to two beautiful fields with almond and olive trees, behind which were more fields and mountains. I made my way up through the fields, to see if there was another path into the mountains. After wading through the last field of freshly ploughed earth, I was rewarded with a tiny track leading up between two hills. I followed it until it was nothing more than the suggestion of itself, before it picked up again, leading down to the main track and a fantastic view of the sea. I have to admit I've rarely felt happier; in the warm February sun, miles from anywhere with just a few little wheatears flying around, wondering who the last person to walk there had been, lost in my thoughts. It was the best meditation.

These three things make my heart sing. But also important are the projects:

Writing

I've just finished developing and teaching an online Creative Writing course which was a success. It's morphed into a fabulous little writers' group, and now I'm back to my own writing—a blog, a memoir and shorter pieces—stories, and essays like this one. Memoir-writing has had unforeseen results: I've reconnected with old friends, one of whom introduced me to the Advantages of Age Group! Ironically, I've also found a Chinese 'step' family in the UK. My father's life-partner was Chinese and writing about them has led me to her nieces and nephews who I knew as a child. It's been exciting!

Learning Spanish

Using NotesinSpanish.com and language 'intercambios' with Spanish friends, I'm hoping to reach a level where I can interact more meaningfully with the Spanish population.

House & Garden Projects

I aim at a job a day. I like the way that small actions can lead to big results.

Volunteering and Helping Others

Before lockdown, I was teaching basic Spanish to Moroccan women in the village. I may be befriending an asylum seeker in London for a daily phone chat soon, and perhaps volunteering in Spain again when my Spanish is good enough.

Last but not least, there are always **surprises** to look forward to.

Reconnecting with my Chinese 'step' family was one surprise. Here are two more:

In 2016, I won a holiday to Jamaica!

And in 2019, a guy came to stay as a Workaway volunteer. After an uncertain start, we got on really well and it was lovely to have someone to bring in the wood, set the fire, get on with the DIY and share the food I made in return. I enjoyed the company, and missed him when he had to go. I don't think we would have made a successful couple, but never say never!

A friend recently introduced me to a new concept, the 'Security of Insecurity.' She said you can never relax when things are 'perfect' because you can be sure they won't stay that way. When your life is more fluid, you know that anything can happen. Perhaps you're more prepared for change. Surprises (and they do seem more plentiful of late) can be great, and they certainly keep me interested in life.

Note—Becca has now moved to London and has become a reggae DJ as part of the Vinyl Sisters as well as a broadcaster.

The Ghosts in the Attic

By Michele Kirsch

Dear Paul,

So we are selling up and have to clear all your stuff from the attic. The boys brought it down from the attic to what used to be Kitty's room. Kitty said, 'Mum, it's like tons of stuff, not all of it Paul's, but literally, it's tons.'

'Do you mean literally in the non-literal sense, as our friend used to tell us she was 'literally bathing in sweat' and it made us laugh and grossed us out at the same time? Or do you mean literally as in truly?' It's a fair question. We are a family of talkers and exaggerators. She tells me wait and see.

So I go to the house to open my daughter's old room and the door is just blocked with wall-to-wall boxes, there is not even a little passageway like you see in those programmes about people with OCD. It's like Charlie Chaplin opening the door to a wall of snow, after a snowstorm. A sea of boxes, each one overstuffed with things from your living life, with your wife, and before your wife. The forecast calls for storms. I feel strangely seasick.

I try to pull out one of the middle boxes, like giant Jenga, and manage to not drop the ones on top, which plonk down on the bottom ones with a heavy thud. I remember when you lived on the top floor as the same block of flats where we lived, when I was pregnant with Kitty, and climbing all these stairs, puffed out with my heavy pregnancy, walking slowly and heavily like an elephant in platform shoes. I called though your letterbox, 'Paul, let me in, I need to pee...' But you were asleep, or not there. You are not here now, not ever. And yet you are everywhere, in these fucking boxes, hundreds of 'em.

I manage to carve out a Michele-sized passageway, opening some of the dusty boxes with bits poking through them. A tripod. A shitload of band flyers for your various bands. Boxfuls of faded Christmas tree decorations and Halloween stuff: your wife was a big fan of both. Big box of home bar equipment. You had beautiful cocktail glasses. Oh God, those cocktails. No, I mustn't. Just for today I am not going to drink. I have to say this every day, to not drink. But those home bars. We did love them. First Eddie got a bar. Then we got one, which proved to be my undoing, our little oval lit up monster maker in the corner, soon to be my favourite toy, a drunk's version of a Wendy House. You had a bar corner and a beautiful black and grey ice bucket. I don't remember the bar, if you had one. If nothing was clean, we'd drink out of Arsenal coffee mugs anyway. Your father said, at your funeral, that you didn't believe in God, you believed in Arsenal. That got a laugh, the sad funereal forced laugh you do when you want to cry.

More stuff. A guitar stand which topples onto my left shoulder. Boxes and boxes of damp ruined red velvet. A strobe light. A vintage effects pedal. Hundreds of unsold CD singles of your band. Bettie Page posters and magazines. A Velvet Underground fanzine I loaned you but you never returned, Now, you are really never returning, which puts the magazine thing in perspective. A box filled with the most awful clothes that are meant to be yours, including your strange Japanese 17 year-old tourist with I Love Kitty everything (not my Kitty, the other Kitty) Camden market style punk clothing. Irony or just plain bad dress sense? You kept me guessing. You and your big girly fun fur coats. The campiest straight guy I knew.

I remember the job lots you used to buy from the BBC costume department, because you'll never know when you need 30 size six dresses in a checked Dolly Parton style, for a Benny Hill episode with a big country Western dance scene at the end. 'The whole lot for a tenner,' you bragged at the time, in your miniscule flat, now filled with dresses no one could wear. I tried one on, and it fitted beautifully. But I didn't want 30 of them. That was 30 years ago, '87, I think. We stayed up all night on speed, playing the same Television album over and over, trying to decide if Tom Verlaine's nasal vocals added or detracted from his guitar playing. We played Glory 50 times at least, just for the opening riff. That was the sort of stuff we'd do not even on speed. Just to make sure we weren't missing anything.

I sniff everything, like a dog, anxious to find something, anything, that faintly smells of you, that strange mixture of sweat, vintage clothing and whatever it was you put in your hair to quiff it up, when you had enough hair to quiff up. But everything smells of dust and damp and shaved wood and rotting cardboard. Those pink and black hounds tooth trousers, price tag still on (20 quid)—something a born-again Christian would wear, with a polo neck and polyester leisure jacket, in the early '60s, on the cover of a knitting pattern magazine, you wally. I am looking for a trace of you, not just your stuff, a trace of the friendship that partially defined me for over 20 years, my best friend, and I think I was your best friend, (you were so loved by so many, I must not be the only one to claim you for BF status) the one who stayed up with you watching a documentary about the Jonestown Massacre on Christmas day, when everyone had gone to sleep, stuffed and drunk, we watched them drink the Kool Aid and become bloated bodies in the forest. It seemed Christmasy to us.

The very thing that defined me and made me feel OK, you, your absence became the new thing that defined me. When you died in 2010, the only thing I knew how to do was be sadder than anyone else, I even had to out-sad your devastated wife and parents. I did this by becoming a raging alcoholic and pill head and walking out on my family, to live in a small room and drink, and think about you. Now, I am somewhat reconciled with the family I so selfishly left, not enough to live there, but enough to be nice and fair. And here I am, wading through boxes of the life you lived so outrageously, so passionately with your wife, with your music, with your strange obsessions with Jimmy Swaggart and other telly evangelists, your nerdiness about Mac computers, even your taped answerphone messages.

You were a curator before everyone became one. I choke as I hear my own, younger voice on your answerphone tape, sounding all warped and watery, the cassettes not swimming well in the attic damp storm. 'Hey Paul, it's Kirschy, are you coming to the Mean Fiddler with me or not, or shall we just meet at the Killer after the gig?' The Killer was our local pub, on average a police incident or at least a glassing a couple of times a week. A girl drunkenly calling your phone, while dancing on a table at your own gig.

'Paul, I'm dancing on the table, at your gig, and ringing you at home. How mad is that?' Then an interview tape, something for your work (the day job—a journalist) with a guy saying the biggest spend of social security will be residential care of the elderly and things like 'medication reminder systems'—an alert to take your pills. You never got to be elderly. I never forget to take my medication.

I am making good progress. I have four piles. One for charity. One for the junkyard, one for me, one for your wife… your widow. I understand the need for tangible memorabilia, that by touching your stuff it will somehow magically bring you back to me, that that smoky glass and steel coffin going behind the curtain never happened, that I didn't get trashed at your funeral and fall down in the disabled toilets, trying to hoist myself up by the emergency cord. But it's all an illusion.

It's just a bunch of stuff sitting in green recycling bags or boxes marked 'Soothing lemon and ginger tea.' Out of date technology that was new, once. Strange, global-shaped Macs and tellys. Stuff that might not work again. When you died, I thought I would not function again. For two years I made myself redundant, a skeleton with a bellyful of vodka and pills, wanting the next best thing to being where you were, which was oblivion.

How dreadful it was to embrace the dead when I had living, loving children and a confused and sad husband who could not understand why I made this crazy choice. I guess at the time, it felt like the choice made me. You know where you are with the dead. The living are a constant unknown, for living people are always undergoing a process, changing. Meanwhile, your stuff gathers damp and dust in the attic. I keep opening things up, clearing things away.

My daughter works from home, the clicking of her keyboards in the other room a strange comfort. There was a time, in my madness, I probably would not have been welcome in the house alone with her. Now we break for tea and biscuits. I do the washing up, just like a normal mum visiting her daughter. I have a fleeting thrill of feeling, well, normal. Looking out at the window at the still intact family next door, two kids, maybe three? The nervy but always on-call for babysitting grandmother, going outside for fag breaks as the kids knock a football around. A kitchen extension in an already enormous house. I ask Kitty, 'When did they build that?' And she tells me ages ago, when I still lived there, as some sort of mother and wife. I can't remember that. I have a hazy memory of the family that lived there before this one. Of people in gigantic houses, their house, the house next door, building, always adding bits, floors, extensions, playrooms, guestrooms. Everybody wants more space. I just want, wanted, more time with you.

Me, I have all this stuff, Paul, your stuff, and no room for it. I finish the washing up and head back upstairs on a caffeine buzz, determined to get the job done.

Then, just like in that Chrissie Hynde song that always makes me well up, I found a picture of you… young, leather jacketed… and my heart leapt into my mouth and I gasped for air. I'm not sure why. I have loads of pictures of you, I just didn't expect to find 'you' here, although you are everywhere… and I am willing myself not to cry, because I've been instructed not to by Mally. I don't how things work in the land of the dead, if you have found each other, but Mally died a few years after you did. Not suddenly like you, but slowly, cancer ravaging his throat and eating him up inside. One day, months before the end, he drove me to work. I didn't know how he could see anything, as his eyes were reduced to slits, his face so swollen from the useless steroids.

He pulled over into a side street and said, 'Look, when I die, don't do that crazy shit you did when Paul died. It's not allowed. Don't fuck things up again, Kirschy, because I will come back to haunt you. Just don't do it.'

And I didn't. But still, here I am, kneeling in the middle of my old front room, sobbing over a picture of you, and then I clock Kitty in the doorway, hands on hips, in a motherly 'What sort of mess do you call this?' sort of way. She says, in a long, exasperated exhale, 'Why are you doing this, again? Why are you…doing this? Don't do this…'

'I'm not doing it, I'm not doing anything,' I lie badly, eyes red-rimmed, a stray tear falling onto the photo.' I stand up quickly and put the picture on a pile. She's rightfully on guard. I did some crazy shit when you died and she's had enough. It's taken ages to get her back on side, just about, so I just need to crack on tidying, and stop crying.

I miss you, but I understand for whatever reason, your number was up. I'm back in my flat now, crammed with a fair bit of your stuff. The strobe light turns my little corner of Hackney into a disco. I can listen to Cosmic Dancer, your funeral music, without crying now.

If you get this, let me know what it's like, where you are. Give me a sign. I'd ask you to look for my dad, for Rita, for Mally, for Lizzy, for Zak, for Josie, for Bowie, for God's sake, he's got to have some dead sightseeing address, but I know there are way more dead people than live ones so it's probably pointless. Right now, just for today, I won't drink, and I will stay in the land of the living.

Love you always,
Michele

After 60 Years, I Found My Cousin
and Auschwitz Survivor

By Eileen Kay

Things can change quickly, even in your 60s and beyond. I was surprised how my looming 60th birthday stood tall, faced me and asked,

'What's the deepest, most heartfelt thing on your Bucket List?'

For me, it was to explore our family mysteries. I grabbed the chance. It was life-changing. The lesson: Seize the Day!

My best, most unexpected birthday gift for my 60th? Eight new cousins, I never knew before—and we actually like each other.

I had wanted to research my Hungarian granddad since I was a small child. I wanted answers to a million questions because my family had a million mysteries. My dad, born in New York, did not want to say a single word about his dad, born in Budapest. The more Dad kept secrets, the more I asked, and the more he said to shut up.

This went on for decades.

A few years ago, when both my parents were dead and gone, there was no one to object. But I was working—I couldn't just pack up and go to Budapest, could I? Actually, I could.

It took some transition time, but I changed all my face-to-face teaching to online teaching. These students don't care where I am, as long as I show up onscreen as agreed.

This allows me to travel.

I travelled to Budapest, to explore The Family Mystery.

I felt bold booking a whole month. I didn't know it would turn into five months, several returns over several years, and eventually establishing residency. My research uncovered far more than I expected. I'd become a genealogy research maniac with a mission to find the real story.

Why the secrecy?

Dad never accepted his parents were from two different religions— his mother Catholic, his father Jewish. He sided with her and wanted to hide him. Our age group is much more open-hearted, by the way.

There was a lot of basic information on the internet, but eventually, I had to follow the trail to Budapest. I am so happy I did. I fell in love with the place.

As for the story, I found so much drama, so many characters, so many ups, downs and surprises, it became the basis of my second published book.

I call my travel memoir series Noodle Trails because although my plans might be straight as an arrow, the actual route looks more like a bowl of noodles.

I was fortunate my ancestry search took me to Budapest, a cool destination in any case, with a groovy international ex-pat world and plenty to eat, drink and see.

I'd encourage readers to consider their own map of 'ancestry tourism.' This idea grabs more people all the time. I can attest, it's a beautiful theme to a trip, wherever your tree leads you.

I was thrilled to see the actual buildings where my family lived, worked, shopped, prayed, got married and where they were buried.

When I saw my great-grandparents' gravestone, with my same name, my whole body shook.

Many of these sites gave me a shiver of excitement, like electricity, head to toe, like the communal DNA was fizzing.

It's a deep experience, to walk near the roots of your tree, or to answer some lifelong question.

Surprises and deep feelings are almost guaranteed.

My most exciting result was meeting real cousins! After WW II, Auschwitz-survivor Andreas Weiss went to live in Vienna, where today he is 91 years old and his family is nearby.

I never knew he existed, until recently.

When I found his 1928 birth record, I could only hope he was still alive.

Next, I found a 1944 document saying he and his parents were sent to the death camp at Auschwitz, so I was upset but did not want to believe it. I kept searching. I wanted proof if he lived or died there, and those Nazis often kept good records.

Soon I found his name on a list of survivors from the camp at Dachau. He survived the war!

I went jumping and dancing all over the room, calling out, 'I have a cousin! He survived the war! One of us got through!' Oh, I cried for joy.

But, was he still alive? If so, where was he? I did not find out for many months. I just kept hunting. The lesson: Keep Going!

I only found him because he left a trail. He wrote some articles, memoirs for a history magazine from his home town Szombatheley.

The magazine helped me contact him and his family. We met. Then we met again and again until we lost count, over the last few years. We plan to meet again, in March 2020. Now it's routine and normal, to meet whenever we can. We're friends now.

Our two branches feuded over a hundred years ago and haven't spoken since, but we just built a bridge.

Leave a trail, build a bridge, find new friends—not bad advice.

Even if you don't find living cousins or a great saga, you'll find history, connections and gossip. I wholeheartedly recommend 'ancestry tourism.' Go walk where your people walked before you. And if you can, eat accordingly.

Letting Go of 40 Years' Worth of Memories

By Clare Cooper

Over the past couple of years, I have had to share—with my partner, sister and other family members—the grim and heart-breaking task of clearing our parents' house, selling it and saying goodbye to well over 40 years of memories. My father bought it as a plot of land, so it has only ever had our family living in it—until last summer.

Dismantling my parents' lives and all that they had built up together over so many years has caused me actual physical pain. Despite never having lived in the house, I felt our family's history seeping from every wall. I was incredibly protective towards it; particularly after my mother had to go into a care home, and the house was standing empty for most of the week. I hated having to leave it every time we stayed there. It felt as though I was abandoning it, and my parents with it (although my dad died 23 years ago), and I would often cry for most of the two-hour journey home. My only consolation is that our buyers are a young couple, keen to put down roots and, most likely (I'm guessing), want to start a family. The place needs another family and all the new life that brings. The last few years have been undeniably sad and tough for us all.

I cried, too, when I saw the skip on the drive for the first time. We had to hire three altogether. It took two solid weekends to clear the garage, shed, loft and airing cupboard alone, never mind any of the actual rooms. When I hired someone to help clear the house of the larger items of furniture in the final week, he had just the one day free that week. He said he had been manically busy, as had all house clearance/van hire people, because of the stamp duty holiday and easing of lockdown rules. This was also the reason why so many of the charities we tried couldn't take our things. They were overrun with surplus items. The world and his wife, it seemed, had been having massive clear outs during lockdown I cried some more when I saw the boxes and boxes of brand-new, never-been-taken-from-their-wrappers Christmas decorations.

Mum had obviously bought them (when?), then someone (who?) had put them away in the loft for her. She must have forgotten about them. But she was clearly ordering for a big family Christmas—the kind we used to have, when our grandparents and other family members came to stay, and when friends and neighbours dropped by. I gave some away to the kind next-door neighbours who had been keeping an eye on the place for us when we weren't there and also to our lovely gardener who was a huge help to us in so many ways. It broke my heart to see them all. She must have spent a small fortune on them; no doubt from one of the many colourful catalogues that dropped through the letterbox on an almost daily basis; her link to the outside world (she couldn't manage a computer, or even a mobile phone, for which, with all the clever scams about, I was heartily thankful). I suspect half the attraction for her was being able to speak to someone on the other end of the line. I hope they understood this and were patient with her.

We tried putting the bigger and better items from the house at the top of the drive for people to take (again, a lot of them were unused and still in their original packaging) and some of them went very quickly. The rest had to go back on the skip, or to charity. My sister's friend helpfully put ads on a local 'free' website and we managed to pass on a lovely big armchair and matching footstool that way. (We all liked it, but none of us had room in our respective homes for it.) The woman who came to pick it up had had a stroke and was walking with a stick. She was very grateful for the chair, and for a couple of other useful items she rescued from the skip.

Someone else came by and asked if we had any houseplants. As it happened, we had 10, all bought by me in an attempt to make the place look lived-in, and I was planning on bringing them all back home with me, then decided I could probably live without most of them, so he walked away with six plants for his wife. He told me he had been living in South Africa for 12 years but decided to return home for his children's sake. He wanted a better education and life for them and it was getting very dangerous out there, he said.

Another man came in to see what bits and pieces of crockery were going begging, saying he was getting them for his daughter, who he and his wife were now living with. Their son had been killed in a road accident on the nearby bypass just a year before and it had made them look at things in a different light. They were living in a seven-bedroom house at the time, with four cars on the drive. He said he had had 47 pairs of jeans and about a hundred Ralph Lauren shirts! After letting the family take what they wanted, he and his wife walked out of the house with just one bag of belongings each—and that was it. He looked so sad as he was telling me all this, I really wanted to hug him, but couldn't (Covid).

Being an avid reader myself, I looked more closely at the books that summed up my parents' lives. Typical of their generation, there was no internet and Google, of course, and so the bookshelves were filled with huge, hefty tomes of advice and information on gardening, family health, cookery, the Royal Family, travel (just how many books on France and Italy did we need?!) and sport (mostly rowing, golf and cricket, which were my dad's interests). There were encyclopedias and atlases, bibles galore (and we're most definitely not a religious family), and sensibly, useful books and pamphlets on making a will and what to do when someone dies.

Having come from a wartime background of 'Make do and mend' my parents kept their furniture for decades. There was the 1950s oak sideboard they bought when they were first married. The big, very old family bureau that I'm hoping will stay in the family, though nobody appears to have the room, is temporarily residing in my sister's living room at her small flat. I know my mother wanted it kept in the family. A few more, smaller items of furniture we managed to share between us without any argument. Oh, yes—ahem—there's also the very old oak dining table and chairs my grandparents bought at auction a very, very long time ago. I looked and looked and looked at it over the weeks and months we stayed in the house and finally decided I just couldn't let it go, so I paid quite a bit of money to have it transported from the house to my own house, where it now resides in the already-rammed-full home office at the bottom of the garden, as there is no room for it anywhere else. I used to enjoy dusting and polishing its chubby, curved legs whenever I stayed with my beloved grandparents. There are so many memories of happy family meals around that table. Though who's going to have it after I've gone is anybody's guess. (Maybe I'll have stopped caring by then. I do hope so. It's exhausting and debilitating, carrying around all this emotional baggage.)

However, surprisingly, despite it being very trendy and sought-after in certain quarters, few people were interested in the G-Plan furniture my parents collected from the '60s and '70s. It was in excellent condition, considering its age (unlike the rest of us), but we were paid a fraction of its worth to have it taken away. It had to go. Though I found an old label for how to put one of the items together, and I've kept it, so there. (You see how difficult all this has been for someone like me?!)

There were LPs galore: musicals and big band sounds, James Last, Frank Sinatra, Tom Jones, Andy Williams and Simon and Garfunkel. Plus many more. The musical history of our family.

There were countless letters and cards to wade through, postcards both used and unused, newspaper clippings, local theatre programmes and brochures for stately homes and gardens visits and, as one who likes to keep these things myself, it has made me see the utter pointlessness of doing so. Have I ever looked at any of mine again? No. Will I, in the next 10 or 20 years? Unlikely. I suppose the answer would be to collate the highlights into scrapbooks but, again, who else would be interested in seeing those?

The ancient family Bible, dated 1817, is so huge and so heavy. I was hoping somebody else in the family would want it, but no, it's landed on my dining table, along with a lot more stuff I have yet to wade through, so I guess it's mine until I can pass it on to whoever in my family would like it. That's the problem with not having children. I don't have anybody to pass all my toot and tat on to, aside from my niece and nephew, and I doubt very much they will welcome it with open arms when the time comes!

Something they might be interested in, though, is my maternal grandfather's diaries. Unfortunately, he didn't keep diaries every year— or, if he did, they've long gone—but I brought home the ones dating 1934 to 1941 (though not consecutive, unfortunately—whatever happened to those?) and have found them riveting reading. I've learned an awful lot I didn't know about my own family and my partner, on reading them, said that he felt he knew my grandad really well, despite never having met him. There's lots about the war, of course: rationing, hiding under the table in the kitchen when bombs were being dropped rather too close for comfort and there's a mention of lots of planes flying overhead one night, which, it turned out, were on their way to bomb the hell out of Coventry. Family and work-related news is in there. They all enjoyed going to the local cinema, and cycled everywhere in the surrounding countryside to visit relatives and friends. The weather is mentioned quite a bit, and it's not nearly so dull as it sounds. If only he hadn't written most of it in pencil, though, bless him.

Don't get me started on the photos. Boxes and boxes, suitcases, albums and bags of them galore—often duplicated, just to add to the confusion. Some of them have careful and helpful explanations and identifications on the back, but many don't. I study their faces for clues. The houses and gardens in the background. The fashions of the day. Someone in the family has attempted to begin the family tree on my mother's side, but I'm still no wiser as to who half the people are in the photographs. My sister, panicking at the encroaching completion deadline, threatened to hurl boxes of slides on to the skip, without going through them first, which I thought unwise, so, guess what? They are my own house now, along with the bulky projector to view them with. And I still haven't looked at them.

There were way too many drinking glasses—who needs that many?! We weren't a family of drinkers. Nor did we give frequent parties. I don't know what was going on, there. The local charity shops have got very picky, these days, and will only take full sets, now, so the rest had to go into recycling.

We had a caravan in the 1970s and, yes, right at the back of one of the kitchen cupboards we found a very bright yellow melamine set of plates and mugs and bowls—the ones we used when we were away. But I'm not keen on bright yellow, and nobody else seemed to want them, so they also went to a charity shop.

There were sets of pristine, unused bedding, blankets and towels. After a bit of research and a few phone calls, we were able to take a lot of those to a local homeless shelter. Again, though, even those places were a bit sniffy about what they were prepared to take, which surprised us. And the tea-towels! I said to my partner: 'Who the hell needs so many tea-towels?!' When I was back in my own home, I opened the drawers under the bed, where we keep spare linens, and guess what? There were about a hundred tea-towels lurking in there. I sorted through them, kept my favourites and the rest (all unused, of course) went to charity. I do like a nice tea-towel, though—I'm drawn to them, then I put them away, because I don't want to get them grubby. Sigh. Clearly, it runs in the family.

I have always thought having lots of storage is A Very Good Thing.

Not any more. Having ample storage just means shoving lots of things away and never looking at them again and my parents' small house was very well served with built-in cupboards in every room—sometimes more than one. All deep and all rammed to bursting.

A friend has just had her loft converted into another bedroom and bathroom, and has found she doesn't miss the extra storage space at all. She says she prefers to have everything to hand; it makes for a much easier life and I can understand that one. It does force you to keep your belongings down and, as far as I'm concerned, this is my new Very Good Thing.

Another friend, who lives in a very small flat, pays storage rental for furniture that belonged to her parents, which she wants to keep but has no room for at the moment. She is currently looking for a larger flat.

This entire, painful, emotional exercise has been a salutary lesson in not hanging on to useless stuff we never even look at again. What is it all *for*?! All the old newspapers and leaflets commemorating some event or other, all carefully saved and filed neatly into plastic folders by my parents, ended up on the skip, or in the recycling bin, simply because there was no time to go through them all first. And that's not including the boxes of papers and other items both my sister and I took to our respective homes to sort through. I have all my mother's old diaries and address books and they, alongside 20 bursting carrier bags, are piled up on a bench in my kitchen—and have been for the past 10 months—because every time I go to look through them, I start to cry. But I have mild OCD and I like my home to look good, so it's a daily niggle for me and I know I have to get on with sorting it all out before an entire year has passed!

I really wish my parents had thought to clear out the loft, and other places, while they still could. Though, of course, nobody expects to have two strokes 12 years apart and die of the second (my dad); nor do they expect to end up physically disabled, and with dementia, in a home (my mother). The wardrobes upstairs were full of the clothes and shoes my mother ordered by phone (she couldn't leave the house in the last few years), then never arranged to have them sent back when they didn't fit her, or whatever—they all still had their labels on. Unable to leave the house at all, not even to go and sit in the garden, I'm not at all sure what she thought she was buying all these things *for*. And the cupboards downstairs were full of brand-new, expensive-looking china, more glassware, kitchen and beauty gadgets still in their boxes and a set of silver-plated cutlery with the receipt still in the box—over 200 pounds, ouch. My theory is that, after spending most of her life being careful with money and making-do, she could finally afford to relax the purse-strings a little and spoil herself with the sorts of treats she would never have considered before. None of us knew about these things whenever we visited; or about the unpaid cheques, bills and backlog of important paperwork, or we could have helped her with it all, of course.

The whole sorry process wasn't helped by me being such a terrible sentimental hoarder. I wish I could have hardened my heart and just tipped the whole lot into the skip. But I couldn't. In fact, I'm still haunted by what we threw out and gave away and regret not keeping more, but our own house isn't that big and is already very full. Sigh. My partner is just as bad: when it came to clearing his parents' house, he took things to the local charity shop one day, and then went and bought them all back the next!

We had been enjoying regular takeaway Sunday roasts and other meals from the local village pub for some months, since they were able to reopen after lockdown. We wanted to support them. The first time we sat down with our lovely lunches in front of us, wafting their appetising scent everywhere, I said to my partner: 'I honestly cannot remember the last time a roast was cooked in this house.' Even my sister, who has a much better memory than me, couldn't remember.

Then there was the garden: a riot of bloom and colour when my parents were fit and able, but sadly gradually deteriorating over the years. I was paying our regular gardener to come out every couple of weeks to keep it all in shape, and put new plants into the patio pots and in the borders, which were looking bare and unloved before. I was also keen to keep up appearances for security's sake. To make the place look cared-for and occupied. Last year, at what turned out to be our last spring at the house, I found it particularly moving to notice all the bulbs emerging from the earth. My parents must have planted these and the garden will continue to flourish; oblivious, of course, as to who will be looking at the plants and flowers and taking care of them from here on. And so the cycle continues…

Saying goodbye to the lovely neighbours, our gardener and his wife and the dear elderly and very sprightly man who has lived in the same house in the village all his life and who very kindly took the bins out for us, and for various neighbours who couldn't manage it themselves (and brought them back in again), was especially hard for me, although we have been invited to tea with all of them—an offer we haven't been able to take up yet, as our trips to see Mum in the home take up the entire day, there and back. After so many years, it feels sad and strange to no longer have a base in the area. Like outcasts. Mum is unaware we have had to sell the house, and thinks it's still ours, with all her things still in it, which makes for some very difficult conversations with her. It would be immensely distressing for her to learn the truth and I hope she never finds out. Naturally, she wants to go back there, which would have been impossible in any case, even if we had somehow been able to hang on to it.

A shout-out to my long-suffering partner, here. I don't know many men who would have done what he did for me, over the past few years. All the driving (I don't drive), the checking and fixing of things in the house and the uncomplaining support he gave me in so many ways, during what was easily one of the worst times of my entire life was over and above and beyond the call of duty. It continues, too, with our regular trips to see Mum in the home. He is a rare gem indeed.

I finally came off the anti-anxiety/depression/sleeping pills I had been taking to get me through all of it. I was crying every day, and barely sleeping for worrying about the place when we weren't there. The funny, plain, ordinary, boxy little house that Dad had built had been a true haven, refuge and sanctuary for me over the years, and never more so than in the last two years of our ownership. I think he would have liked that, though I'm not so sure he would be so happy with, or approve of the way things have turned out. I hated that our last few weeks there were so stressful, fraught, panicky and emotional, and I'm still feeling wretchedly guilty, grief-stricken and regretful at what we threw into those skips, and gave away to charity and the neighbours—it haunts me every single day. Sorry, Dad. Sorry, Mum. Though, as someone pointed out to me last year, I'd have most likely felt sad every time I looked at anything I'd kept. He said it's not always healthy to be reminded. He has a point, though I have kept some things, of course. Just not *everything*.

And when I do think of what we had to leave behind, I find it helps me a little to imagine that at least some of those things belonging to our family are still residing in the area and, especially, in the village we loved and were very happy to call our home for so many years.

The Benefits of Having Friends
Waay Younger Than You

By Michele Kirsch

My young friend Chloe (23) was sobbing after watching a viral YouTube video about the elderly talking about loneliness. Some old biddy with all her tchotchkes and doilies and you know, those things that cover the arms of armchairs that no one ever sits on, cos she has no visitors, saying how some days she talks to nobody, and then the advert bit comes on, and it's something like, make a difference! Ring an old person! Chat shite. They will love you for it. Not exactly, but that's the gist. While you youngwhippesnappers are snappy chatting on the interweb, or eating raw fish, or going to discos, whatever it is young people do, old people are at home, rotting in front of their stuff, feeling dead sorry for themselves. Call 'em. Tell 'em about your sushi. It will make their day.

And Chloe said to me, 'I really want to ring my nan, but she says never during *Emmerdale.*'

And I thought, I'll have that. Never during *Emmerdale.* So I says to Chloe, you know, you must never ring me during *Emmerdale*, either.

Chloe goes, 'But our Michele, you don't have a telly.'

'Don't care. We have to establish boundaries, Clo…'

Chloe is one of my Bright Young Friends in Jobs that have Nothing to Do With Their Degree And Are in Shitloads of Debt. I have many, because after coming out of a treatment centre for tranquiliser addiction in 2012, I found myself gravitating towards the sort of dumbass jobs I did at the beginning of my working life. Cleaning. Washing glasses, FOR A YEAR, at a big chicken and steak restaurant. Positioning myself as the strange granny type with a bit of a rock and roll past.

After a few conversations, after establishing that English was my first language (in most of the jobs I do, it's not even essential) and

93

actually, some time ago, I sorta made a living from this language, I started to get young people coming up to me, for love advice, to ask what music I listened to in the olden days. New York Dolls, I would say, waiting for a glint of recognition. Always a pause, and then, 'Wow,' the implication to me being, how can someone so very fucking old, as old as my mum, have liked something I've had my eye on in the vintage record shop?

When I was at the chicken and steak place, the young, usually beautiful waiters and waitresses would come in and between gasps for breath or bitching about a difficult customer, would tell me something personal, something a little deep, or a little lovelorn, something to which I could be of some sort of matronly assistance.

And I loved it.

I loved, for the first time in my long life, being mistaken for the wise and sensible one. You fake it long enough, you actually begin to feel it. I found myself telling all of them, 'You are young, you are free, friggin' Supergrass wrote a song about you, (Who are Supergrass, they say) this job will be nothing to you next year, when you are modelling for Topshop, or representing refugees in your law surgery, or filling out mid-sized venues with your indie band (I said mid-size to manage their expectations).'

And I really like, for years after being a sort a chaos queen, being scatty in my personal life at best, downright deranged at worst, I was finally at a peaceful, sensible place where kids the same age as my kids (who were not talking to me at the time: they are now) would ring me up, ask me out, hang out with me after work. I saw with sober eyes how very hard it is to be young these days, much more so now than when I was young and you could have a crap job, live in a bedsit, buy very cheap drugs and have a really good work/life/drug balance.

Now I work in a café where all the staff, most of 'em still young enough to be my kids, including my boss—are in recovery. They are drug and drink free, and very sorted. They have dreams they still have oodles of time to fulfil. I am now the one with no plan B, happy to flip eggs for the rest of my working life, but I can vicariously enjoy their hopes and visions and dreams. I love it that my expectations are extremely managed, and they are still in grit and determination mode. And every day I look forward to hearing about their lives, their loves, their dreams, their possibilities. But never during *Emmerdale*.

On Being a Grandmother

By Lili Free

I don't wish to gloat but being a grandparent is the best. To be honest, compared to parenting it's a breeze. All I have to do is follow the orders from my son and daughter-in-law. If I bend the rules a little when I've got the grandchildren to myself, well nobody needs to know. As long as I get them home without a major injury, it's all good.

I wasn't given a manual when raising my sons and I bumbled along, saving for the therapy I knew they'd probably need down the road. My youngest has gone one step further and actually *become* a therapist. That's when you know you've messed them up. In all fairness, he's wiser than me now and we're the best of friends, having worked steadfastly through the long list of my mistakes.

It took two to three years, some hefty walks and talks, a fair few tears, me saying sorry a lot, the whole process peppered with moments of laughter, humour being something we do thankfully possess in this family. My older son doesn't seem to have a list. If he did compile one, he's certainly too busy now to think about it, indeed he probably can't remember much before the birth of his first daughter. As the second one's arrived now his brain is mush and he thinks I'm the bee's knees because I show up and take the three year-old out. This leaves two bewildered adults free to tackle the endless To-Do list and give the baby some attention. God, I remember those days, in a sort of hazy, '*how did I not end up in an insane asylum?*' kind of a way.

Back then I was attempting to be at least a slightly better parent than mine had been. This was before the internet had come into our house. I read a few books but quite frankly words on a page just don't help when you're against the wall, fighting for breath and wondering why you had kids in the first place.

This generation of young parents have an infinite resource at their fingertips. My son and daughter-in-law have already hired a Sleep Trainer and a Mummy-and-Daddy trainer, both certified psychologists, both hugely helpful. All we had were two sets of parents who thought we were doing *everything* wrong and didn't hold back in letting us know.

Against all odds, I've ended up living in the same town as the kids. Having been a witness to the grandma on my dad's side ruining my mother's marriage to my father in an almost psychopathic manner while I was growing up, I'm determined to break the mould. I could easily fall into the stereotype of interfering, know-it-all, old school grandma, which would inevitably have been my destiny if I didn't have a fiercely questioning mind and a determination to cauterise ancestrally-inherited bad behaviour at the root.

Ten years ago, I left Kings Langley, where my ex and I had co-parented for 23 years in the same village but living apart, both sacrificing a lot to put them through Steiner education. He'd remarried and I was extremely lucky that his new wife was keen to be involved. She became a wonderful stepmother. It was a challenging and rewarding time for all of us. Because of the commitment to the school, we were all forced to stay in one place for a very, very long time. There were periods when I felt trapped, but that's parenting, I guess. I'm not sure why nobody tells you about the trapped part before you agree to the job—it's a conspiracy of silence we're all indoctrinated into in order to keep producing more humans. Do I regret having children? No—I adore my boys and am hugely proud of them. Am I knackered? Yes.

When I stored my stuff and set off, I had no idea where life would take me. My main goal was to shed as many family responsibilities as I could. Life had been a juggling act for as long as I could remember and it was your classic burn-out situation. I imagined I might be on the road for a year, choose somewhere to live and carry on building my career as a tantra teacher and therapist, which was going fairly well at that point.

It didn't work out quite the way I'd imagined. I split up from my long-term partner, escaped to Australia during the worst part of the menopause and fell madly in love with New Zealand, returning three times over the next three years. I wrote two books while flitting about and did odd jobs to get by. It was the freest and gloriously unencumbered I've ever felt. If I think about my carbon footprint, I used up *all* my quota during that crazy time. I excused the long-haul flights with the reasoning that I'd never travelled when I was young, never had a gap year. In actual fact, there had been no gaps at all in four decades of hard work.

On one trip back to England I was given the news that I was going to be a grandmother and all my fantasies about settling in New Zealand evaporated. I returned for one last time, bid a reluctant farewell to the verdant valleys of the North Island, said goodbye to all my kiwi friends and returned home, a little sad but excited for the birth.

So here I am, settled in Brighton and I'm loving it. The adjustment from being a nomad for 10 years to paying rent and working for a living was tough for the first few months, but it was sweetened by the knowledge that I'm living down the road from the loveliest little girls I've ever known. I had boys so, of course, the girly thing is a complete novelty.

I'll confess that in those early years I had a lot going on. I was distracted as a parent. I did my best, as does everyone. Now, there's nothing that takes my attention away when I'm spending time with my granddaughters. It's not my job to worry about whether or not they're getting a balanced diet. We can thoroughly enjoy that ice cream (and flake!) in the Big Beach café, taking our time to introduce ourselves to each and every dog who frequents it. If we want to spend an extra half an hour wandering down a street because it has '*windows in the ground, Grandma Lili!*' we can. There's nothing to rush for. I can find myself bouncing the baby on my knee, making gurgly sounds for an entire hour and not want to be anywhere else, doing anything else.

But I've given myself a good talking to. As excited as I am to be a granny, I'm going to wait until I'm invited, wait until I'm asked, wait, wait, wait and keep my nose out of their business. I shall get on with my life.

I'm going to be the grandma who's appreciated rather than dreaded.
I'm going to be good.
Wish me luck.

SECTION FOUR
HEALTH TALES

Dirty Blood and My Still Born Boy

By Serena Constance

Blood has been such a massive part of my life for the last 37 years. Every month, from the age of 12, I've bled like a stuck pig. One of my best friends recently said how much she enjoyed her periods. My jaw just dropped. I've always hated mine violently. From the first drop. Bleeding pints, great big fat clots the size of my fists, soaking up ultra-maxi pads in one gush, spilling over the sides, through my black pants and through my dark trousers, leaving a bloody puddle leaching into my chair in the middle of a business meeting. The shame of discreetly trying to wipe it off, waiting for everyone else to leave first and hoping no one would notice.

And the pain, don't talk to me about period pain. That time I was 15, curled up on the bed in my first boyfriend's bedsit, then him calling out the GP (in the days when they would do home visits) to give me a massive shot of morphine to take away the most incredible pain I'd ever experienced. The morphine felt good.

That time in my early 20s on a rural bus in Java, when I was writhing in pain on the plastic seats, silently crying big fat tears down my cheeks. I had no sanitary protection as I'd been taken by surprise. A kind Javanese lady took me off the bus and into her home to clean me up, give me painkillers, wash my clothes and let me rest before making sure I got home. A good Samaritan.

The only respite I ever got was going on the pill as a teenager for seven years.

'You're not to use it as a play pill,' my mother scolded. Little did she know. Too little, too late.

Numerous tests showed nothing—no endometriosis, no fibroids, no this, no that.

101

'Dirty blood,' a Javanese reflexologist told me, prescribing a thick black liquid brew that tasted putrid. But I downed it every day, desperate to have clean, light, easy blood.

Trying to get pregnant in my mid-30s (my mother had me at 39, I thought it would be easy—too little, too late), how I hated my blood even more. Every month obsessing over cycle lengths, daily temperature charts, and urine samples. More tests.

'You have an unusually long womb and a tight vagina,' the gynaecologist said. Dirty sod.

Then a miracle. Just as I had almost given up—a missed period and a positive test. Excitement, elation, at 37 I was going to have a baby. Not my first pregnancy, but this time I wasn't afraid, I was older. This time much coveted. Oh, but then the blood came. Hang on, that's not right. Is it? 'Go home, don't worry about it, everything is normal.' Three months came and went. Blood came and went. Still the baby grew. Clinging on. Heart beating somersault twists and little kicks. Until the clots started coming. As big as a fist. No, no, no. This isn't right. This can't be happening. Please God, no.

'Your placenta is coming away—see that shadow there—a large clot of blood,' the consultant said. 'Very touch and go. Go home, rest, and wait.' A death star lurking in the lining of my womb. There is no God.

My waters broke at five months—ah, what a gush that was. Forty-eight hours later I went into labour, was whisked into the Royal Sussex, sirens blaring. My beautiful perfect, tiny Tom Thumb of a son was born on 2 May 2006. The sun was shining on a glorious bank holiday. But everything was black. My world stopped turning. For the next three years.

'Dirty blood,' said the woman at the nutritional supplement centre, 'full of copper, no wonder you lost your baby.'

The cow. So tactless—so unprofessional. I was furious. Bereft. Obsessed.

Then my first husband fucked off. Sick at the sight of my dirty blood. Wanting new blood—fresh and young.

Then I hit my roaring 40s. And how I roared, and wept, and bled some more—a whole lot more—as if my whole insides were falling out. Has someone just been murdered? Has someone slit their throat?

The period pain is minimal now. Almost non-existent. My cycles are starting to dither about but my sex drive has gone through the roof—the sex-surge they call it—do keep up; all that testosterone. The hot flushes come thick and fast (always carry a fan), night sweats come and go. My short-term memory is hopeless, and I'm forever losing things. Ah, the perimenopause. Bring it on—I want it to stop. No more bleeding at long, bloody last. No more packing spare sets of clothes, wearing two pairs of black pants, no more shoving a MoonCup up myself (I care about the environment) and yet still having to wear a maxi-pad, so what's the point? Dear MoonCup, please can you make a bucket size cup—the size of the blood red moon?

Oh, hang on a minute. When my periods stop, that will finally be it. The finality of my fertility. And I will grieve all over again. Not as intensely, but it will still happen. Lurking in the shadows, popping up on Mother's Day (will someone please send me a frickin' card?), popping up when siblings start to become grandparents, all those life stages and milestones that my second husband, friends and family celebrate as their children grow. Of course, I celebrate with them.

The joy of being an aunt, a great aunt, a fairy godmother...the magical, mysterious, marvellous elder that comes bearing gifts. The exotic elder that always plays and dances, makes up stories, dresses up, hides and seeks. They all clammer to try on my jewels and trinkets. The elder that still goes clubbing in Cardiff nightclubs and gets crowned Queen; the elder that takes a drag, and does all the things their parents can't as the responsible adults. I am fun personified. I'll settle for that.

'Aunty I love you.' The best thing a child could say to me, as he gives me a big fat cuddle. 'I love you too darling.' So much love—a bottomless well of it.

There was a time when I had to grit my teeth and sob behind dark glasses, closed doors, and in the loo at work. Although that time has gone now, I'm still a mother, and it was still a birth—however invisible, however silent. Always there. Always loved.

Dirty blood. I'll be glad to see the back of you.

An imagined 11-year-old.

Somewhere, in a parallel Universe, there is a bold young boy playing with his vorpal sword that goes snicker-snack. His name is Vincent. He has blonde hair, and blue eyes; he's very creative and loves to dress up. He wears feather boas, and glitter. He's a glam rock star in the making. He loves to fly kites. He can ride a horse and swim the ocean.

He loves physics, art and dance like his mother. And English literature and New Wave films, like his dad. He's a brave young boy, playing in a field full of sunflowers.

Every October there is a National Baby Loss Awareness Week. I light a candle and dance—a wild dance, shedding skins in celebration of a short life but whose soul lives on in my imagination, making me feel more, laugh more and love more.

SANDS, an organization devoted to Saving Babies' Lives, Supporting Bereaved Families threw me an umbilical lifeline when my world stopped. You can support them at www.sands.org.uk .

Why I Love Cold Water Swimming

By Nadia Chambers

I have loved being either in or on the sea ever since I learned to swim off the sandy beach at Margate. I was four years old and these summer Sunday trips on the train from London Bridge station, were a highlight of my young urban life.

I can recall the sheer excitement of seeing the first glimpses of the shining sea, the squeals of joy as the salty air rushed up to my nostrils and the utter happiness of splashing about in the water, riding on my dad's sandy back as he swam out and then being towed back in towards the shore. My dad encouraged me to kick and swim as he confidently held me, letting go a little bit more each time until I could float and propel myself. The feeling I associate with being in the sea is one of glee. Yes, sea swimming is a really gleeful activity for me and continues to be so.

Of course, lockdown in these pandemic times has seen scores of people taking the plunge into the briny for the first time, and many of them continuing to swim through the summer into the autumn and onwards into the winter. People who are, somehow, now captivated by that increasingly popular lockdown activity—the Cold Water/Outdoor/Open Water/Wild Swim.

A great deal of attention has been given to something that—only a year ago—was the province of a relatively small group of oddballs who maybe commanded a column inch or two on New Year's Day.

Two thousand twenty saw the rise of the Outdoor Swimmer, the cataloguing of the many health and wellbeing benefits of immersion in cold (15 degrees or below) water.

Looking for an improvement in your mental health? Get in the water! Eager to strengthen your immune system? Get in the water! Want to fix whatever ails you? You get my drift. Open water swimming has been chronicled, critiqued and analysed from a dozen perspectives and yet, for every article written, there remains a weird mystique attached to the lets face it, the relatively uncomplicated act of getting undressed and getting wet.

This is my personal account of taking my existing relationship with the sea, one that has included scuba diving as well as swimming, to a new and unexpected level.

Cold Water

In January 2020, when the notion of a pandemic and the chaos that would ensue seemed quite preposterous to me, I found myself following a friend and local sporting hero on social media who had been swimming through the winter. She, along with a group of (mostly) women, regularly swam off our local Portsmouth beach, right through the coldest months of the year. It looked great, if slightly unhinged and I really wanted to join in. Then Covid and lockdown entered our lives and vocabulary and, for a while, I forgot about everything except trying not to catch the virus. Easter came and went and I hardly ventured outside of the house, not least because we had my elderly mum staying with us for several weeks and I became a full-time carer.

However, once mum was able to move back into her flat, I started going to the beach and found myself desperate to get into the sea. It was now the beginning of May and yes, the water was fresh!

The body has a clearly defined and well-documented response to immersion in cold water. It is, at once, an assault and an energising stimulant. Your blood pressure goes up, your breathing becomes gasps, your nerves zing and I swear you can feel your internal organs contract (well, maybe that's just me!) But, and this is the thing, you can learn to accommodate this reaction, to acclimatize your body, to control your breathing (it really is all about the breath, the exhale), to relax your tensed muscles, to embrace the cold and then welcome it, wallow in it, love it.

All that is required is for you to be present, focused, alert and surrendered all at once.

The biggest benefit for me, in all of this, was not, however, the physical sense of wellbeing. It was the fact that, in going swimming in the sea, I was able to maintain contact—in real life—with my best friend, because she came too.

Since last May we have swum together several times a week, always socially distanced—she is a senior nurse in ICU and I am clinically extremely vulnerable. We're both healthcare professionals (I'm retired) and we both understand the principles of infection control. The act of going swimming moved beyond mere exercise and getting some fresh air, it became more than a routine, providing a focus and structure in this chaotic and dystopian world. It has become a ritual, a celebration and an anchor.

The Process

Each swim begins the day before when we are in contact via WhatsApp, exchanging details of tide times, sea state, weather conditions and work commitments. We agree on a time to meet on the beach and then we prepare. Swim kit is packed. Swimsuit (our personal challenge is to avoid wearing a wetsuit), goggles, hats, tow-float, swim watches, towels, a flask of hot drink, hot water bottle, extra warm layers of clothing, waterproof changing robe all organised into a bag ready to go.

There is a methodical wonderfulness in the way we first wave to one another, then chatter briefly before setting onto the shingle, shedding clothes down to our swim gear and then striding—we always stride—down to the water's edge and then walk straight in—without hesitation. I like to start jumping up and down in the water, laughing or shrieking, as the water gets deeper. I whoosh my out breath forcefully and inhale deeply, overriding my gasp reflex. It calms and strengthens me as I immerse myself to swim.

Catriona simply slips her shoulders beneath the waves and exhales. I watch the stress melt away from her dear face, the world's biggest smile taking its place. We remain several feet apart as we swim, talk, take photos, marvel at nature, sing or cry. We keep an eye on how our hands and fingers are feeling—a loss of dexterity is an indicator that your body is pretty cold and you need to be getting out. During the summer months, we were swimming for anything up to two hours at a time. Now, in January, the water temperature is around six degrees and we manage 10-15 minutes before our fingers start to seize up and it's time to exit.

The ritual extends to emerging from the sea, beaming and burnished, getting dried, dressed and warmed up as quickly as we can whilst continuing to bask in the heady mix of endorphins and companionship.

The Bond

We have both noticed how much we enjoy the view of the world from sea level, in the water. It is time out of time when the world and its business stand still. The water that holds us suspended in its cold depths connects us to one another. On Christmas Eve we enjoyed singing carols as we bobbed in the waves and then on Christmas Day, we exchanged gifts before donning novelty hats to swim in.

As I write this—I'm thinking about the swim we have planned for tomorrow. It has been a week since our last swim, Catriona's work schedule has been punishing to say the least, and storm Cristoph laid waste to the few possibilities of getting into the water safely.

It's okay though. The sea isn't going anywhere anytime soon. It'll be there tomorrow to welcome us. We're both hoping that the water temperature will have fallen further—another boundary to push at, another day of feeling very alive.

Discovering I had ADHD at 57

By Ivan Pope

I have spent most of my life in creative pursuits, drifting from one thing to another without ever clearly understanding what I was doing. I certainly never had a plan, much less a career and—although I had some notable successes along the way, and am not unhappy with my life—I always felt something was wrong. I just couldn't put my finger on it.

The revelation of attention-deficit to me was a classic epiphany. I was trying to work out some issues that we had with our son who, although a very intelligent boy, seemed incapable of working at university and had just extricated himself from Oxford in the most painful and seemingly pointless fashion. Someone suggested ADHD (Attention Deficit Hyperactivity Disorder), the full name of this syndrome. I was both dismissive and uninterested, believing at that point that ADHD was a term applied only to annoying children who would not sit still. Nevertheless, I went to Google and searched the term. Immediately I came across a list of ADHD attributes and these brought me up so sharply that my life changed in that instant. I was 57 and, while I wouldn't say my life had been a disaster, I seemed to have always stood on the edge of normality. 'That's my life, I thought.' I was alone but I may even have spoken out loud. It became as obvious as it could be: almost every way that ADHD was said to manifest was familiar to me. In that instant, I understood myself better than I had ever done.

Since then, I have come to see attention deficit as both the driver of creativity and the author of my strange unfocused life. I have not been formally diagnosed, I am self-diagnosed. I have read a lot about it and also, more importantly, listened in to a growing community online who discuss, challenge and inform each other about how attention deficit works in their lives. This syndrome seems to explain a lot about the strangenesses of our lives: why are we like this and also like that. It is a strange and shape-shifting disorder which is comorbid with a range of other neuro-diversities and some even more strange issues like hypermobility and digestive issues.

Attention Deficit Hyperactivity Disorder is not named well. It's not really about hyperactivity (although to be fair, there is a hyperactive version, and it is said that for many of us, the hyperactivity is internal). It's not even really a disorder. It seems to be more of an attention surfeit, we pay too much attention to too many things. It also creates a strange relationship with time. I've known these attributes my whole life, but I never considered them strange. I assumed everyone had them to some degree and that my creativity, my way with ideas, was just something I was a bit better at. Then I found ADHD and suddenly I could see myself in operation, I could anticipate how I might react and understand what I was doing, and why I was doing it. This 'disorder' (as I don't like to call it) is well scientifically and medically documented, but still hard to put into words. The notion that it is about an inability to sit still is nonsense in most of us, though the hyperactivity may be considered to be internal, a driver of our restless lives. We have huge issues with procrastination, an inability to get started, and then we have hyperfocus, the ability to spend hours in a different world, undertaking a single task.

I started looking, as I so often did, at art and literature for answers. In her book *Flights*, the Nobel author, Olga Tokarczuk, describes a condition that she calls Lazy Venus syndrome. Although she never uses the term attention deficit, she describes someone with ADHD perfectly and beautifully.

The result of this situation is that I have, as I see it, Lazy Venus syndrome. In this case, we're dealing with a Person whose fortune has gifted generously, but who has entirely failed to use their potential. Such people are bright and intelligent, but don't apply themselves to their studies, and use their intelligence to play card games or patience instead.

This… induces a strange kind of laziness—lifetime opportunities are missed because you overslept because you didn't feel like going, because you were late because you were neglectful. It's a tendency to be sybaritic, to live in a state of mild consciousness, to fritter your life away on petty pleasures, to dislike effort and be devoid of any penchant for competition. Long mornings, unopened letters, things put off for later, abandoned projects. A dislike of any authority and a refusal to submit to it, going your own way in a taciturn idle manner.

It is interesting to compare Tokarczuk's description with a more conventional list of attributes of ADHD:

- Easily bored, Gets frustrated, Anxious
- Does not meet goals, Easily distracted, Searches for stimulation,
- Sense of underachievement, Restive
- Disorganised, Can't get started (Time blindness)
- Resistance to authority, Impulsive, Doesn't follow procedure
- Impatient, Procrastinates, Lots of hobbies
- Called dreamy. Hyperfocuses.
- Has an aversion to paperwork

People I talk to, especially artists, often recognise this sort of language because it has been applied to them. Indeed, it reads like my own school reports. They (and my mother) constantly told me I lived in a dream world *'to live in a state of mild-consciousness.'* We are often categorised as lazy *'a strange kind of laziness'* despite being intelligent and highly creative. We tend not to finish things, getting distracted or starting something new. We tend to be impulsive, getting into trouble and resisting authority in different ways. *A dislike of any authority and a refusal to submit to it.* People with ADHD will often ask themselves how they can be lazy when they spend so much time being busy, starting and getting on with multiple interests *abandoned projects.* We tend to have a dislike of paperwork *unopened letters, things put off for later.* ADHD can drive fierce creativity but it can also ensure that creativity never finds lasting expression.

In his book *Adult ADHD: How to succeed as a Hunter in a Farmer's world*, Thom Hartmann says that the forgetfulness, disorganisation, impulsivity and boredom that ADHD brings can be as constructive as they can be destructive. To be fair, attention deficit can be hugely destructive and far more intense than I have experienced. It is a formal medical condition that can ruin lives and there is a lot of disagreement currently (especially in the US) about over-diagnosis and medicalisation. My interest is not in the medical side or in the politics of this, but in understanding how or whether attention deficit relates to creativity. In this, I mean all forms of creativity, the ability to come up with new ideas, to execute creative work within any field. It is clear that this is an ability that not everyone has—not everyone wants it—again, creativity could be seen as a curse as in the Chinese saying, *May you live in interesting times.* There is a double edgeness to creativity, an understanding that true artists stand close to some edge, that they may pay heavily for their talent—and not everyone wants that.

I have become fascinated by the double-edged sword of this syndrome which gives great creativity through the restless search for stimulation while undermining it repeatedly with distraction. Impulsivity is important for creativity, as is a resistance to a normal way of doing things, and a willingness to experiment, but finding disorganisation and frustration will often destroy what has been started. I used to fear that my creativity would leave me, while at the same time having no understanding of what drove it. Now I can look at myself and my behaviour and see what I am doing. I haven't changed in how I operate in life, but I am more at ease with why I am as I am. When I was an entrepreneur, my advisors would demand consistency—and consistency is the exact opposite of attention deficit. I even came up with a phrase to refute them: consistency is the last refuge of the unimaginative. Now, with my new knowledge, I look back at that time and that attitude and understand that I precisely understood my way of being in the world even when I had no way of thinking about it. Now I do.

If you have read this far and are now thinking what I describe is just the description of normal people, of a certain creative type, or of human behaviour, then consider that maybe you are looking at the world from within attention deficit, that you yourself have Tokarczuk's Lazy Venus syndrome. Welcome to the club.

I Was Like a Man Falling Off a Ferry—I had MS

By Peter Marriott

Sometimes I think Job has nothing on me. All he had to contend with was a questioning of his faith in God in the face of all the evidence to the contrary. I have been faced with much more existential dilemmas than that.

I took early retirement about seven years ago, at the age of 55, due to various ailments that I couldn't put my finger on. Ironically, it was my finger that first clued me into what was wrong. Just the very tip of my right index finger was sore and plagued by a painful numbness, if that doesn't sound like too much of a contradiction. I was beginning to find it difficult to type and my work as a lecturer and researcher was being affected as a result. The pain gradually extended further down my finger and then into my other hand followed by my toes and my feet and it was becoming clear that something was seriously amiss.

The next thing was the tests and the MRI scans, until eventually the GP sat me down and handed me the letter he had received from the hospital and said '*maybe you had better read this.*'

And there it was: a diagnosis of demyelination (myelin is the fatty covering on your nerves) and the strong possibility that it was Multiple Sclerosis. Bit of a hammer blow. I struggled on at work, of course, that's what we are meant to do, isn't it? We pretend that everything will be alright. But, of course, it wasn't.

I found it more and more difficult to get upstairs and the fatigue was so bad that I made a little bed under my desk. Often students would knock and find me rubbing my eyes and coming back to life to answer their questions about essays and coursework. Within a few months the brilliant HR department at Sheffield was offering me early retirement on a full pension and even though I still did not feel as though I was disabled, I took it. As with all retirement, it is necessary to take a good run up at it and think your way into a new purpose in life. But rather than having several years to get used to the idea, I was pitched into it like a man falling off a ferry.

I had joined the army at 16 with no school qualifications, had left at 21 and become a lorry driver, before studying German as a mature student. If the army gave me nothing else then the ability to speak German and drive lorries turned out to be worth their weight in Bitcoin. After that I got a job as a lecturer in post-45 German history and it was all downhill from there. In that sense, my entire adult life was consumed with either physical or intellectual labour and it has proven really difficult to break that habit.

I have largely got there now—as anyone who knows me will be able to tell you—but still I feel as though I should be writing books, if not rushing up and down the highways of Britain delivering concrete or tarmac. The initial anxiety dreams of having lost some important piece of military kit or misplacing my lorry have largely faded now and I sleep a largely untroubled sleep. My ex-wife and I used to talk about how we were both so brilliant that somebody should pay us just to be ourselves. Well, now they are. It's called a pension. The problem is that I am not myself anymore.

It's amazing how quickly I dropped any pretence at academic work and when I now read the research I did, I feel as though it was a different person writing it. That's because it was, and I don't really understand most of what I wrote or why I wrote it. Not because of any cognitive decline on my part but simply because I was so much older then and I'm younger than that now.

Since that first MS diagnosis, there have been plenty of others as well, so that it becomes difficult to disentangle all the symptoms. I have also had sepsis in my arm from a cat bite, which needed quite a nasty operation (I have pictures if you need proof). When they investigated why I was getting such serious infections they found that my blood was basically empty. It had hardly any of the things in it that it needs to do its job. Pancytopenic, they called it. When they investigated the reasons for that they found in turn that I had a very rare form of leukaemia; hairy cell leukaemia. No, I hadn't heard of it either.

The doctor said to me '*Oh well if you are going to have cancer then this is the type that you want. It's not even proper leukaemia.*' I think that was meant to be reassuring. It kind of was, in a way. Anyway, a series of injections and infusions (the first of which sent me into a spiral of reaction in which I thought I was definitely a goner) and a couple of weeks lying down and all was fixed. Full remission. If it comes back in another 15 years—which is possible—they will simply give me the injections and infusions again. Mind you, by then they will have probably invented something else and all will be well. I'm hoping that by then they will have also found a cure for MS.

Because that's just what one does, isn't it? It's the principle of hope. One hangs on for dear life, squeezing every drop you can out of it, trying to have experiences and to fill up the empty hours you have suddenly been gifted. The empty hours are there because of illnesses. But had I not had these things and had I struggled on for a few more years until I was 67 (another five years of work—inconceivable—and I do sometimes wake in a cold sweat wondering whether they will make me go back to work if a cure for MS is found) then I would still be doing better than my father, (who died at 62—the same age as me now—which seems to have some deep significance that I can't quite explain) or my uncle—his brother—who also died in his 60s. My younger cousin has just died of the dreaded c-word as well and I have reached that age we are all familiar with when all around me people are beginning to drop off the perch. Although at the same time, I feel freer and more in control now than I ever have in my life and I have also become Zen-like in my appreciation of what is around me—to the extent that I can do nothing all day and think it good—there is still a big hole where the whole should be.

I taught German philosophy as well as history at university and I spend a lot of time—probably far too much time—looking out of the window and thinking about Heidegger and Hegel and Being and Nothingness. Although that is all great fun, and something to bore my grandchildren with, it doesn't butter many parsnips. But life is funny like that. Camus recognised the absurd nature of our existence and the randomness of the things that befall us and I find it difficult to think of it in terms other than that. I even invented a term for it during some extended discussions at a particularly drunken conference; namely, the metaphysics of contingency.

In other words, stuff happens and then we make grand stories up about why it had to happen, how it is all part of some great plan for us both as individuals and as a species. But there is no plan, of course.

Heidegger adapted Descartes' famous *cogito ergo sum* (I think therefore I am) into *sum moribundus* (I die therefore I am) to explain our purpose and, as the old army song has it, we're here because we're here because we're here because we're here, and as retirement shows us, our existence is completely pointless. It's what I call an unnecessary necessity.

Everything that has happened to me over these years has been necessary to make the person that I am now, but my existence was not necessary *per se*. If I had not been born the world would have carried on—indeed, my poor, mismatched shotgun parents would have gone their separate ways as they should have done—and the universe would have carried on expanding without even a blink of the eye.

I don't know what the advantages of age actually are other than a recognition that nothing really matters and that it becomes much easier to accept the banality of life than when one was young and everything mattered so very much. *Life is what it is*, as they say today, but you only pass this way once so it is important to make the most of it, etc.

The worst thing would be to lie on your deathbed feeling and knowing that it was all for nothing. Despite all the things that have befallen me I am neither desperate or unhappy. Sometimes life feels like the trials of Job crossed with the labours of Sisyphus and Hercules thrown in for good measure. But it has been a hell of a ride and it's not over yet.

How I (a 66 year old man) Transformed My Health

By Phil Oswald

This is about change, personal change, the desire for it, the need for it, the context of it, the possibility of it, and the experience of it.

I don't want to come across as preachy, self-obsessed, needy, screechy, and so on, (as if!) and I am NOT a therapist, medical practitioner, psychoanalyst or expert in any way. I can only describe my experience.

I was born in 1951, a baby boy, in what was then Cumberland, a lovely part of the world. With friendly, open people, a strong sense of mysticism rooted in the dark hills, unpredictable weather, open countryside, the lakes, the moors, the ruins, the legacy of the Lakeland poets, standing stones, Roman occupation and invasion attempts from beyond Hadrian's Wall. There was also immense potential for drama and isolation.

Black Sabbath lived in my hometown Carlisle for a while. Their doomy oeuvre is usually analysed in terms of bleak industrialism, soul-crushing factory work but I also hear their banshee call of the wild deserted moors that they would have crossed late at night in their van. There's also the thrill of local supernatural legends, like the Croglin Hall vampire in their songs.

My childhood was spent in a society emerging from post-war shortages, attempting to rebuild Britain, with its new heroes, James Bond, Doctor Who, the rise of television and radio, the early days of multiculturalism. Into this world, shockingly to my parents' generation, came the revolutionary force of teenage culture, rock 'n' roll, hippies, drugs, permissiveness, Swinging London (it sounds so quaint now, it was so exciting then), and into this world, I emerged as a young adult, longing to be part of it, but not quite sure how to achieve that, and blundering along through a very large part of my life, a spoiled only child who threw himself at the brave new land.

Alcohol played a large part of my life. I regret that. But this is all history now but then there was a backdrop to a life of bingeing, yo-yoing weight, car crash relationships, divorces, rock 'n' roll, stressful work, money worries (yes, I know, it's the same for pretty well all of us, but, of course, the world revolves around MEEEEEE), and a gradual slomo glide towards a final crisis. There was the slow dawning that I'd got a lot of things wrong, and harmed people I really cared about.

I had a full breakdown, lots of medical intervention (the NHS were brilliant). It was described as clinical depression, something I regard as different from morbid melancholia. My physical symptoms were— trembling hands, racing heart, gasping for breath, overwhelming feebleness (no driving, no socialising, crawling to the toilet, friends doing errands for me, even driving me to the GP), long, long periods of motionless sleep, hands folded over chest, periods of staring blankly into space for hours, no reading, no TV, no work, nothing achieved, no sorrow, no joy, nothing, but sudden attacks of helpless sobbing, coming out of the blue.

It wasn't hell, or misery; it was just nothing. Nothing mentally, zoned out, blank, gone, withdrawn inside a feeble, trembling body overdosing on adrenalin. That was a few years ago. I recovered as my GP told me I would. She was brilliant, and she was right. But it didn't dawn on me that the real underlying problem was still there. The horrible sense of guilt and regret that I'd conducted my life badly. I did share this with friends, but they dismissed my fears, kindly, compassionately.

I felt I was stuck in an inescapable prison, I just accepted it, and carried on with life, busying myself as my strength returned, business as usual, telling myself I'm okay. Really, I'm okay. And so it went on. With that lurking black cloud of guilt over divorce, financial loss. Things that would affect my son, not just me, but were caused by me. (I'm okay, really, I'm okay).

Still bingeing, still chaotic. My mother died, I had to look after my very old father for several years. That was pretty tough, but it did teach me that, well, sometimes, you have to face your destiny, and that life isn't one long joke. He passed away in 2017, after years of decline. He was in the RAF in WW II, born during WW I. Imagine the difference between us; he actually had moral courage.

In March 2018, something happened. My son sent me a wounding, angry email (he lives with me, but he used email to communicate this message). He told me it was time I stopped messing around, harming people, blowing hot and cold, complaining endlessly but never doing anything to improve things. Brattish behaviour. Spoiled child behaviour. He said in no uncertain terms that if I didn't sort myself out, within a week, then things would be unpleasant between us.

I love my son. He is everything to me, and I hadn't realised how bad things had got, how oblivious I had been. He told me that he was worried about me, that other people were worried too, even though I thought everything was fine. So I did what he said. It was brutal, it was hard, but I tidied up a lot of loose ends. Actually, it was laughably easy. It occurred to me then that a metamorphosis can be easy. Even should be easy. Even actually is really pleasurable.

But how could I do it? I'd been on diets, I'd been to gyms, I'd cycled, I'd been slim, I'd been fat, up and down, round and round, precious little willpower (it seemed to me, making excuses yet again), I'd be drunk, I'd be dry—there was no consistency, no sense of real, long-term gain, just knee-jerk quick fixes, including lying, deception, secrecy, all those little monsters scurrying around in the spoiled little boy's psyche, neglecting friends, disappointing people I cared about, losing their respect, all that stuff.

So how to go about it? Some lights started to go on. I read, I googled, I YouTubed, I sought out the things I'd missed or sneered at, the pinnacles of human achievement, inspiration, courage and liberation. I reflected on the notion of self-reinvention, like Bowie or Madonna. If they could do it, even in the context of the music world, then why couldn't I? I'd remember seeing a movie, with Anthony Hopkins and Alec Baldwin, who were trying to survive in the wilderness. And Hopkins' repeated mantra was: 'If one man can do it, another man can.'

It stayed with me. But here's the problem: I have got fit, then slid back; I have dieted, then gone back to large fries and chocolate shakes. It's not just how to do it, but how to keep on doing it. So I YouTubed, I read, I Googled… self-help stuff, motivational stuff, this diet, that diet, and still I was blundering along, but things were slowly becoming clearer.

I knew I'd been very unhappy for a long, long time, and I couldn't break the binge cycle of action and reaction, or so I thought. How to go about it? I'd look at drawers full of clothes that were too small and think I'd never be able to wear them, but not want to get rid of them, because that would signal the acceptance of final capitulation to a chaotic lifestyle, and its aftermath. I'd waste money, miss golden opportunities, break up good relationships. It was as though I was frightened of success.

It all came to a head because that same weekend I'd seen Don Giovanni in Southampton, and I'd checked the dates. Strange that it was THAT opera. THAT weekend. Synchronistic, one might reflect.

In the course of YouTubing, something clicked. Motivational clips are often quite boring, predictable, and usually they are angling to sell you something, but amongst all of that there was something. Two things, in fact. One was transformation. The other was toxicity.

Let's do toxicity first. What my son was really telling me was—get rid of poison in your life! Get rid of it. Toxicity isn't just about substances like alcohol, tobacco and so on. There is also social toxicity, emotional toxicity, moral toxicity and, for me the biggie: psychic toxicity. I've listened to people moralise about young people self-harming, and, yes, it is a terrible thing, but those judging these young people might be grossly unhealthy themselves, without realising that they are self-harming too, in a terrible, terrible way, blindly, with good intentions, and, (the most horrible thought of all), that I was like it myself. *Quis custodiet ipsos custodiens*? Is that how it goes? So true. I was poisoning myself with guilt, regret, overwork, dark thoughts, melancholia, rejection of society, negativity, introversion. I was a psychic self-harmer. We all are, to a greater or lesser extent. It was suddenly so clear and obvious to me. I could not become well, or at least better, until I stopped poisoning myself.

It seems to me that toxicity is very BAD for us, to put it simply, tritely even. But let's think about it. Psychic toxicity is BAD too, banal though that might sound. You know, and you feel, how your body reacts to toxic junk food. That's a given, I think, so… why did I do it? Some kind of post-Freudian self-flagellation thing? Probably. Nice flavour? Something like that. It's the same with junk emotions, junk mindsets, junk values, junk irrationality, they poison you, and lead you to real self-harm, to comfort eating, to retail therapy, as it's jokingly called. To waste, to anger, embitterment, resentment, excess. Whatever. I became bloated, and limited in my choice of clothing. It was shit. Because of self-poisoning. Why? One thing is for sure: ultimately, you are the one who will pay for it. So don't do it. It sounds banal and crude, and I do apologise for this, but I'll still continue, even though you are already thinking about things you do to yourselves that are toxic. Do I need to name them? Do you need to throw them out, push them away like a raft that once brought you to safety, but is now allowed to drift off because it isn't needed anymore?

It seems so obvious to stop. We beat ourselves up, and it is counterproductive. At this point I have to say this especially includes toxic relationships. Sorry. I apologise again for being preachy, I am truly sorry, but I am describing a life-changing experience. I am NOT telling you what to do.

Now is when you are really going to hate me. There is one thing that is not optional. We all know that, don't we? Again, it's obvious, so simple, but it seems so hard to keep going. Let's think of it this way: not exercising is in itself a form of toxicity. You have the option. And all of this can be done at home. It is an incredibly exciting thing to experience, trust me. I'd say one of the most exciting things I've ever experienced, (in a very clunky, bedraggled life that has included clinging terrified onto a horse bolting through strange woodland), is to see the world this way, then react accordingly. You're NOT on a diet, you're NOT slogging painfully away. You are relaxing, and you are not beating yourself up any more. THIS IS THE KEY.

Soooooooo easy, soooo obvious, really. I'm ranting. Forgive me, I don't want to piss you off. It gets worse though. It's almost like—well, it actually is—a psychedelic experience. Seriously, your perception alters, things just seem to intensify. This is just what happened to me, between the ages of 66 and 67. I dropped from XL to M, waist from 44 to 36. Without feeling I had to do something, had to join a gym, had to get on a bike, had to limit what I ate, had to take supplements—once I stopped agonising (i.e. psychically poisoning myself), I just did these things naturally, with really very little effort, as though they were happening to me, and all I had to do was go with the flow, let it wash over me.

It's boring to read this, I'm sure. I have zero willpower, but something stirred inside me (honestly, stop laughing) and I found myself going to a gym, then, imagine it, cycling nearly every day, off-road, in open countryside, along Route 23 on the Isle of Wight, amongst rabbits, squirrels, herons, jays, woodpeckers—stopping for a pot of tea at Pedallers' cafe (highly recommended). It was utter, utter, joy. It just was, and it still is. I even whistle sometimes. But exercise doesn't seem like a task, it's more like a pleasing ritual for me, doing crunches with music or a lecture playing, so I'm not exercising, I'm listening, and learning. I just do this and that while I'm listening. This has been my journey since March 2018. At some points before that, I did lose track, but life seems better now.

The Hidden Power of the Climbing Wall!

By Asanga Judge

A few years ago, at 76 years old (I'm 80 now and I'm still going to the wall and the rocks), I was about to hang up my climbing shoes and call it a day. The effort of carrying a heavy rucksack filled with climbing gear into the hills to a crag was getting too much. Even places close to the road often required a steep, albeit short, slog. And then, there were various bits of equipment to carry on the climb.

In fact, for the previous two years, I had hardly managed to get out at all. In any case, most climbers give up before reaching their 70s. And for the last 20 years, I have had to cope with a chronic pain condition from a severe injury after being hit by a large falling rock while climbing on a sea cliff. Even so, there was sadness about letting go of what had been an enduring passion in my life.

Although I started climbing when I went to university in my late teens, once I qualified and was working as a young hospital doctor, I didn't keep it up. It wasn't until my mid-40s that I started again. My most active and successful climbing period was from 44 to 50. I was very competitive and quite obsessive. I remember spending hours poring over guide books, creating 'tick lists' and aspiring to 'better my grades.'

I usually climbed with a partner who was either equally matched or a bit less accomplished. This meant I would frequently lead on the rope, which is what I preferred. I have also soloed where a single fall would have been fatal. This requires a certain level of confidence, rather than recklessness. The element of danger and excitement is what produces the adrenaline rush, which is addictive.

I moved to Snowdonia during the early 90s in order to be in the mountains and joined the local climbing club. I climbed every weekend, and midweek if I could. This was usually on home ground but there were special away meets to other areas in the UK. Climbing trips abroad would be arranged with another climber from the club. I worked as a locum GP, never wanting to commit to joining a partnership as I wanted as much time as possible to climb. My motto was—*I work so that I can climb.* I was an all-rounder, climbing on snow and ice as well as rock. Gym training was part of keeping fit although another saying was—*the best training for climbing is climbing.* With fitness came confidence and that led to a lack of fear and feeling of invincibility. Pushing myself to the physical and mental edge meant there were falls. Without the ability to factor in falling, climbers are held back from improving, by their fear of falling. These days it is possible to take courses, which address this.

All this came to an abrupt end a few weeks before my 51st birthday. I was climbing on a vertical limestone cliff in Pembrokeshire, South Wales when I was hit by a falling rock. I have no memory of it to this day and woke up in an intensive care ward three days later. The rock had shattered my ribs puncturing a lung, fractured and dislocated one ankle and shattered one side of my pelvis, splitting open the roof of the hip joint and removing a significant amount of the pelvis and overlying structures. Since then, I have needed to walk with the aid of a stick and have chronic pain. I managed to return to work in under five months but couldn't even look at a rock face for years.

When I was 65, I had an urge to climb again. I started climbing with a friend that I had a good partnership with pre-accident. I became passionately involved again, enjoying regular climbing to a reasonable standard, even spending many ecstatic hours bouldering on the rocks above my local beach, as training. Then my friend pulled off a loose rock while I was climbing with him and fell. The rock shattered into pieces on its way down and I was in its line of fire, although I wasn't injured. He suffered an injury to one elbow, which stopped him climbing. However, it was like a deja vu scenario for me and triggered an emotional response. That was eight years ago and at that point, I lost motivation and when I did go out climbing with another old friend, I was not enjoying it and even felt a bit scared. Although I carried on doing bits and pieces.

Recently and now at the age of 76, I heard enthusiastic accounts, from several old climbing friends, of the recently revamped and re-sited Beacon climbing wall in Caernarfon about 14 miles from where I live. Before the accident, I had looked down upon indoor sport climbing. I thought that it wasn't the real thing and lacked the adventure and danger that went with being on a natural rock face, involving route finding, placing your own protective gear and dealing with changing weather, loose rock and more, in the 'great outdoors.' I thought it was for young gymnasts who had never climbed outdoors and never would. However, since then, it has evolved its own identity as a competitive sport, as well as becoming a popular pastime for a wide range of participants from children to men and women of all ages, many of whom also climb outdoors.

Finally, I agreed to meet an old climbing buddy there, after filling out an online questionnaire about previous experience and following their safety rules (all basically common sense) and signing up to membership. On stepping inside the building, it was a colourful space that transported me back to the wonder and magic of my many climbing times and memories. Memories of wanting nothing more than to feel rock under my fingers and space below my feet while executing the balletic upward dance when in 'the zone.' However, the enormous advantage of an indoor wall is there is no heavy gear to haul around. All I needed was a pair of light special climbing shoes, I own several pairs, and a chalk bag—in other words, freedom!!

The general vibe was a friendly and family-oriented—from pre-teen kids having fun in the 'crazy climb' area watched by proud parents, to 60+-year-old men and women vets testing their skill and stamina. As well as trendy-looking climbers, teens and younger adults—male and female, impressively ascending bulging walls or swinging acrobatically in outrageous positions in the bouldering area. I was transfixed by these different climbing feats.

My previously held judgments were blown out of the air—I loved it and had come home! And now I am a regular visitor, enthusiastically anticipating my next projects. At the moment, they are running a lead climber competition during the winter, divided into age categories. Mine is the mega-vet at 70+. Maybe I'm in with a good chance as there can't be many in this category. That itself is stepping outside my comfort zone, which is what it has always been about for me—the challenge.

My Relationship with My Weight

By Cheryl Reum

I was born feet first at midnight with a caul which was said to indicate a child of mystery and magic. A puny miserable lactose intolerant creature, I spent the first year of my life in hospital, puking and unable to thrive.

My mother had a wonderful statuesque figure and after selling her rings to pay bills decided to be a nude photographer's model in order to be able to keep me alive. As I reached 12 months, she was told to take me home as they did not believe I would survive. She met a woman on the steps of the hospital who recommended unpasteurised donkey's milk and that turned out to be the nectar of life for me.

Like many children of the '50s, we ate dinner plus a pudding. And my Mom was a good wholesome yummy cook. Macaroni cheese, cottage pie, French toast and syrup, white bread with butter and apricot jam and peanut butter. Rice pudding, trifles, ice cream and chocolate sauce. A starch, a protein and a veg then pudding and lots of full cream milk to drink.

We were fairly active and played outside, as well as cards and board games, drawing and painting. We also did cultural activities and had weekend drives and generally a good family life with mom, dad, three siblings and a bunch of assorted pets.

A shilling a week provided for sweets on a Friday at the local café. Penny chocolates were my personal favourite. Everything went well up until my 13th Birthday when I was sent away to boarding school.

I thought it was going to be a great adventure but loathed every second of it. The restrictions, the rules and the emotional trauma which took place around leaving my family.

So I filled the empty spaces in my heart with Romany creams and gained 15 kg in one term. During a three-month period, I became a little barrel on legs. In addition, my skin stretched suddenly and I had livid stretch marks on my breasts, stomach and thighs.

Although outwardly the comic and the card, inwardly I was deeply unhappy. Alas, the more I expanded the less visible and loveable I felt. I fell for a gorgeous Portuguese young man but it was unrequited and that made me feel even worse.

Sport was a nightmare as was the gym. Chafing thighs and plus I felt like a mammoth. A year later, my family moved to the area and I was released from prison but continued on through my teenage years being plump.

Around 15 when I left school, I started smoking and taking Nobese, a diet appetite suppressant and Veinoids to lose weight. And so began the see-saw and metabolism destroying journey of the next 30 years. Weight Watchers, Weighless, the Dr. Atkins diet revolution. Bran and yoghurt.

Yes, I did lose weight. I also fainted often and regained those same 15 kgs over and over again. I got married at 23, stopped smoking and entered a new phase of more-than-plump. My husband loved me and we were social. I worked hard in the beauty sales industry and we built a life and everything that goes with it.

My mom, my gran and my aunt came and co-lived with us and everything was hunky-dory. At 36 I fell pregnant with our first and only child. Fast forward with motherhood and a career and an extended family. I gradually got heavier year by year. I had already decided that was it, no more dieting. Thirty years followed with me holding onto my 'baby fat' and eventually weighing in at just under 100 kg which was way too heavy for a small 163 cm frame.

I moved to Cape Town, got divorced six years ago after 39 years, and my former husband died three years ago. Had seven moves and then on my 64th Birthday, my new partner and I set a goal to lose 10 kilos as an incentive to go on a cruise. The biggest loser would sponsor the other. Being competitive by nature, this turned out to be a grand idea.

I had also been to a seminar when I was 61 and set a five-year ahead goal to reach a target 30 kilos or almost five stone lighter. We did a firewalk which helped imprint this intention.

How did I lose these 30 kilos? First of all, I took a product called Wondernut that is an emetic. Because I had lost the same 15 kilos again and again. I started noticing my clothes were looser on me. I felt more energetic so I started walking every other day—5,000 steps on my phone.

As well as drinking warm lemon juice every day and consciously drinking more water.

I found that my sweet tooth started to go away. And I was eating three meals a day rather than snacking. That helped with weight loss and stabilised my moods. The latter was slow as I travel and socialise a lot.

A year later, I had lost 10 kilos even with an erratic lifestyle. I feel so much more comfortable in my body.

After a few more months of losing weight, I went out and bought new clothes from exchange shops. At the end of 18 months, I could swap size 22 clothes for size 12 ones.

This was just fantastic. I started yoga and Body20, a modality with an electrode enhanced jacket that gives the equivalent to a five-hour work out in 20 minutes. I am a star pupil!

I just enjoy my life so much more. And my relationship with my body is so enhanced. No chafing thighs, no puddles under my breasts. I buy new underwear and feel so much sexier.

Have I changed as a person? Am I happier? Did I have body shame? No—to all of those. I just feel healthier and better. I eat what I like without the devouring urge. Hurrah.

The end result is at 67, I am now 30 kilos lighter, exactly the amount, I wrote down in my forward vision. That partner is no more, the body is lean and gorgeously toned. I have been at this weight for several years now, I walk, hike, I love life and wear stylish clothes. I am fit and healthy. My inner being is now my outer JOY. For me, everyone is perfect just the way they are but for me, this does feel better.

Tides in the Body—Menopause

By Ursula Troche

I'm still on the edge, and not often there, as yet. Yesterday is only the second time I've had an encounter with the menopause. The first time was two years ago, when I didn't have my 'bloody days' for three months in a row—after which I wrote the 'Celebration of the Circle' poem, published here on advantagesofage.com and at the end of this piece—and the second time is now. Now is when the blood is still not coming. I've been waiting for my period after what I thought were typical premenstrual symptoms. It's that strain and unnerved-ness, which ends when the period begins.

Period-experience had taught me that when blood comes, the tensions cease. It's just that I had not been as conscious of this relationship as I am at this moment when it's not here and I am still waiting! I have realised that it's the blood-flow which actually brings healing to the body. The sight of the blood signals the transition from the lowest state of 'ebb' back to 'flow.' So one can say that there are tides inside the body, and for a long time in a woman's life it's our blood-flow, which enables the flow of things—and we go with it! We all go with it, we all 'go with the flow,' when we are at ease! So our period enables and teaches us this.

Flow, tide, ebb, flow, ebbflowebbflowebb: I think that as women, as long as we flow, we are like rivers. When we stop flowing, it might be because we have reached the sea. All rivers, as we know, flow into the sea! So we will all get there eventually.

There are tides by the sea as well, of course, and even more obviously so—tides in a river are more likely to be overlooked than they are by the sea—and it matches how we, as women, are overlooked; and also how we, as women, neglect the significance of our tides, our periods.

Sign of the times, sign of the tide, precisely, it is! Period! We are Zeitgeist! We are time and space, within!

Once we flow into the sea, we merge with a greater body of water, and merge with the oceans, a taste of greater expansion. But this body of ocean is not a male or female body, it's universal. The ocean is both male and female (and 'other' too, as the sea is fluid!). More evidence that the sea is not just male is that it 'answers' to the moon. That's another aspect of us, and of us all!

A gender-politics note of caution: I do not consider this to be a 'women and nature' story: rather it is about 'geography and the body.' It's embodied psychogeography.

Psychogeography is, traditionally (though it's at odds with 'tradition'!) a radical/alternative/ transformative exploration of urban (and non-urban) environments. It developed around the Situationist International, highlighting the constraints of capitalism on our life-experience, space, place, time, boundaries. It's about us and space then—landscape, and the effect that has on us: what industrial landscapes do to us, or housing, urban planning, coastal edges, and more. And in this tradition too, I have looked at my body in itself as a geographical space, and what our bodies do to us, and what that means.

I think traditional cultures often say that rivers are female, and the ocean is male—though some rivers are male too. My experience echoes the idea of women as rivers, to start with, though. This leaves more space for gender 'fluidity' as well. How would you write a male version of this? I am curious to hear other interpretations and experiences, with perhaps other 'elemental' immersions and configurations. My geo-spatial body experience (and my choice of elemental signification) is that I am not in the sea yet, but I have reached the river-mouth, I am still on my way to the beach, and happily taking my time, doing loops and turns rather than moving in a straight line towards the sea. But despite all of my twists and turns: the menopause is not too far off—the sea is out there! As of now, my period will most likely come back again—rolling down the river!

There's one more thing I realised from this experience of period-intermission: the idea that the onset of the blood, as long as it comes, brings healing. It's healing because it brings about a release of that premenstrual tension in the body, signalling that body is ready for another cycle-turning. What blood can do! And that makes me think of Christianity in an inverted way. The church uses the symbolism of blood as a means of healing, during communion. The way the church sees it, however, seems taken out of context. From my experience here it's a woman's blood that brings healing, not that of Jesus—unless, of course, Jesus was a woman! And that now, seems more and more inevitable to me.

Celebration of the Circle

I'm not menopausal anymore
I am bleeding again for now
So it's just been a temporary stop
A foretaste of what is to come
My age has reversed
So it's not always linear
There are circles, U-turns and diversions
Every now and then
Age comes and goes
In roundabout ways
And for now I just got younger
But age will come and catch me again
And the bleeding will stop
For the circles I go around in
Are not endless
It's not always anticlockwise
Though there might be timeless wisdom
Inside that time-thing somewhere
And I love going round in circles
And ignore the line that moves
Me and my age onwards and upwards
But one day I know
That that line will win over the circle
And age will get me
Even if I dance
Though dance I will
As a resistance to the linear
A kind of circular opposition
And a celebration of the circle
That allows me to come and go

Postscript

Since moving to the coast, I came up with a question, wanting to find out whether periods and tides coincide. From then onwards, I checked the timetable for the tides every time my period started—and found out that the beginning of my period always coincided with the high tide mark.

I checked every month, but then our Covid-pandemic and lockdown happened, which seemed to induce a lockdown in my period: nothing came, there was a standstill. Months later, some periods did came but soon after the menopause took over: another standstill. So now I am blood-less, period...

I enjoyed finding out that there was an association between tides and periods. It also has made me see the sea more female than I had done before: now there weren't just female rivers, but a female sea as well! Or at least a sea which is feminine as much as it may be masculine. Both sides now, seasides now, ocean flow.

I'd be really interested to hear other's experiences about how your periods might coincide with the tide. If you are by the sea and have a period, check the tide: if it starts during low tide, I'd be amazed to hear about that, as I never started at the low tide—and if your period starts at the high tide, I'd be interested as well, as that was my experience. Do we all start at high tide and finish at low tide?

What I Learned about My Gut

By Nikki Kenward

I have had a lifetime of learning about my gut, in particular my bowels, and I know that I am not alone! I am quite sure many of you reading this will have had debilitating and hard to understand issues with your gut at some point in your lives. Like me, you have probably tried all kinds of supplements, nutrition adjustments and food restrictions to help your gut work in a comfortable and effective way.

Like me, you may have become frustrated with how little impact all this has had and not know what to try next. Maybe like me, you have discovered that talking about mental health and bowels in the same breath is a good way of ending a conversation.

It was only when I realised that my gut was illustrating and responding to my emotional status, both current and historical, that I began to have some understanding of what was going on. It was only when I began to understand that in Eastern traditions the lower belly is considered the centre of emotional and spiritual growth, that I began to see the potential there and to feel the emotions there. It was only when I studied the anatomy and physiology of the gut that I developed awe and wonder for its incredible beauty and complexity. And it was only when I read some of the recent research into the gut microbiome and the enteric nervous system (aka the second brain) that I began to understand how the different tissues in the gut were able to hold onto difficult experiences in the past that impacted our gut function from that moment onwards, that this all started to fit together into one huge puzzle.

If I tell you that every moment of every day, your gut is responding to how safe you feel, that every moment it is remembering times when you did not feel safe and sometimes this all gets mixed up together into a tangled experience that is hard to fathom. Does that resonate with you?

My gut has memories of a traumatic childhood and then a near-death experience later in life (I was scuba diving in cold water and started breathing in seawater) which left me with Post Traumatic Stress Disorder, or as I like to call it now Post Traumatic Gut. Many nights were spent waking with palpitations, nausea, dizziness, cramps, diarrhoea, then days feeling depleted and sore and only just functioning.

I was feeling isolated and helpless often and not knowing where to turn for help.

Our bowels and our mental health are intimately connected, one reflecting the other all the time. As a child not able nor allowed to talk about how I felt whilst witnessing the emotional explosions of others, my gut was often constipated and its enteric nervous system moved beyond fight and flight and into freeze as I dissociated from the people and the world around me. As a teenager with anxiety and depression, I remained emotionally stuck. Later in life, and after my accident, I began to do my emotional work and my gut came on that journey with me. I am still travelling, but I know I am not alone.

As a CranioSacral Therapist, I was also seeing many people with mysterious chronic gut issues in my practice. I decided to take action. After a long period of research and trying out strategies and bodywork techniques for myself and clients, I wrote a new curriculum for the Upledger Institute, 'CranioSacral Therapy and Listening to the Enteric Nervous System' which I now teach internationally to support other practitioners help the people coming to them.

I also wrote my book, published by Upledger Productions in the USA and UK, *It's All in the Gut* which is for anyone interested in emotional stress and the gut. This is written through my personal story in an effort to make it engaging and relevant but also contains much of the recent research, the anatomy and physiology and, of course, strategies and meditations to help anyone reading with a gut issue.

Alongside this, I have a YouTube Channel Colon to Cosmos, which has some visualisations and meditations to support people on their journey of exploration with their gut.

So what can you do? The fundamental way to help yourself is to do your emotional work, through CranioSacral Therapy, talking therapy or any therapeutic practice that works for you. Emotional stress is the number one thing that has a negative impact on our microbiome and our enteric nervous system and all the layers and cell populations in the small and large intestines. This includes stress from the past as well as the present. It doesn't matter how many avocados you eat, it will make little difference if you do not address these fundamental issues.

Alongside this work, you can support your gut health by being active, especially outside in nature. Your gut bacteria love being taken for a walk, just 30 minutes a day will help them. Learn to breathe. Eat a clean diet (avoid processed anything or anything with a list of ingredients as much as possible!) and drink plenty of water.

Make time to do anything that makes you happy whether that is singing, yoga, knitting, cooking, gardening or anything at all that you love.

All of this will support your gut health and your vagal tone which is also important for healthy and happy gut function. We have so much more power to help ourselves than we may think.

So is my gut health perfect now? No more than my mental health. I am still anxious often and my bowels can be fast and uncomfortable. I also have periods of calm and normal function. The difference is that I now listen to the message my gut is sending me and do my best to deal with the emotional issue if I can or at least recognise it, as well as doing the things that help. For me these are yoga, weight training, walking by the river, talking to friends and so on. Like I said, I am still travelling.

SECTION FIVE
INTO-ME-SEE

My Sexy 70s

Dr. Eva Chapman

I joined Instagram thinking that it would be a good way of promoting my book. My goal was to reach 10,000 followers. Then I got really scared. Did I dare to come out as a sexy, older woman on a platform like Instagram? I thought everyone would laugh at me and say; 'How can someone over 70, be sexy?'

I dared.

The response has been amazing. It seems that most people love it. They say it gives them hope. So, I have reached 10K followers and it has been great fun. And is also how I found my publisher, Publishing Push.

This book follows me from the misery of menopause, through my 50s and 60s, to 70. It has been a life-changing journey. I was so happy to finally really wake up. I have written the book for people, especially women, who think that menopause might be the end of the road. For many years, I really believed that my days as an attractive, interesting and sexy woman were well and truly over.

Especially, when I knew that my quota of eggs had run out. I believed Cher when she said: 'Fifty sucks. Men don't look at you anymore.' I bought into all the societal messages that I was a dried out old husk, heading for withered crone-dome. I hated getting old. Cruise ships were full of ageing wives whose husbands had left them for a younger model. The world seemed grim. I ate too much and my evening quotient of wine rose steadily. I developed more chins. I became an apple shape as my middle expanded. I started to wear loose floppy tops.

Annoyingly my husband, Jake, got better looking with age. I railed and railed that it was totally unfair. Men got more debonair as they got older. I hated getting wrinkles. I became obsessed with having a facelift. 'I will leave if you do,' said Jake. My interest in sex dwindled to almost zero. I gobbled yam pills and a herb, suitably or unsuitably, called 'horny goat,' but to no avail. I read Germaine Greer and Leslie Kenton who talked me out of HRT. 'Was that right?' I wondered on a bad day. 'Surely estrogen rollicking through my veins might make me look younger and sexier.' Germaine said she was happy that men didn't look at her as a sexual object anymore, but appreciated her brain. I personally would have happily traded in my PhD for just one wolf whistle.

Things came to a head when my husband was smitten by another woman who was half my age. I was devastated. But what could I do? Especially when I was being stalked by the Dowager of Decrepitude. Well, I turned and faced that Dowager head-on. I kicked myself up my sorry backside, dyed my hair black and had a spiky cut. I bought a black leather jacket and leather pants, and out I went to claim my man back. This is described dramatically in the book and with it came an intriguing twist that I hadn't expected. The best outcome was that my sexuality came back like a tsunami.

Little did I know that this blast of sexual awakening, after several years of being a dried-out husk of a woman, would launch me into a fearsome self-evaluation. I would become to my total surprise, a sexy, rampant flirt in my 60s. And with this came a re-emergence of my spiritual self. Really? Sexy at 70 and spiritual? I had engaged in many spiritual practices for over 30 years but had not yet learned one of the fundamental principles of those practices—which is to accept and love oneself totally.

With the aid of some tough self-inspection, deep inner exploration and openness to new experiences, I faced down my negative spectre of cronedom. Jake and I found some younger friends who introduced us to a whole, buzzing, new party world and I started to learn to flirt. Jake enjoyed flirting too and encouraged me. The book describes some of my early woeful flirting experiences, but I persevered. What I discovered was it had little to do with wrinkles and sagging skin, but all to do with inner confidence and self-belief. It was transformational and I had a blast.

I also explored different gurus and different spiritual paths, which all helped me see what was in the way of me truly accepting myself. I also explored the therapeutic effects of drugs, which helped me overcome limiting self-beliefs. My mother was destroyed by severe schizophrenia, which caused havoc in my childhood and teenage years, as I watched her descend into a drooling vegetable. She had never overcome growing up in Stalinist Ukraine and then at age 17 was taken as a prisoner by the Nazis, and forced to work as a slave in Germany. One of my powerful beliefs was that I would also go mad. So, I went to Peru to face my fear of madness, once and for all. With the help of my husband, Shamans and the jungle drug, ayahuasca, I managed to put my mad demons into cages where I could keep them in order. That was incredibly freeing.

There were other tough lessons along the way and many tests, especially physical. Debilitating sciatica nearly ended my marriage and cancer spread its dark shadow over our lives; as well as claiming the life of a dear friend. My husband got lung cancer and I developed a rare cancer of the blood.

The book describes how we dealt with these misfortunes and fell more and more deeply in love with each other. By dealing with my unruly unconscious, and as a result of further meditation, I made a startling discovery at age 64. Inside me was a Russian Bar Girl waiting to come out. This was not easy to accept. Russian bar girls are young and beautiful, they stereotypically pick up men in bars. Here I was supposedly on the way to becoming a wise old crone, and instead, I had to come to terms with this voluptuous, seductive inner woman, chomping at the bit. I started to do sexy dances for my husband. I said to him; 'Aren't I too old for this?' 'No,' he answered, 'I have been waiting patiently for years.' So at least once a week I put on a sexy outfit, some music, and dance; such fun and so liberating.

When the Wild Adventures Stop and a Real Relationship Happens Later in Life

By Lena Semaan

Sometimes he sneaks up behind me when I'm in the kitchen and puts an arm in the small of my back. I take a breath or jump, kitchen knife in hand. Of course, it's Andrew, however, somehow it hasn't registered that he's the person saying hello. So far nobody has been injured, however, there have been lectures on kitchen safety. Yes, I do know we live together and I'm not expecting anyone else but maybe I'm not expecting him either. We've lived together for around three years now and I love it. So, why the hell do I react like this almost every time?

I can only surmise that it's the legacy of living alone for around 16 years. Ok, maybe 17 but however long it's been, it's patently obvious it's had a profound effect on me.

First, you should know, I love living with him. Unequivocally. I was never a serial monogamist and he's really only the second person I've loved. In between the two, there has been a wild series of adventures which, as well as being diversions with all the fun and frustration those bring, only served to make me more aware not just of what I wanted in a man but what I needed as well.

Our meeting was the most serendipitous and I've never enjoyed being around someone so much. For one thing, it's helped to address my cuddle/hug deficit which was in the negatives before he came along. I mean—we are talking serious minus numbers here. I think that subconsciously while I was having those mad affairs in my 40s, I knew I needed hugs but unlike my 20s when I had sex hoping I'd get a cuddle as well, I never expected them. Unless they were the pre or post-sex kind.

Besides living alone, I'd been brought up to be utterly independent. There wasn't much choice when you were part of a migrant generation in a

140

new country with both parents working and trying to figure out how life worked. At nine, I was taking the tram to Melbourne's CBD with my sister and buying clothes. At 14, I was doing it by myself and by 15, I could sit in a café with a cappuccino as if it were the most normal thing. I loved travelling alone around Europe in my 20s and while I would have liked some help in making big life decisions, the way things were—I just made them.

Meeting Andrew was huge for me, but then on another level, it was absolutely the right time. The other day, musing about it I said, 'I was ready to meet you.' He agreed. And yet when I make a cup of tea, I still don't ask him if he wants one. Same goes when I raid the chocolate stash on level two of the upper kitchen cupboards. (He could if he wanted to put it on level three out of my reach but he doesn't.)

He asks me what I'm going to do on a Saturday and I'll say I'm off to trawl my favourite charity shops. Now I know he likes doing this. I consciously know this however instead of saying: 'Why don't we…' I, well, I still say: 'I.'

I've improved a little bit over time. He does get a hot beverage sometimes, even when he doesn't want one. And he doesn't miss out on the important things. If I cook dinner, I do it very much with him in mind. His guitar mates marvel at the compliments I give him just because I say what's on my mind. They tell me they'd have to work very hard to get anything like that.

When we're at home, we're two introverts in a toybox, a world of our own. Sometimes he'll go off and play guitar but not before checking in and letting me know he's off to make noise and may not return for some time. I've told him he doesn't need to ask me because that's just plain wrong. I don't own him. My mother always told me that. When he tells me, I appreciate him even more, however, I don't think I'd appreciate him less if he didn't. I just take it as two adults who understand each other doing what they do. I must be infuriating sometimes.

I'm utterly delighted when he walks in the door even though I might be in the writing zone. I just don't want to talk right then. I love it when he picks me up from the train. For me, these are moments of excitement. Perhaps, just perhaps, the little girl in me is happy he's returned and can't believe it. Because I actually never expected to meet a man I love being with later in life, and I know many readers probably felt or feel the same way. Occasionally, I'd accept the idea that I'd be alone, but the enormity of that didn't ever register.

And if you're not going 'aw shucks' by now, I will tell you what changed us from being friends into lovers. It was a moment when we were all with our late friend Bob and Andrew was leaving the weekend party early. For some reason, he stopped and said, 'Behind those passionate eyes is a lost little girl.' He hugged me, then left. Luckily, that was the beginning of a whole new conversation the next day.

Touch Me Not

An interview with the lead actress, Laura Benson,
about her character who has difficulty with sex and intimacy

Laura Benson is a British actress based in Paris—she was in *Dangerous Liaisons*—who plays a lead role in the controversial and challenging new film *Touch Me Not* (which also features Seani Love as a male escort and Seani also appeared in the AofA Tantra Hot Tub Salon which went FB Live). *Touch Me Not* follows three characters, one of which is called Laura, a 50 something woman, who is out of touch with her sexuality and takes some radical steps to address this situation. The film coasts a fluid line between reality and fiction. It won the Golden Bear in Berlin 2018.

How were you cast in *Touch Me Not*?
Through a casting agent, who works with the French co-producer. They were casting in several countries. I was asked to send something that I had shot recently. The film I had just done wasn't out yet and I didn't have anything recent in stock. So they sent me five pages about the subject of the film and I was asked to do an exercise: a video diary for my lover. I thought about it for a week and then did it and sent it, like a bottle in the ocean. The next week I was asked if I could go to Bucharest to meet the director, Adina Pintille. I obviously agreed. We had a four-hour meeting. I had understood what the director wanted from this meeting. It wasn't going to be a chit-chat… she wanted to feel who was in front of her and what I was made of. So my challenge was to go and not contain myself and be as free as possible.

What were your initial thoughts about playing this character, Laura who has difficulty with sex and intimacy?
What I had read gave little insight into her feelings and her struggle.

She seemed cold and terribly cut off from herself… dead in a way. I didn't know how I was going to bring her to life.

Were you excited by the original script in that you were playing a woman in her 50s who is the main character in this revealing/naked about vulnerability way? It's unusual to get this opportunity, isn't it?

I would say that what is unusual is to have a lovely part to explore (which has nothing to do with the age) and to work with an inspiring director that you get on with and understand in a way as well as on a project you like. All those ingredients are not always present all at once! I never actually considered that I had the main character and her vulnerability appeared during the process. I didn't know before we started working that this would emerge. And yes yes, it was a lovely opportunity, which came out of the blue! I feel very lucky. I think that Laura could be 40, 45, 50, 55…

Obviously, it was a wonderful opportunity to have an interesting important part to play, considering that most important characters in film are under-45! A casting agent friend of mine told me that in France when they suggest actors over 50, the producers and TV say '*no, menopaused*'! But I do more theatre than film, and a female actor's age doesn't have the same significance on stage, because there aren't close-ups—the body and how you move and your energy are more important than the reality of your age. I've seen some Commedia dell 'Arte where the character is 20 and the actor behind the mask 80. So to answer your question, I didn't realise really how lucky I was.

What were you challenged by in the process as an actress where it sounds like you had to get in touch with your own vulnerabilities?

For me, the challenge wasn't as much about being in touch with my vulnerabilities than it was about dealing with my fear of the unknown, my lack of confidence and my doubts.

And how did the improvisation go? Do you enjoy this way of working?

The script was just a starting point, like a trampoline that we could bounce off. A kind of skeleton, if you like. It acted as a kind of safety net. There was very little dialogue. A great deal of the material, the nature of the interaction, came from what was happening on set and how it was happening. Doing a scene when you have no idea where it is going to go, and more to the point—if it is going to go anywhere at all can be very uncomfortable. I would say that 'exploring a situation' rather than 'acting a prewritten scène' is a lovely way of working when you have a director that you can understand (and can understand you) and with whom you share the same vocabulary. There is a certain amount of preparation needed in that kind of approach. Adina has her way of working that takes you into a profound process, so you're not lost and you are pretty charged. What was nice about the relationship on set, was that she was as worried and excited as us. So we all worked together (technicians included because for the camera and sound people, it wasn't easy either) to do the best we could. The work was about being in the present moment, being spontaneous and authentic.

What did you discover personally?

I discovered how little I knew! How much there is to experiment with! I think the most surprising thing I discovered was when I was filming myself on a day off. It was a way of staying involved in the process and not losing touch with the film. It was something that spontaneously came to me when I woke up that morning. I put my body in the window frame (the window was very big) and I pushed and pushed against the structure. The architecture became my prison. And since I had voluntarily put myself in that space—that I wasn't a victim—my frustration and anger transformed into pleasure. Close to a sexual pleasure. It was very empowering. When Seani Love talks about 'conscious kink changing the world and plays a male escort in the film, I understand how some sexual activities can release and transform very powerful negative energies. And that changed my outlook on BDSM.

What kind of dialogue about sex and intimacy was going on between you and the director, Adina Pintilie? This is also included in the film?

We spoke about many many things; I don't remember it being focused on sex. But the conversations, when we weren't talking about work, were generally intimate I think they contributed to creating a particular dynamic based on trust.

Did it make a difference having a female director?

I have often worked with women. Doing this film with a man would no doubt have been very different... but how, I cannot exactly say.

145

Do you think it is valid not to explore why the character Laura has ended up with such difficulty in her sex and intimacy life? Anger with her father is intimated but not explored.

I think that Adina is more interested in looking at someone's attempt and struggle to change than explaining where the problem comes from. As far as I am concerned, we don't need to know where Laura's problem comes from—what is important is that she can move towards going beyond it. A young couple at a film festival said that it was the only 'positive' and 'uplifting' film they had seen in the film festival.

What was your interaction with Seani Love like? He was in our AoA FB Live Hot Tub event on Tantra and we loved him. He's playing himself in the film? A sex worker, who deals with intimacy issues.

Seani's work is really interesting and I would say that the interaction we had is what you see in the film. We didn't meet and talk before, my only interaction with him is when we were on set filming. I didn't even see his face before he came into my sitting room!

Were there moments when you had to say 'No' to the director?

No.

Adina was very respectful of limits even though wanting everything! She never—or rarely—asked for anything precise. So the limits were where you yourself put them. I asked her at the beginning of the film, when we were preparing the escort scenes: 'Are you expecting me to sleep with them?' She said: 'you do what you want.' Things were generally not decided before. It was more organic than that.

The film's reviews have been very mixed, I read *The Guardian* one by Peter Bradshaw and laughed. I wondered if this is because these reviewers have difficulty themselves with intimacy issues?

I think the reactions correspond to the anger someone can feel when they are going out to have fun and escape reality, then find out that someone is forcing them to have a therapy session and that they weren't asked if they wanted, let alone warned that they were going to have one (whether they like it or not).

What kind of conversations has come out of it for you?

People have shared some lovely things. One young man said that he spent his first night with his girlfriend just after they had both seen the film and that it totally changed his way of relating with her and changed both of their approaches to their intimacy. I am surprised because a lot of people have thanked me and given me hugs. I recently spoke to a woman who said she was happy to meet me because she had been worried about me during the film. I think it is a film that is a relief for a lot of people who have suffered feelings of inadequacy. In Kiev, a young woman had been thrown out of a café three weeks earlier because she suffered from cerebral palsy. She was so pleased to see the film. It gave her courage and hope.

What did you enjoy about making this kind of film? And the responses?

I enjoyed the complicity with Adina, the challenge and adventure and am relieved that I managed to overcome any fears and doubts, or at least deal with them. I am pleased to have managed to be spontaneous. So I guess that I have grown up a bit!

Going Back to Rio's

By Suzanne Portnoy

I went back to Rio's this week, the naturist sauna club, in Northwest London. I'd spent half a decade there, hanging out, getting laid, getting warm and then suddenly stopped five years ago when I met a guy who didn't like me going there. I'd said, 'OK, I won't go back,' because I loved him and figured I'd had enough of being a swinger; it was time to settle down.

I'd thought about it often over the years, especially on the days when the weather was so cold and miserable, that it felt like my bones were freezing over. On those days, I missed Rio's steam room and of being able to lie in there, often alone, for hours, until I was so warm, I could walk outside with my jacket half undone on a five-degree day.

Other times, I thought about going back for the sex and the camaraderie. I wanted to be with other like-minded people, naked and free. Rio's was a place I could always count on for a chat with a stranger and a fuck on the side, if I wanted it. I could have a steam, a sauna and go home. I always thought of it not so much as a swinging club but an erotic leisure centre. Even standing next to a naked man with a semi-hard on, showering, was a turn-on. How many other places could provide so much for the £8 entrance fee?

From time to time, I'd find myself in Kentish Town and I'd pass the place and I'd wonder whether it had changed. Would there still be a tin of McVities digestive biscuits at the bar? Could I still order a tuna sweet corn sandwich? I'd wonder if they'd tarted it up, got a new steam room, whether there was still fake grass in the garden to lie upon. I'd reminisce in my head about the fun times I'd had, the laughs, the horny sex, and all the people I'd met.

For some long, it was my refuge. I'd pop my clothes and mobile phone in the yellow locker by the entrance and then forget about everything. It was like being dropped onto an alien planet where I could be and do just what I wanted and everyone was accepting. OK, maybe not the woman behind the bar, that always seemed to be wearing Marigolds, but all the rest didn't seem to mind what I did. For the few hours that I was there, I wasn't anyone's mother, or boss, or friend; I was just a naked middle-aged woman, usually amongst a sea of men.

Admittedly, the place was not for everyone. I tried to bring a girlfriend once and she wasn't having any of it. 'I get why you like it here,' she said, sitting in the steam room in a bikini while a guy opposite us leered at her. 'But it's not for me.'

In any case, now I'm single again, I figured, why not? I'd know soon enough, once I got inside, whether I really had moved on. I checked the weather report and it looked like being a glorious, hot day. I wanted to lie naked in a garden, soaking up the sun, and I couldn't think of anywhere else in London where that was possible—besides Rios. Maybe I was looking for an excuse to go back too.

I checked Citymapper and it said I could be there in 40 minutes. A bus was leaving in five minutes. That was all the reason I needed. A small part of me was scared so I grabbed a bikini bottom before I left. In the past, I'd always gone completely naked because, after all, it was a *naturist* club but this time I didn't feel so bold; I wanted some protection. And I'd taken one further precaution by enlisting someone to come with me, a local guy who was on a swinging site and seemed nice and attractive enough. I knew, if worse came to worse, we could ditch each other.

I went up to the door and paid the entrance fee, grateful that the woman taking my money was not the same one I remembered from my past. That woman always used to give me the up and down with her eyes as if to say, 'I know what *you* get up to here.' Despite being five years since I'd last passed over that threshold, I half expected everything to be just as I'd left it.

I grabbed my towel, was buzzed through the door, noticing the new shiny, black mirrors in the changing area. Then I saw the familiar lockers with their key on a wide elastic strap. There was the same bin in the corner for our wet towels and the one, lone chair in the other. The rest was familiar too, although now in the garden there were rows of green plastic chairs where none had been years earlier, many of them broken. Some building supplies were tucked in a corner too like they always had been. Funny how some things never change.

I met my new friend and it turned out we had a lot in common, both being media folk and from North London. We were grateful when it turned out that our children, around the same ago, *did not* know each other. Conversation flowed easily. I went out and brought back a couple of beers from the shop across the street. A Hungarian guy came and sat down next to us and told us about the swinging club he used to run near Budapest. A guy opposite heard my American accent and asked my views on Trump, of course. Later, a man came round with some ice cream he had bought nearby and offered us each one. 'What's a hot day without ice cream?' he said. My companion was smiling from ear to ear. "I can't believe I've passed this place every day and never been inside."

We struck up a conversation with a nice couple and, before too long, we were all playing together in one of the small side rooms. Sweat pouring off our bodies (the room was very small), we kissed and licked and fucked until the heat became unbearable. They were cute and fun. I hadn't kissed a woman in a while; I'd forgotten how much I enjoyed it. How soft and small a woman's mouth always felt in comparison to a man's. Her boyfriend was well hung, horny and hard.

'I guess you're back on the horse,' said my new friend.

'Yes, I guess I am,' I said.

Something tells me I'll be going back again soon.

Eco-Sexuality and Annie Sprinkle

By Nancy Jainhill

Annie Sprinkle, a golden era porn star cum environmental activist, and her partner, Beth Stephens, a queer artist/activist, and professor, have always been all about sex and sharing their enthusiasm publicly. Now, as ecosexuals, they're skinny dipping for the environment. *Water Makes Us Wet: An Ecosexual Adventure* that they directed and produced, is a documentary about water which conveys its message through the ecosexual gaze. Together, Sprinkle and Stephens, with their art, are shifting the metaphor 'Earth as Mother' to 'Earth as Lover.' They've married the Earth, Sky, Sea, Moon, Appalachian Mountains, the Sun, and other non-human entities in nine different countries. Experiencing nature (human and non-human) as sensual and erotic, they aim to make the conservation movement sexy, pleasurable, and diverse. Their partnership reflects a merging of concerns about the environment, broadening definitions of sexuality, and an expansion of radical feminist art.

From tree hugging to dirty sex—orgasmic mud baths for example— the ecosexual approach to battling climate change is more fun and maybe even more effective than mainstream, dry-mouthed techniques. Sprinkle and Stephens, the co-creators of the ecosexual movement, which teaches that humans aren't separate from, but are part of nature, use ecosexuality as a platform for environmental discourse. 'Ecosexuality is a new sexual identity, an environmental activist strategy, and an expanded concept of what sex is (and can be) in our culture. What most ecosexuals have in common is a love, passion, and interest in the well-being of the Earth, and they find 'nature' sensually pleasurable.' Today they estimate 12,000 to 50,000 people identify as ecosexuals. The relationship between Annie and Beth, playful and sexual throughout, provides the medium to appreciate the erotic interplay between humans and nature embraced by ecosexuality. Their sensuality thrives in the watery milieus of *Water Makes Us Wet.*

The subject matter of the film is significant, yet there's plenty of opportunities to smile and even laugh. Social issues are presented in a playful, performative and humorous way. Sprinkle and Stephens, are free spirits, which also characterizes the ecosexual movement. Working collaboratively with E.A.R.T.H. Lab, a nomadic institute situated in the University of Santa Cruz (UCSC) Arts Division with a mission to create new forms of environmental art, conduct research, develop theory, and produce happenings, Stephens, Sprinkle and their dog, Butch, embark on a performance art journey in their 'E.A.R.T.H. Lab mobile Unit' around California, investigating the pleasures and politics of water. As viewers, we're taken along for the ride. Sprinkle, about to turn 65 at this point and 69 now, and about be a full-on senior citizen, and Stephens, 58 then, 62 now, in keeping with their past, briefly appear naked in the film, feeling that it was important to be naked older women countering a taboo.

Performance, Calderwood Pavilion, November 13, 2009

This documentary is part of their film trilogy to raise awareness about the environment. In *Goodbye Gauley Mountain—An Ecosexual Love Story (GGM)* (distributed by Kino Lorber), they raise performance art hell in West Virginia to help save the region from mountaintop removal destruction, which climaxes with their wedding to the Appalachian Mountains.

A porn actress and pleasure activist in the 1970s and 1980s, Annie Sprinkle was a key player in the sex-positive feminist movement, her art projects a vehicle for promoting sex education and equal rights. Now, an ecosexual, she's enlarged the scope of her efforts, approaching her mission with the enthusiasm with which she embraced her life as a porn star and pleasure activist. 'My work is still very much about sex, and I've done work about sex for almost five decades. Just that now my ecosexuality and love for the Earth comes into play.'

Beth Stephens, her partner, and collaborator for 18 years, realised her connection to nature growing up in West Virginia, spitting distance from Gauley Mountain. An interdisciplinary artist and activist, she's explored themes of sexuality, gender, queerness, and feminism through art since the eighties. Currently, a professor, Chair of the UCSC Art Department, and founding director of the E.A.R.T.H. Lab, Stephens' visual art, performance pieces, and films, have been shown extensively, nationally and internationally.

Initially, I didn't take ecosexuality seriously, but I've learned it can be very serious and may be a surprisingly successful conduit to express crucial messages about the natural world. The environmental ethic suggests that survival requires a mutual relationship of respect and care between humans and the Earth. Who can argue with that? (See Sexecology.org)

'Why water?' I asked.

Living in California after their wedding to the Earth, the state was experiencing a severe drought.

'So not having water, being on water restrictions, and reading about places where over 100,000 people don't have good drinking water, like the central valley in California, we got worried. We just love water. Plus we depend upon it for life.'

To some extent, the water problems of California provide a paradigm for water crises occurring elsewhere in the United States and globally. The U.S. is technically water-rich; however our usage is outpacing our resources. For the past few years, the effects of serious drought have been extensive throughout the west—not just in California.

In 2016, when Sprinkle and Stephens set out on their road trip, the reservoirs, rivers, and aquifers in California had dried up. Narrated by the Earth, *Water Makes Us Wet* is informative, funny and engaging—and focal.

What started their quest? The drought was a factor, but it was a clogged toilet at home that made them ask, 'Where does it all go?', leading to their investigation into what happens to San Francisco's wastewater. The education they received was the impetus for their journey. Blending the scientific with the spiritual, their exploration into the ways of water include visits to research labs and field stations, conversations with a wildlife biologist and a Director of Public Works, and meetings with others of a more spiritual bend.

At Big Sur they swam in the perennial stream, Big Creek. 'When you spend a lot of time in nature you don't need to know the name of the thing,' their biologist guide, said. 'You just need to know its place in the environment, stop talking all the time, see where your mind goes'—an ecosexual message.

A visit to Annie's family home and pool where they stop to swim provides the opportunity to share details about the water burden associated with pools. Annie gave her first blow job in this pool which is why she picked the name Sprinkle when she got into the sex industry—she loved it wet. Here, Annie and Beth cavort naked talking about water magic, against the backdrop of information about the burden of the more than 1.2 million residential pools in California, 250,000 in Los Angeles County. Thirty-thousand gallons are required to fill most pools: California water usage varies according to the socioeconomics of a region. For example, the daily average for residents of Compton—a community with few pools and below average median incomes—is 106 gallons, compared with Beverly Hills where residents average 284 gallons.

Informational screenshots about the ocean are sobering, letting us know the consequences of greenhouse gases on ocean waters, and that between 1970 and 2012 there's been almost a 50 percent decline in marine life populations. Poignant and humorous images, such as their communication with elephant seals, capture the sexuality omnipresent in nature.

In the mountains east of Los Angeles, Stephens and Sprinkle learn how Nestle is mining water off the mountain, depleting the water supply, endangering more than half a dozen animal species, and creating a shortage for people living there.

Annie succumbs to eating a Big Mac that she says, 'is more embarrassing than making porn,' which never embarrassed her. This moment, the film's editor, Keith Wilson feels, reflects the complicated relationship many have to water and consumerism, to food and humour, and our ability to handle and juggle that complexity. Annie's downfall provides the opportunity to explore the relationship between water and beef, resulting in a trip to stockyards: 1799 gallons of water are needed to make one pound of beef in California.

One of the last places visited is Lake Tenaya, where Annie's dad had wanted his ashes sprinkled. Tenaya is an alpine lake in Yosemite National Park, and problems associated with high visitor use have been increasing, information that would have been good to include. This is one of the scenes which best reflects the sensuality of their relationship with nature, and an understanding of ecosexuality.

The interplay of the sexual with the ecological, the personal and the informational, the mixing of levity with significance, is successful. At the end of the film Annie and Beth "crash" the San Francisco Pride Parade, add an "E" to GLBTQI, reflecting the integration of sexuality and ecology, and the connection to their earlier lives.

To respect, love and be kind to the environment, to realise that we are part of a beautiful ecological cycle and every move counts—are ecosexual messages delivered by Sprinkle and Stephens, by the experts they meet, and the photography which reinforces the magical dynamics of nature. Screenshots of facts are effective, as are visuals such as endless shelves of bottled water and the stockyards. However, depending on the target audience, moments such as the baptism of a childhood friend, Beth learning how to use a netipot, or the extent of time spent at the San Francisco parade, were distracting.

What's next for Stephens and Sprinkle? 'As the Earth is our love, we are in an intergenerational relationship with the Earth. We are just a few decades old. The Earth is millions of years old. We are very young by these standards.'

And, they are completing a book, *Assuming the Ecosexual Position*, University of Minnesota Press, chronicling their ongoing art collaboration and exploring their ecosexual work, combining sex and gender activism with environmental activism. To quote Annie, 'We expect the book to make a big splash in the academic world.'

SECTION SIX
THE LAST TABOO

Dreaming of Death

By Caroline Bobby

I've always been preoccupied by death. As a child I worried a lot about dying in the night. I worried about being suffocated or split in two by a speeding train. The psychotherapist I grew up to become has some thoughts about those fantasies, but that's another riff.

It hasn't been the easiest journey to reach what I call 'the fields of kindness.' It has taken most of my life so far, to truly start to soften and relax. By that, I mean relax with who I am and where I find myself. Surprising, just how elusive simplicity can be. Simplicity was patiently waiting for me all this time.

I offer this preamble, because I want to talk about my relationship to and with death. It would be reductive to say something like—she's had a broken life and lives with depression, therefore a self-confessed longing for death is suicidal ideation.

I have been suicidal. I tried to die for the first time when I was 13 and for the last time when I was 30. I didn't understand why I kept failing. I was desperate. I tried every which way. Plastic bags on my head, razor blades, hanging, overdoses. I couldn't quite let go.

Now I get it. I was in unutterable pain and death called me long and loud. Now I get that life was calling long and loud too. I love life, though it has taken a long time to arrive. I can love life and long for death at the same time.

I don't know if I long for death just because living with baseline depression is unforgiving, and every morning is a shock. I don't think it's just that. This human and embodied world has never, quite felt like my natural habitat. At a cellular level I am aching to go home.

Seven years ago, I started sending Postcards from the Window Ledge and it has proved the most redemptive writing I have ever tapped

159

out. It was time for me to forgive myself for being depressed. Even more radical, it was time to welcome the one I am, rather than keep chasing down the one I think I need to be. Oh my, what a homecoming.

And now, I live, more or less, in The Fields of Kindness. Kindness to what is, rather than a sanitizsed, feel good version. It can be fierce. My fields are situated on a cliff top overlooking the ocean. The winds blow in and waves crash on the rocks. The grass in my fields always tastes of salt.

Because I have been blessed to find this wellspring of compassion, inside me, for myself and for this crazy, broken and beautiful world, my longing for death is now much clearer to see. It has become simple, like so many things have. Some people long to meet a human partner in this world and I long to leave it. I make that comparison because this longing has a very particular quality. I think it is the same longing. A universal longing.

It is more usual to discuss a longing to meet a soul mate, at a social gathering, than to bring up a longing for death. So, I am rather chuffed, that over the last couple of years, partly by blogging from the window ledge and by talking about something unspeakable, this longing of mine has become visible, included and even loved. Last weekend I was at a gathering of my home dance group and our teacher ended a teaching point with the words: *Unless you want to be dead…* she added *No, not you Caroline.* The group chuckled. Oh, how much I loved that comedic lightness of touch and acceptance.

I spend a lot of time imagining my dying and death. Not unlike the wistful dreaming of meeting a beloved. I riff on it in my mind. It's a narrative I visit often. I add detail and follow threads, like writing a song. I know it's slightly off-key to daydream about getting a terminal illness, but it's not off-key to me. I find it deeply soothing, even as I know that fantasy and reality are different and accept that I have no control over how and when I die. If God's a joker and I suspect he/she/it is, then I'll probably die in a car crash. I'll be gone in an instant and miss the whole thing. I don't want to miss it. I want to experience every last drop of it. I think I'd die well, if life gives me the opportunity to test my thesis.

Death has a bad press, but what if it was as tender as birth? Having been privileged to welcome a daughter, and to say goodbye to a sister, I know it to be the very same border. The first breath, as we enter the embodied world and the very last one as we slip out of human form and back into the mystery.

One of my roads not travelled, is a heart-house funeral service. I see it quite vividly: big house, gardens, bodies received and tended to, families and friends cared for, groups, prayers and rituals of all and no denomination, community, art, music. Above all else, space held for the ravaged beauty of death and dying: a kind, compassionate and human space, for this utterly human experience. I'm a death wife in my soul. And a birth wife, so to speak, because that borderland of first and last breath, is my kind of land. I like it there. It's simple and quiet. And intimate. And when you're there, there's nowhere else you can be.

I'm not one of those dynamo types, the ones that make dreams and visions happen in the actual world.

I'm unlikely to build my Heart House of Death. So maybe my contribution to the death conversation is just this: my notes, the odd riff, a postcard or two, and a tendency to bring up death at dinner parties.

My First Death

By Lena Semaan

Unlike many people of my vintage, I'd never experienced dying up close. Last year the universe sent me on a crash course, reuniting me with my friend Bob whom I'd met at university in 1979. This isn't just a story of death. It's one of friendship, the kind that doesn't need Facebook Likes to remind it. I hadn't seen or spoken to Bob in 26 years but it seems he'd been sitting in my subconscious. 'Bob' is how I've always introduced myself at parties when I don't really know anyone. It sorts the dull men from the potential. I bought a cult toy back from New York years ago. It had a name but I renamed it Bob. For some unknown reason my godchildren call several of their toys Bob.

I wasn't meant to be in Melbourne last August. I was meant to be working in Qatar. I didn't care for the place but, unusually, I'd taken a contract purely for the money. They took the job away the day I arrived so I flew to Australia. Three weeks later as I was suggesting to a policeman he should close Melbourne's meth labs, instead of fining me for my inability to cross at the lights, my sister switched on her car radio and heard an interview with Bob who'd become a famous children's screenwriter. And then she heard the words 'brain tumour.' Bob had a Stage Four Glioblastoma Multiforme.

'Fancy name,' he said when me met. 'Basically, it means Mr. Imminent is at the door.'

The boy from Western Australia wasn't just my friend. He was my Lebanese mother's adopted Jewish son and a favoured guest at family gatherings. It took us one three-hour conversation to reignite our friendship. After that we were inseparable. I stayed at his flat and looked after him. People said later 'You're amazing for doing that.' I told them I was fortunate to be with Bob again. I wasn't there because he was dying.

162

I wanted to be with my intelligent, incendiary and incredibly funny friend.

'I've taken up smoking again Leens,' he said when we met. 'I figured I'd die from lung cancer instead. That way people won't feel sorry for me, they'll just say I deserved it.'

These past months have been a time of fierce joy shadowed by despair and tears. Joy generally doesn't turn up without conditions. There were times we both knew we'd never be more alive: I can't recall rolling on the kitchen floor with laughter in many, many years. Bob looked after me as much as I cared for him, reconnecting me to people from our mutual past and introducing me to the parcel of scriptwriters, cyclists and musicians who coloured his life. At night feasting on Lebanese food parcels from my mum with a film primed to go, he'd grab my hand and say, 'It doesn't get better than this Leens. We're living like kings.' Bob liked a ritual. We sat at the kitchen table as he smoked his evening cigarettes, then hugged each other before he wobbled off to bed. As people heard our story, they shook their heads in disbelief. 'You're meant to be together for this time.'

Somehow I found strength when he needed it, shoring him up before hospital visits and distracting him from the demons who inconveniently popped up when we were trying to enjoy the moment. In January 2016, the Glioblastoma brought out the heavies. The seizures started and his left side was no longer his. I kept telling myself it would be okay. As aggressive as the tumour was, he wasn't in pain. I didn't figure on the emotional suffering, the anguish of having a lucid brain in better working order than most healthy people ever have. Very early on he'd told me he wasn't going to let the cancer decide. Following his diagnosis, he'd done copious amounts of reading on the Glioblastoma and joined Exit International. 'I've got Nembutal,' he told me. He'd bought it from China. 'When the time is right, I'll use it.' We knew it would be more difficult when he went into palliative care, but Bob knew all the legalities as did a close circle of friends. As long as we weren't there, he could do whatever he wished. Endless discussions were held about how to get around the first part of that sentence, but it wasn't possible. We all hoped he wouldn't do it but we also knew that was just the living being selfish.

Those eight weeks Bob spent in palliative care—far longer than most people—showed me why we need to be able to make choices about what we think is a good death. Opposite Bob lay Graham, drugged to the eyeballs and getting increasingly foetal every day. Quality of life is an individual issue and Bob knew this wasn't the dignified manner in which he wished to die. He'd pushed himself mentally and physically all his life, and to be reduced to whimpering in the manner of a wounded kangaroo wasn't in his plans. It was his wish and mine that I'd be rubbing his head when he died. Instead, along with a few other confidantes, I was reduced to distant bystander, wondering when it would be. The deadline kept shifting but two weeks ago it was patently obvious he'd had enough. Earlier that week he'd had a huge setback when his right hand seized, as he was playing his beloved harmonica. The last thing he liked doing was now out of reach.

I saw him 24 hours before he died. I'd already been to see him that day but at 6:00 p.m. I was struck by a sudden urgency to be with him. When I arrived, he was in his wheelchair staring at the wall. He looked so vulnerable, confused and childlike.

'Hello,' I said, coming up behind him. He was startled.

'Who's that?'

'Me, Bobby. What are you doing?'

'Dreaming. I think I was dreaming.' It was the way he said it but watching this huge character, this giant of a man suddenly dissolve into a lost child was too much for me.

I put my arms around him. He sparked up for a while, he asked me if I had plans because he was worried that I didn't plan enough and then he was tired. We hugged which we always did and he played with my hair not wanting to let go. Because I was trying to be grown-up and strong, the sobbing accelerated. Now he was comforting me. 'I don't say I love you enough Leens, but it sounds trite.' I told him it wasn't but trite itself was highly overused and beneath him. He laughed. I cried all through the night and into the next morning. I figured we'd have a few more days but his calmness worried me. They put him on watch the night he died because he'd yelled at the psychiatrist but he was a clever bastard. He found a window around 10:00 p.m. It was time enough to wheel himself into the toilet, mix up the bitter powder, drink it and get back into bed. He fell asleep for the last time.

Bob detested the smiley cancer industry. Like Hitchens, the idea that he was fighting a brave battle was swatted aside. 'It's a fucking illness,' he said. The prevailing narrative of survivors and bravery overlooks the reality that most people diminish and die in the most painful circumstances. From the moment you're diagnosed as terminal, death becomes a process based on a collective view of what is best. I'm not questioning palliative care: it's one of the only alternatives we have. But it's not for everyone (and by the way how many doctors do you see curled up in palliative care?) While we ramp up the fetishisation of cancer and parade those who've fought the good battle, it seems to me we're avoiding the hard discussion, the one about most people dying horrible deaths and being unable to die the way they choose.

All Bob wanted was a few people to be around him at the end. But because he didn't follow the script, he had to die alone. It's not so much his death that upsets me: it's that I wasn't allowed to be there to rub his head.

Nadja's Death—My Second Wife

By Luke Ball

Nadja was my second wife, and I was her second husband. We were very happy together for 30 years when she was diagnosed with uterine cancer in India. We had gone there, as we did every year, for a three-month stay to avoid the rigours of the English winter, and we loved the climate, the friendliness and our band of friends who gathered around a spiritual teacher there. We rented a small house and left enough belongings there to live a simple meditative life, exploring the locality and our inner feelings as we examined our values and what we wanted out of life.

We found that what fulfilled us most was being in the company of like-minded souls and gradually discarding past and future to live as contentedly as possible. As anyone who has watched *The Marigold Hotel* will know, India has its own way of imposing alternative values on those who persevere long enough to become hooked.

After the initial operation came lockdown and no further treatment was possible for a while. But I have to say that our care in the hospital in Pondicherry was exemplary and the convalescence very smooth. However, it was a little alarming not to be able to book a flight home, and we were relieved when we finally were able to leave three months later. We spent the time examining our feelings towards death and talking about it openly, and it was clear that chemotherapy raised more forebodings of alarm than accepting the likelihood of dying, so we focused on celebrating our unity in love in spiritual surroundings. And here I should explain that I'm a retired GP so I had some awareness of what to expect, having dealt with end-of life scenarios for many years. I was determined that dying should happen at home in Devon if it came to that, and be in a loving environment.

Entering the complex protocols of the NHS was a little tricky but eventually we were seen by the consultant who sent us for a scan which indicated that the cancer was steadily spreading but we still had a year or so together. As Nadja had no symptoms our life was perfectly normal, until one day she realised she could not see out of her left eye.

It only took a few weeks before the brain metastases brought on confusion and confinement to a hospital bed which the nurse arranged to have placed in our front room. Shortly afterwards, the tubes appeared for pain relief and sedation. We were fortunate to have excellent nursing care, and over the ensuing three weeks I was able to look after her at home and administer the drugs as she required them.

I would lie next to her listening to her breathing, which became intermittent after a while and she stopped squeezing my hand. I waited for the breath to stop, and spoke to her quietly urging her to let go. But for days she persisted, lost in another world, until one night I went to make a cup of tea for myself. When I came back, she had gone! I felt a flood of relief that I could now stop waiting and relax. There were no tears then, just emptiness.

After the funeral—which was a very moving ceremony during which we played clips from her experiences with her teacher in India and her feelings about dying—came the practicalities. My sons refused to leave me for several days, until eventually I had to tell them I needed to be alone to process my grief. When I was alone, I allowed the tears to flow, and was surprised at how many there were. In between I wrote poetry, which was an enormous emotional relief.

The Leaves of Autumn

The leaves of autumn sweep across my heart
To heap like memories against the outer wall
The wind that tears the empty trees apart
Lends but the echo of a life's recall.
To set the match which will ignite their pyre,
Consign a lifetime's story to its past,
The conflagration's all-consuming fire
Incinerates the grief of love so vast
Converting it to ash and fading chatter
That smoulders in the courtyard of a time
When nothing but your presence seemed to matter

167

And now reduced to metaphor and rhyme.
The souvenirs we shared in summer's sun
Slide into winter's vision of decay
Where heavy-lidded skies weigh down upon
The now diminished remnants of a day.
The curling smoke contains our testament
To joyous life joined by a reckless chance
When destiny was but an accident
Of careless love deciding on the dance.
The Gardener comes to separate the embers
And spread the balm of distance on events
So time will come when no-one quite remembers
The dramas on the far side of the fence.

I went to stay with family, but the return to an empty house was worse. The tears seemed unending, but in between life was returning to normal. It took many weeks for the grief to subside, but eventually I was able to turn to face the future and felt as though that chapter of my life was over and a new one beginning. I had to make a real effort not to look back at the past and focus on where I was going and throw myself into new ideas and meeting new people.

Many years ago, before I met my wife, I had left London and moved to a small village in Devon as I had the urge to return to rural life. Now being a member of a small village community helped enormously, as I feel surrounded by friends and neighbours on whom I can call on for mutual support. Daily walks in the country around, meeting people and being part of a tribe, has meant that I even have to close the door on company sometimes to ensure I have enough solitude to gather my thoughts and write my poems.

The Spreading

Today I took the last of you to where we used to sit, upon that old stump facing north along the track.

You are not so heavy now, death has diminished your stature so your grainy remnants fit in this small sack.

A treasured intimacy strokes my hip beneath the pillars of nature's tall cathedrals, urging

Their misty-fingered boughs to bend a last farewell and send you to your final merging,

While overhead the rooks give their assent to welcome you to their domain and bid you sleep

In their harsh hands. No sadness now, the raging grief subsided into nature's gentle keep,

And all emotion now dissolved in tranquil earth and sounds of wind and rain.

Your like will never stroke these fingers with their gentle touch or come this way again.

The weighted space within my breast contains your whispered sighs the trees repeat

In earnest of their promise to embrace you for safekeeping, as now you bend and gently touch their feet.

My Business—Planning the end of your life!

By Jane Duncan Rogers

My worst fear had just happened—my husband was dead, we'd had no kids, and I was left alone in the world. Age 54, too old to be a young widow, too young to be an old one.

That was how my 2012 started. Not a good place, and certainly not a place where I could ever have imagined what has happened since.

In those early months, I knew, in theory, there would be a blessing somewhere in his death, but I wasn't in the least interested in finding it. As grief took its grip on me, and I was tossed and turned by its waves, I just hung on, doing my best to trust that I would survive. And at that time, I wasn't even interested in surviving that much—I didn't actively want to die, I just didn't want to be alive.

But now, I can honestly say I am grateful for my husband's life AND his death. For without them both, nothing of what I am doing now would be happening.

Three years after he died, I published my memoir, *Gifted by Grief*. By this time, the blessing in disguise had shown itself, the writing of the book had proved cathartic, and I was in a good place in myself.

Readers' reaction to the book showed that they too wanted to answer the questions I had asked my husband a few months before he died. Things like 'what are your passwords,' 'what kind of coffin do you want,' and 'how do you want your body dressed.' Not easy to answer at the best of times and certainly not when you know you are on the way out. But we had plucked up the courage and amazingly, had enjoyed working on what turned out to be our last project together, despite the title being 'Philip's end of life plan.'

Little did I know it, but this was the start of what has become a fully-fledged social enterprise Before I Go Solutions, a training organisation where we train others to become accredited End of Life Plan Facilitators and provide products and programmes to help people put a good end of life plan in place.

I had previously run training courses and had in the back of my mind to train others, but this was brought forward a year when several people asked if they could train in what I was doing. Hence our pilot in 2018 for what is now our End of Life Plan Facilitators Programme, with the eighth intake for the training about to start as I write.

I had a lot to learn about being a social enterprise though. Despite being eligible for grant funding because of our status, it took a while to get my head around the fact that there are funding opportunities, and what social impact really meant in the eyes of possible funders.

I thought that by the very nature of the business, we were making a social impact—after all, everyone has to die, it's a community event, and therefore an impact on society. But funders needed to see a more specific benefit than that. Eventually, we were successful with a lottery-funded bid for £10K to bring Dead Good events to Scotland, and the development of a pack of End of Life Planning cards.

We have also developed the Philip Rogers Scholarship Fund, enabling those from disadvantaged backgrounds to become Facilitators, bringing this work to their communities too.

One of the ongoing challenges with this business has been the need to educate people about the importance of doing this work at all, and specifically what an end of life plan actually is. Most know about wills and funerals and the importance of doing them, and at the very least knowing if you want to be buried or cremated. And even then, a significant number have not attended to these matters (fewer than four in 10 adults in the UK still do not have a will in place, with statistics showing that there's has been only a one percent increase in will-making between 2019 and 2020, despite the pandemic).

But an actual end of life plan means you not only have a will sorted, but also both powers of attorney; your funeral organised in all its details; your digital life planned (because you'll still be alive online years later unless you state otherwise beforehand); your house decluttered (aka death cleaning); your advance care plan in place (your preference for treatment towards the end of your life); and the way your finances and household run—all documented and in one place.

And even when people realise that actually, this is a big project (after all, planning a funeral can be at least as big an event as a wedding, and yet we are supposed to plan that in a few days, compared to at least a few months for a wedding), they often just don't do it.

Like Susan, who told me 'I bought your second book, *Before I Go,* intending to go through it and complete everything. But six months later and I haven't touched it. I need help'

Or Regina who said 'I've started but I've got stuck with what to decide about how I want my end of life to be ideally, especially as my family are not forthcoming in talking about this with me.'

Or Saul, who shyly attended one of our courses as a lone man, and expressed his overwhelm in beginning about how to deal with the increase of possessions over the past 40 years, leading to anxiety, indecision, and worrying about what would happen amongst his kids when he was gone.

These are some of the scenarios that our facilitators now help with.

This journey so far has been one of ups and downs, with a lot of dogged determination on my part to fulfil our mission of having an end of life plans become as commonplace as birth plans.

Now, my time is focused on developing the Facilitators Programme, working with organisations to help their staff become more at ease with talking about end of life to their customers, and learning how to scale a young business so it becomes sustainable for long after I have gone.

This is quite a challenge for someone who has been used to being a solo professional for most of her life! We now have a team of administrative staff, all working part-time, and a crucial part of the workings behind the scenes.

Plus a growing international community of licensed facilitators (we've trained over 70 now, and about 25 of those are actually practising).

For me personally, I feel as if Philip and I are still in the business together somehow. As a psychotherapist, he was intent on helping others have a better life—and in a strange sort of way, he is still doing this from beyond the grave. This is definitely an unforeseen blessing!

Death Dinner

By Rose Rouse

After the soaring, a peace
like swans settling on a lake.
After the tumult and the roaring winds,
Silence.

—Sheila Kitzinger,
a natural childbirth activist

I am entering into the terrain of my own drawing-closer mortality—yet talking about death is still forbidden. Sex is so much more out in the open. Death is the last taboo. We do not talk about dying, how we'd like to die, or how others have died.

My mother nearly died of sepsis when she was 90—her organs had begun to close down but being the Yorkshire woman she was and still is, she battled through—and then by chance, I saw there was a death café at the Dissenter's Chapel in Kensal Green Cemetery as part of their October Month of the Dead.

I invited a close friend who presumed erroneously that Death was the incidental name of a café, and that we were meeting for Saturday morning tea and a natter. Instead we found ourselves in a circle of 12 discussing—the feelings that are evoked when a family member dies, the nature of a good death and different funereal rituals.

It was simply incredible to have this space to reflect on death and dying. There was a palpable sense of closeness and connection between us all at the end. Amanda and I definitely felt more alive as a result of the extraordinary conversations. One man admitted he'd never really expressed the grief around his mother dying. Another woman talked about the terrible suicide of someone close to her in detail. There was the death/life paradox in action. Plus it took place in this simple chapel created for non-conformists in 1834. Perfect. It sounds weird to say but we loved it, and vowed we would visit more. Forget bars and restaurants, death cafes are the place for truly, deeply, madly meeting.

A few months later, I found myself having the idea for a Death Dinner as part of our Advantages of Age OUTage series of events supported by the Arts Council England. It would also take place at the Dissenter's Chapel and was a performance and a film. The aim was to invite 10 people from deathworld—from mortician and author Carla Valentine to Soul Midwife Patrick Ardagh-Walter, to academic and expert in death rituals, Professor Douglas Davies to coffin plate aficionado, Hannah Gosh who happens to have a tattoo of one on her leg—to dialogue openly about their interests in death and dying, then dig a little deeper. We, at Advantages of Age, are keen to open up this last taboo as well as helping to form a Death Community, supporting the Assisted Dying movement, and also facing the nitty gritty of what we might personally want in terms death and dying.

I also thought it would be fascinating to invite the guests to come dressed as they would like to be buried or burnt. As well to bring objects with them that they'd like to go alongside them on the onward journey. This personal DeathStyle fascinated me.

Our aim was to turn the death stereotypes on their head. The guests arrived to a big red neon sign declaring Welcome to Death and then had their photos taken in or out of a deliberately kitsch Lachapelle-influenced gold frame with a leopard skin backdrop! By the wonderful photographer, Elainea Emmott. Of course, not everyone was so keen to be snapped in this Day of the Dead type Momento Mori and we let them off the hook. Professor Davies wore his grey suit but had a rather extravagant cravat with it. Patrick, the soul midwife, was in his suit and photographed with his white miniature rose, the object he had chosen to take with him into the next world, which he felt crossed over between earth and spirit, a living rose. Others were keener to step into the frame, Liz Rothschild who runs a woodland burial ground, had turned up in her cream nightie and had chocolates to munch in the after-life. Suzanne, co-founder of Advantages of Age, was wearing a sexy scarlet dress clasping a photo of her beloved boys. Caroline Rosie Dent dazzled with her gold and black Victorian dress, black shawl and headband covered with ivory roses. In fact, she was the style star of the Death Dinner.

Everyone was welcomed over that liminal threshold into Deathland by the Queen of the Night (Ingrid Stone), all in white, of course, rather than black, with her purifying burning sage sticks. In silence, we made our way to our seats at the table accompanied by the haunting, ethereal sounds of Fran Loze's cello. An abundant feast—from tomato and goats' cheese tartlets to Parma ham and the remarkable broken heart cake—had been prepared by Caroline Bobby, our magnificent cook and a guest.

During the first half of the dinner, I invited the guests to tell us a little about their relationship with death and how they were linked to Deathworld.

Charlie Phillips, photographer, has documented Afro-Caribbean funerals at Kensal Green cemetery for years. He explained how Afro-Caribbean funerals are changing and that the emphasis is on paying out a lot of money and having songs like *I Did It My Way* by Frank Sinatra these days. He had brought along his camera, of course, as his death object because he is referred to as 'the dead man photographer'.

Liz Rothschild is a celebrant, started the Kicking the Bucket Festival in Oxford, owns a woodland burial ground and has a show called Out Of The Box about death. Liz explained how when a friend of hers died, her group of friends gathered in such an intimate DIY way, it inspired her to want to support others create this kind of a ceremony.

Hannah Gosh makes modern mourning jewellery and told us why she is so taken with coffin plates. She had also brought along a pug's skull as her object, but not her pug's skull!

Caroline Rosie Dent is an end-of-life doula and a death café host. She told us about her death anxiety as a child, and why she'd brought along a part of her son's umbilical cord to take with her on the ancestral trip.

John Constable aka John Crow wrote The Southwark Mysteries, a series of poems which became a play. It is the story of the Winchester Goose, one of the medieval sex workers in the area who were condoned by the Bishop of Winchester but forced to have unconsecrated graves. John has been a campaigner around the Cross Bones graveyard for many years and holds a monthly vigil there on the 23rd of every month.

Caroline Bobby is a writer and psychotherapist. She had brought with her *The Book of Longing* by Leonard Cohen and her favoured piece of fine woollen cloth, that she would like to be wrapped in when she goes. She sees herself becoming ash and being blown away.

Patrick Ardagh-Walter is a soul midwife, which he describes as being simply alongside someone as they approach this last stage of their lives.

Carla Valentine is an author, mortician and the Technical Assistant Curator at Barts Pathology Museum where she looks after 5,000 body parts in bottles. She describes herself as being quite an unusual child who was interested in death and whose grandfather died when she was seven, in front of her.

Professor David Davies lectures in Death Studies, His most recent book is *Mors Britannica: Lifestyle and Death-Style in Britain Today*. He explained that he's fascinated by different groups and their attitudes to death, some like their lives and deaths to cohere, others are just the opposite. He said he hadn't brought an object because he's never thought of having an object with him at that time.

Liz Hoggard is a journalist who admits to feeling like a bit of a death tourist in our midst. She sports pearls that might act as some sort of collateral in a future existence and has brought along two lipsticks, one of them is black, the other red. Max Ernst described the latter apparently as 'the red badge of courage.'

During the break, we listen to Caroline Bobby's recorded version of her piece, Dreaming of Death. It is precious and moving. In it, she says: 'I don't know if I long for death just because living with baseline depression is unforgiving, and every morning is a shock. I don't think it's just that. This human and embodied world has never, quite felt like my natural habitat. At a cellular level I am aching to go home.'

After this raw and vulnerable piece, we entered a discussion about death led by Suzanne. We looked at whether there is a revolution in death going on, whether death is really trending, how we could welcome death into our daily lives in conversation and what sort of funerals we would like. Some of it was funny, other parts were poignant. Professor Douglas Davies declared controversially that the only revolution going on is amongst middle-class women. 'The Death Chattering classes,' he asserted.

Finally, Charlie Phillips declared that ideally, he would go while making love. And that he'd like 'Lucky Motherfucker' on his gravestone as well as 'Came and Went at the same time.' As you can imagine, laughter rippled through the chapel.

I announced that natural birth activist and then death activist, Sheila Kitzinger had inspired me. She had a death plan, managed to stay at home to die surrounded by her close family despite doctors trying to get her to hospital because she had cancer, then she was put in a simple cardboard coffin decorated by family and friends, and eventually taken in the back of a car for a small woodland burial. The more flamboyant memorial service came later.

Goodbye My Lovely Friend

By Suzanne Noble

There comes a point in life and I'm sure it's different for everyone when one becomes aware of one's mortality. I can't pinpoint when, exactly, it was for me but one day I became scared of climbing up or down steep staircases, thinking I might fall. I stopped driving about 10 years ago when my little Fiat 500 was taken back by the leasing company and, since then, when I get in the passenger seat of a car, I'm aware that my heart beats a bit faster than usual. I avoid looking out from tall buildings. These may all be totally unrelated or, as I suspect, they're just my brain sending out a warning signal that life is full of dangers that I'm not quite as resilient as I was in my youth and that death may come upon me suddenly.

I have also spent the past year becoming more interested in death and specifically, how I'd like to die and my funeral. A lot of this has come from putting together the film *Death Dinner* which Rose Rouse and I created last year with the help of an Arts Council grant.

Prior to making the film, I hadn't really given death much thought, but the dialogue over dinner made me realise that there are many different sorts of funerals and ceremonial aspects, as well as various ways of body disposal.

Recently, I attended a Thanksgiving for the Life of Nigel Castle, held at the Rosslyn Hill Unitarian Chapel in the heart of Hampstead. Nigel was someone who had been in and out of my life for the past decade, thanks to an introduction made by his closest friend, Rob Norris.

A keen gardener, skilled healer, acupuncturist, osteopath, masseur plus being a good musician, Nigel was multi-talented. At various times, he had tended to my garden, worked his magic on my back and danced with me and others at 5 Rhythms, another passion of his. My children, now grown up, remember us all sitting in a circle and singing together while Nigel and Rob played guitars. He was a familiar face around Maida Vale and Queens Park, driving around in his beaten up Volvo. I never knew how he kept that car on the road but he did. Nigel was always around and then, one day, I found out, via Rob, that he had lymphoma and two months later he was gone. He was 67. I never got a chance to say goodbye but there were plenty of people that did. Nigel was much loved by everyone that met him.

If funerals could come with ratings, then Nigel's would have been a five star one. I'm by no means an expert on what constitutes a good or bad funeral, but Nigel went out in a way that will leave a lasting memory for me and, I'm sure, for many others.

The service itself lasted two hours. And, let's face it, it's hard enough to find a table in a restaurant that will let you sit there for two hours, much less a chapel. The service presided over by Anja Saunders, Nigel's old friend and an Interfaith Minister, wove together music, poetry, tributes, recollections and finally Nigel's own voice. At various points during this unconventional and beautiful service, we danced around the beautiful wicker casket to 'Dance Me to the End of Love' by Leonard Cohen, and then we were invited to come up and weave flowers into it or write tributes to Nigel on small, brown labels which would be buried with him.

There were tears and laughter as friends and family recounted their memories of Nigel. A pianist had written a song for him. A guitarist wrote another one. His friends from 5 Rhythms read out a series of poems.

Rob and I particularly liked White Owl Flies in and out of the Field by Mary Oliver, which seemed to sum up Nigel perfectly, https://www.saltproject.org/progressive-christian-blog/2022/2/14/white-owl-flies-into-and-out-of-the-field-by-mary-oliver

The length of the service felt like we were all able to collectively grieve, and by the end, I felt my spirits lighten as we all said goodbye to him. It was an amazing tribute to a wonderful person and I couldn't help thinking that the world would be a richer place if everyone chose such an intimate departure ceremony.

Afterwards, I spoke to Anja to thank her for the way she managed to oversee the service and its host of participants in such an effortless manner. She was so fittingly graceful in the way she provided just the right amount of space and time between tributes for us to absorb what Nigel had meant to those he loved and just how much of an impact he had had on so many people. At the end, she encouraged us all to breathe and we did.

179

Leaning Into Death

By Caroline Bobby

As some of you know, I am deeply interested in death and dying.

Some time ago, I released the beginning of a film collaboration with my friend Andrew Hassenruck. Its intent was to keep some kind of record as I explored the possibility and option of taking my life.

When I say released, I don't mean in a major way. I'm not a media star, and neither is my little film trending. Nevertheless, I have come out into the public domain with my enquiry. Everyone to whom I matter has seen it. Many people I don't personally know, some who kindly follow my blog, friends of friends, friends of strangers, have seen it too.

Over the last decade, I have chosen to write from an undefended place. It serves me well as a connective measure, and if on occasion it can serve someone else, well, that is a cherry on the cake.

Although I'd become comfortable with the process of working like this, putting this piece out there—still put my heart in my mouth. My close friends were already in the loop. I had had fulsome conversations (you know who you are) and felt into what it would mean, and what it would ask of me, to go public.

It's an emotive and taboo terrain. It's an unusual proposal. It's likely I'll trigger some people to anger, fear, judgment, or argument. Most difficult of all is when others want to fix me. I get the good heart of it, but that triggers me.

Don't get me wrong, if I were offered private health care that would take me out of the six months between appointments and praying to get to talk to the same surgeon as last time, groove, I'd say an unreserved, yes, please and thank you. They are the facts of the matter—alongside the time it takes to journey through the necessary hoops. I'd prefer a shorter route to finding out if the surgery to fuse two discs in my spine, either alleviated pain enough to make a difference to my quality of life, didn't work at all, or indeed made it worse. These are the possible outcomes.

It's the intense level of generous but onerous offers to fix that sees me off. The endless treatments and practitioners that have worked miracles for someone else. I want to say: don't you think I've tried a lot of different remedies over many years? Don't you reckon I might have some people in place? Don't you realize that my disposable income is very small and may well be allocated already? My low tolerance for such efforts may not be fair, or very graceful, but I also want to say: what if you don't have to offer me anything, and neither one of us needs fixing? My point being that these old narratives make distance happen, and I'd rather hang out in the fields of helpless humanity, where tears and laughter are buddies, and it is as it is.

Death compels me, and always has done, though this last decade of my little life has been the kindest. Kindness found me when I gave up looking for redemption. It was always there. Do I regret how long I didn't know that for? Yes, I do.

I wonder about the duet of my depression and physical pain. If I were of a lighter disposition, would it seem such a viable option to choose death in the face of increasing disability and pain? The truth is I don't have and won't find a categorical answer to such wondering. A simple thread of truth is this: if there isn't a way to reduce the degree of pain in my back, hips and groin, the pain that is my constant companion, I don't want to stay in the world. It's survival. It's both too much and not enough.

My specialist subjects of death and enduring depression are not always easy to speak about. I feel deep in my blood and bones that doesn't serve us, and that the unspeakable needs a voice. Many voices. Being a tiny thread in that conversation matters to me. What if depression responds better to being welcomed than banished? What if suicide is not by definition a tragedy? (Though of course it often is). What if choosing to die, is for some of us, the optimum option? What if death itself is not a tragedy, but could be more of a sweet human event to be thought, talked about and walked towards, differently? What if the mirror twins of entering embodied life with the first breath, and slipping out on the last, were equally blessed? What if more of us could turn our faces into dying with awareness and kindness?

I know, that's a lot of what ifs.

181

Here's a thing, I feel a least some gratitude to this opportunity for sincere enquiry. I enjoy, yes enjoy, thinking it through, imagining and creating details. I can feel my integrity and my love of beauty, ritual and intimate communication in the harness. I would put my heart and soul into giving it my best, passionate effort. That must mean at least some part of me, however small, would be disappointed if the surgery is effective and I get to stay in my little life for a while longer.

In the few weeks since setting my film loose, I have received so much kindness and understanding. I am truly humbled by some Herculean stretching to empathy instead of opposition. Gratitude especially to my brother Paul, sister-in-law, Maureen and precious niece, Genna.

When I started sending Postcards from the Window Ledge seven years ago, my first blog post ended with these words.

Somewhere between a daughter being born and a sister dying,

I have found that I can love life and long for death at the same time.

That both are true, and I am as full of tenderness as of despair.

As Leonard Cohen says in the lyrics of Famous Blue Raincoat: *I hope you're keeping some kind of record.* For me, the taking of a few notes along the road never fails to crack my heart open. With my heart open I always remember we are in it together. All our little lives rolling on and running out, in a ravaged and beautiful world, that in my humble opinion—is also dying.

Note—this was an enquiry that Caroline did at a particular time and is part of her long-term enquiry into death dying, and her back operation was successful.

How Rituals Helped Me Grieve for my Mother

By Serena Constance

I'm a skeleton collector. I have a large sea-washed radius from a sperm whale beached on the sands in Orkney. Part of its flipper, its hand. One of my most treasured possessions is an early Victorian piece of scrimshaw, engraved with portraits of two women—maybe the whaler's wife and daughter or maybe his lovers in different ports—made from a sperm whale's tooth which I inherited from my father.

In fact, I have a whole collection of teeth, ranging from a 50,000-year-old European cave bear's molar to all my baby milk teeth kept by my mother alongside my four adult wisdom teeth taken out when I was 21. I can now keep my wisdom in my pocket.

Bones and teeth survive. Bones remind us of the transformation that occurs at death. I have a bunch of my hair too, literally a fist full of matted dreadlock strands woven with strips of fabric and beads, remnants of my thankfully brief 'crusty grunge' phase in 1991—hair which has lasted nearly 30 years. Like bones, hair lives on. I've come to understand I'm a bone worker. Bones have worked their way into my 'medicine basket' of ritual tools that have helped me navigate a year filled with death. From the sudden death of my mother at the end of 2017, to the sudden death of my mother-in-law within two weeks of that anniversary in December 2018, to the sudden death of a yoga friend who tragically took her own life. Their bones now are ash; only fragments of bone remain, returned to the earth to sit with ancestral bones or waiting, resting, keeping family company whilst loved ones adjust to the massive, unexpected earthquake of transformation that's hit them. The dead have to adjust too. Sometimes their souls need help crossing the mythic river in the Underworld. There lies the role of the shaman, the psychopomp, the death doula, the soul midwife, the priest or priestess and the Irish mna caointe and baen-shea in the-end-of-life and soul-crossing rituals they perform.

Through all of this, more than ever before, I've come to understand the value of ritual in our natural cycle of life and death. Ritual makes us human. Ritual connects us to our animal, secular and spiritual selves. We know many species have ritualistic behaviours. Corvids have been observed participating in mourning rituals, and I still have the vivid picture in my mind of a London raven jumping up and down on a dead bird's body, cawing as if were singing an intense keening in St James's Park as I walked to work. **We now know that ritual increases the likelihood of species survival as it binds groups together**. I wonder if this large, black bird was performing a ritualistic death dance to warn the rest of the flock, or was it in mourning? Ravens have long since been associated with death in folklore and myth.

Part of being human is coming to terms with death. Ritual has its place in helping us negotiate that final transformation—from ashes to ashes, dust to dust. In our increasingly secular society long focused on prizing youth above elderhood, spending vast amounts of money on maintaining a youthful veneer, we have developed an unhealthy relationship with death. Death and its rituals have been pushed to the side lines in this relentless pursuit of youth, of living as long as possible, even if the quality of that life is often questionable. Death has been taken out of the home and medicalised. So many people want to deny death, they fear death; by doing so death has gone underground until it rears its inevitable skeleton head. Death is all around us, there is no escaping; delaying possibly, but let's face it, it's not going away. The planet is at the precipice of the sixth mass extinction, yet still so many of us are ill-equipped for death. We've forgotten how to greet it, to sit with it, and ultimately how to mourn and grieve. However, many of us do instinctively know that ritual has its place when it comes to death. Even if that instinct is sometimes more unconscious than conscious.

Death demands ritual. Not just the physical death of our loved ones: our partners, our elders, our families, our friends, our babies, our children, leading ultimately to our own death, but other symbolic deaths too. The end of our bleeding (if we're a woman), our marriages, our jobs, our old, worn-out selves, all these transformations involve a final goodbye which deserves to be marked and mourned. Ritual and ceremony can provide a framework to do just that. Underlying all ritual (and myth) is a universal pattern: the death and rebirth of a god or divinity that ensures the fertility of the land as well as social order and harmony. When we place ourselves at the heart of ritual we connect back into that universal pattern. I think that's the key to ritual unlocking whatever transformation and change we are marking, honouring, letting go of or celebrating.

You don't have to be religious to create ritual. As I've discovered, consciously creating your own personal rituals can be very cathartic and freeing. There can often be a sense of drama to ritual, and there is the idea that theatre itself emerged out of ritual. The performer in me, having created improvised theatre and dance over many decades, has been naturally drawn to creating ritual in recent years, particularly in this year of major loss. The death of the mother is one of the most fundamental deaths to grieve, since not only do we come into the world from our mothers, they represent the fertility of our land, of our society, of our ancestors. No wonder 2017/2018 was an earthquake year when I lost both my mother and my mother-in- law. At the same time, I've been losing my periods—the ultimate ending of my fertility, although an ending I'm finally glad to embrace after giving birth to death. It's taking me 13 years, and many deaths in between to reach this place of acceptance.

Through all of these griefs, I've found myself creating ritual. I'm not religious; but I am spiritual. For many years I was a card-carrying atheist, rejecting the dogma and ingrained patriarchy of most monotheistic organised religions. Christian mythology never really did it for me anyway. I just couldn't relate to Jesus, and as a mythologist, I couldn't understand how people actually believed the Bible as a gospel truth, not as a loose collection of stories written down many hundreds of years after the grains of various historical events had become mythologised and spun into stories. I enjoyed the story telling aspect at Sunday School (I voluntarily went when I was seven for a brief period) and at 14 easily gained an A in compulsory O level Religious Education. I guess it's because I'm a storyteller.

When my baby died, I found myself craving ritual. I remember going into churches just to create my own rituals focused around Mary, lighting candles for her and my son. The archetypal mother who had also lost a son. To me she was the only remnant of an ancient fertility goddess left, sanitised into a virgin by a male dominated institution. I found Catholic or High Church of England churches always good for some goddess veneration in the form of Mary. Their churches really do the best smells and bells—because they understand the theatre of ritual.

The three cores aspects of ritual being:

- blood sacrifice (the blood of Christ in a cup)
- a natural process or mythic historical narrative (the Christian mythology), and
- an act of magic (the Christian symbol of transformation, the Holy Communion)

Thirteen years on from that earthquake birth, I'm exploring and creating my own rituals which have been particularly helpful during my year of mother grief. I have organically gathered together my 'medicine' basket with my tools of ritual. My bones, my incense, my core oracles—the runes and roses—and various other objects of meaning and personal importance. My horse skin drum 'Paskadi', my rattle, my cloak, my hood, and my 1940s fox fur cape. The elements of ritualistic transformation. I've started inviting others to join my rituals and offer rune and rose reading rituals.

I created my rune set after being called to work with runes in three dreams within three months of my mother's death. This became a ritual in itself; collecting the wood to complete the set (I'd been given the first nine), carving, sanding, polishing and then anointing them with the last vestiges of my own menstrual blood (the blood sacrifice), into a tool that can help others transform (the magic), underpinned as they are with a Norse mythological framework (the narrative).

By working intuitively and instinctively, I've found that creating rituals both personal and shared, has really helped me through my grief. It's provided a focus and an outlet for my grief. When my mother was close to death (she died 24 hours after having a major stroke whilst out shopping), I somehow knew what to do. I didn't consult a book; I wasn't a member of a church, but I knew that ritual was important. In the year that's passed, I've also discovered I have a natural ability to do what I now know as soul journey work. I've found I have 'psychopomp' abilities—I had to look this up—after experiencing very strong and vivid dreams and vision journeys with drumming, where I've helped dead or dying people (and trees) 'cross over' to the other side.

Birds too, back to the corvids, are said in many cultures to have a psychopomp nature, carrying the dead to the afterlife. A few days before I lost my son, I was lying in my old bedroom at my mother's house, clinging on for dear life looking out at the sycamore tree at an unusual gathering of at least 15 magpies in the tree. There had not been one before or since. My mother and I were both struck by the strange occurrence. The magpie is my death bird and my magician. I don't try to explain this psychopomp phenomenon, as ultimately I don't think it matters. I simply accept it. All I know is the role of the psychopomp is known in myth, in folklore and in ancient spiritual practices, down through the millennia. I've also starting exploring the power of singing laments and keening from the Celtic Scottish and Irish traditions—coming as I do from strong Celtic stock as well as Norman Viking—using my drum to access these songs as they emerge. They are a powerful way to bring voice to death and grief.

I'm beginning to see there is a place for all this work—as we enter into a new, more open and frank relationship with death. Death is coming out of the shadows. Ritual most definitely has its place and new death rituals are emerging, rooted in our landscape, in a way that is meaningful for us today.

The growth of the death cafe is one example of communities coming together to talk about death and break some of the taboos that have grown up in our youth-obsessed world. I went to one in Plymouth the week before I led a small family ceremony to inter my mother's ashes in her family grave. The cafe was well-facilitated, we all sat round tables talking about our experiences of death, dying and grieving, and it was actually very light hearted. There was much more laughter than I expected. Ultimately, I think that's the trick—to laugh with death, even in the midst of the tears, the anger and the whole gamut of emotion death wrings out of us. Gallows humour, morbid humour is there for a reason. Death doesn't want us to be deathly serious…all of the time.

I'll continue to collect my bones, read my runes and bang my drum whilst I carry my increasingly heavy medicine basket around the country singing to the land and telling stories to birds in the trees, laughing along the way like some crazy Sacred Fool literally dancing with Death. And strangely as I sit here in my mother's easy chair finishing this article, the voice on a radio play I'm listening to drifts over, and says: *She deserves a good death.*

Resources and further reading

Chi In—my poem about death and the Sacred Fool
For rune and rose readings, rituals, poetry, stories and my blog visit www.runesnroses.com

For more on ritual, the book *Ritual—A Very Short Introduction*—by Barry Stephenson
For information on death cafes, https://deathcafe.com/
For information on psychopomps, https://en.wikipedia.org/wiki/Psychopomp

Welcome Aboard the Funeral Revolution

By Kate Tym and Kate Dyer,
the founders of the UK's first **Coffin Club**

It's a sunny morning in September in a room above an art gallery in Hastings. There is laughter, chat and a feeling of warmth and camaraderie which seems slightly odd considering each of the five people involved are busily decorating their coffins. This is Coffin Club UK where death is always top of the agenda and yet no one seems very sad!

Kate Tym and Kate Dyer, the founders of the charity, encourage clubbers to plan their perfect send-off and, if they like, bling up their coffins too. 'We go through life planning each step of the way and then, when it comes to our funerals, we seem quite happy to just leave them completely up to chance,' says Kate Dyer, cheerfully. 'Yes,' adds Kate Tym, 'families find themselves, at a point of bereavement, having to make decisions about what mum or dad or sister might want and they're not in the right place, emotionally, to start asking questions or thinking creatively. Coffin Club removes that anxiety as it means you get exactly the end-of-life celebration you want and you know exactly where every penny's going.'

Funeral Directors, generally, like to offer a range of packages—it's 20 minutes up the cremation, or a religious place of worship, to a very set format. 'People don't realise that funerals are actually very unregulated,' says Kate Tym, 'you can separate the cremation or burial from the celebration of life.' 'We've had send-offs in barns, village halls and even the upstairs room of a pub,' Kate D says. 'Simply by changing the setting, the whole atmosphere changes, too,' she enthuses.

Kate T says that by putting a brightly-decorated coffin into the mix it becomes part of the proceedings. 'Guests aren't afraid of it—they come up and look at it, touch it, pat it, have a chat with the person inside.

Sometimes we leave a space where people can write messages to the person inside—they're involved right up to the last moment.'

Coffin Club runs over six weeks, for one morning a week, and each week there is an invited speaker—forward-thinking, independent funeral directors, the manager of the local crematorium, a representative from the local hospice, the manager of a natural burial ground and a lady who did her own DIY ceremony for her husband just over a year ago. 'She kept him at home for five days after he'd died,' Kate T says cheerfully. 'She really is our poster girl!' Each clubber is given a funeral wish list right at the beginning and fills it in as the weeks go by. So, from burial or cremation to music choices, to venues and readings and anything else they might fancy, not a stone is left unturned.

'The reasons people come to Coffin Club are all different,' says Kate D. 'Some are all about practicality, they want to cost their funeral and have it all organised before they go, so that their family aren't left with the job. For others, it's more about coming to terms with the inevitable and finding that in itself empowering,' Kate T adds.

Currently, in the UK, the average cost of a funeral is around the £4000 mark (https://www.sunlife.co.uk/how-much-does-a-funeral-cost-in-the-uk-today) and that's not including the 'do' afterward, the flowers or the catering or any legal costs around settling an estate. Coffin Club wants to deal with funeral poverty, too, 'We can get a much more personally tailored funeral to come in at around the £2,500 mark. It can be done even more cheaply if you don't use a funeral director at all, but that's not for everyone,' says Kate D.

'Each time we've run the club we've had one person attend who is terminally ill,' Kate T says. 'That's really hard, but also means a lot to us. Ashley came along wanting to be buried in the field at the back of his house, but wasn't sure if that was even legal. It is legal and it's really not difficult to arrange. Coffin Club enabled him to get exactly what he wanted.'

'He had the most fantastic celebration of his life,' says Kate D. 'We started in the village hall, which was packed. The service itself was full of music and lots of people stood up and told personal stories of their memories of Ashley.'

Without the crematorium time limit hanging over us, we were able to let the service take as long as it took, and at the end that was about an hour and a half. Then he was drummed across to the field where he was buried with family members helping to lower his coffin into the grave. 'Ashley had actually been too poorly to decorate his coffin,' Kate T explains, 'so his family did it for him after he'd died. They covered it in maps of places he'd travelled to and tickets from gigs he'd been to. I think they found it a nice experience, talking about things he'd done and sharing memories.'

Kate D takes over, 'Everyone came up and touched his coffin, wrote messages, talked to him—it was really very lovely.' That's the true validation of Coffin Club—someone who came along and got exactly the send-off they wanted and for it to not cost a fortune.

The coffins Coffin Club that uses are really innovative. They are flat-packed ply coffins that come in 10 sections that are then put together with an Allen key. The Kates get them from a Dutch company called Coffin in a Box. 'They have a really low-carbon footprint,' says Kate T. 'They're made with virtually no waste, have low-emissions in combustion and biodegrade really easily. Putting them together is pretty funny, too. Having been involved in making and decorating the coffin gives people a feeling of taking control.'

'We've had people's kids come and help them, they laugh together whilst decorating their box, it's a truly bonding experience and makes the whole thing less frightening. Of course, there is a very deep sadness when someone dies,' says Kate T, 'but celebrating their life and trying to capture some of the joy and energy they had when they were alive is about love and respect, too. It's not about making light of it, it's about caring deeply enough to give them a send-off that is totally about them.'

The decorated coffins have ranged from simple—painted white with a Star of David to much more decorative, for example, hot pink with unicorns and Elvis, to the jokey, for example, a plain box with This Way Up and Handle with Care stickers on it. 'It's not about how good they are, artistically,' says Kate D. 'It's more the process... the thought behind them. It gets our Clubbers thinking about what's been important to them during their lifetime.'

They range from an elderly Quaker who had a Quaker Oats themed coffin to Bev, who loves purple and went for a vibrant violet base coat. 'A lot of the conversations happen while we're decorating,' says Kate D. 'It's a time when people share some of their deepest feelings because thinking about dying—brings these emotions sharply into focus.'

'Coffin Club was born out of frustration,' says Kate T. 'We're funeral celebrants and we were so depressed by the one-size-fits-all formula of most funerals that we thought there must be a better way. We want everyone to know that there's a vast choice of send-offs available to them from the traditional Victorian gent in front of a limo hearse to skipping naked through a field with dancing girls and fire eaters!! If you know you can do anything at all and still want to go the totally conventional route, we'll support everyone 100 percent. However we don't want people having 20 minutes up the cremation because they had no idea they could do anything else. Coffin Club is all about choices.'

Ultimately, Coffin Club is about people taking back ownership of their end of life celebrations. 'We can't believe the children of the '50s and '60s generations are going to go for the formulaic way!' The Kates really believe, as a nation, we're on the brink of a funeral revolution. 'We've run three Coffin Club Master Classes so that people in other areas can learn how to set-up and run Coffin Clubs and are certain they will grow all over the UK.'

Coffin Club has been followed by a local documentary maker, Whalebone Films, for over a year and the BBC came and filmed in September too—there is a definite feeling of the tide turning. 'We don't believe respect is about how much you paid or what you wear. it can be about getting out a pot of paint and doing something that's a labour of love.'

Coffin Club really is a fabulous initiative. As the Kates say: 'We've got to start talking about death again as a nation. From the moment we're born, we're all terminally ill. We need to bring death back into day-to-day and out of the scary, taboo place that it's been for a long time now. If you talk about sex, you're not going to get pregnant and if you talk about death, you're not going to die. You'll just be well prepared—Coffin Club is really just about thinking outside the box!'

SECTION SEVEN
VOYAGES

The Importance of a Good Travelling Companion

By Rose Rouse

One's destination is never a place but a new way of seeing things
—Henry Miller

I'm not one of those people who like to travel alone. I like to share my experiences with someone else. However, I don't underestimate the difficulties of being with someone else for 24 hours a day. I know it's a testing experience. There are many areas for conflict. It can break a close friendship.

After two years of not just Covid-prevented trips but also working on projects that needed all of my attention, I was keen to go away. I'm always interested in exploring new places and I'd loved going to Senegal in West Africa with my son a couple of years ago. I wanted to do more in that part of Africa. Ghana arrived by chance—I was chatting to someone who worked for the same charity as me. He happened to have built an eco-lodge on the coast in the Volta area of Ghana called Meet Me There. I looked at their website and decided then and there that Ghana would be my new destination.

That was summer 2021 and of course, I had no idea what would be happening with Covid and it was pre-Omi. I invited my partner, Asanga to come along. January is always my favourite time to get away, a long way away; to flee the pervasive grey, the post-Xmas blues, to lighten the emergent year.

Eventually, Asanga declined. A few years ago, he and I faced our differences on this front. He declared that he was no longer—he was 78 at this point and is 80 now, has a major climbing injury and is happy with the heavenly landscape of sea and mountains in North Wales—interested in long haul trips abroad. But he was supportive of my continuing enthusiasm.

I was stumped because none of my usual travelling companions were available. And then I happened to be talking to an old friend, Ruby Millington—we met when we both worked as freelance journalists for the *Evening Standard's* Metropolis 30 years ago—and she confessed that she'd wanted to go to Accra for some time to check out the style and the art. That she'd read it was the new New York.

We'd never been anywhere at all together that lasted longer than an afternoon but in September, we booked the plane tickets. It was a commitment and a leap into the Covid unknown. We booked a recommended hotel/hostel in Accra and the eco-lodge for a few nights and then we did nothing except rest in a kind of uneasy contentment about our future plans.

There was a flurry of worry amongst my friends as Omicron arrived in South Africa. I explained that South Africa was a long way from Ghana. Ghana, in fact, had very low Covid deaths—just over 1,000 according to their official figures. For some reason, I had faith.

In mid-December, I realised that I needed not only my Booster Covid vaccination but also diphtheria/typhoid, tetanus and yellow fever. Not just one vaccination but three. I tried to get out of the yellow fever one—I managed to find proof that I'd had it in 1978 in New Orleans and these days, it's meant to last for life—but Ghanaian regulations stipulate that you need to have it in the last 10 years. I had it. I have survived so far.

This was the beginning of the tenaciousness that was required before we even set foot in Ghana. A whole trip in itself. There was the visa situation. There were umpteen conditions to fulfil—a written invitation from our host, proof of a hotel, proof of money, flights, a vaccination pass, etc. Ruby and I almost lost the will to live trying to fill it in online. And then we had to get the Ghanaian High Commission in Archway— after a lateral flow test in the morning.

Finally, just before Xmas, we had our visas. Hurrah.

Ruby looks after her incredible 96-year-old mum, Maria—who (bless her) was really keen for her daughter to get away for 18 days—and was organising for a lovely local woman to go in every day, as well as preparing meals for the freezer and a multitude of other tasks. I hadn't realised what a superwoman Ruby was. She actually managed to ring her mum every day while we were away—from petrol stations (Ghana's petrol stations are often like palaces, they have oil and are proud of it), from the side of busy roads with a Pentecostal choir singing nearby. It was one of her many travelling feats.

And then there were the British Airway requirements. As well as the PCR test to do. Uploading vaccination passes, Travel Codes that took hours to obtain from a Ghanaian-approved website—we spent hours trying to work it all out. We failed to upload them and arrived on Jan 6th 2022 at Heathrow feeling weary and anxious.

It was a good sign that it was a pretty smooth check-in, after all. A six-hour flight and then there was a mini-crisis for me. I could hardly walk as I arrived in Accra. My ankle had been affected by sitting in one position on the flight, I wasn't sure what was going on. But I had to hobble up and down the airport getting the incredibly expensive lateral flow test and the results. And then my bag was one of the last to arrive. Luckily Ruby was there to help out. We both took it as a good sign that a holy man from Senegal was arriving at the same time to chants and hoots from a group of local Muslims.

WE HAD ARRIVED IN ACCRA. We celebrated with a beer at midnight amidst the gorgeous equatorial heat next to the pool at our hotel/hostel. We had booked separate rooms aware that we hadn't voyaged anywhere together and as a space precaution. In other words, we might need that space from one another.

I really liked Somewhere Nice—mostly occupied by young people backpacking or working for NGOs—there was a big breakfast table for the sharing of tales and I found out from a couple of Parisian-Cameroonian women some good local places to eat—but Ruby wasn't so keen. She saw the layers of untended dust and dirt, I saw the communal thing.

Accra was confusing to navigate at first—not to mention my difficulty walking which thankfully only lasted a day—lots of duel carriageways and I am not sure Ruby was convinced by the 'new New York' description. But something happened on the second day that cemented our travelling relationship. We had decided to look at art galleries; in the evening, I suggested we go to the 1957 Gallery (the year of independence, Ghana was the first African country to leave its colonisers under the socialist vision of President Nkrumah in 1957) which was located in the five-star bling Kempinsky Hotel. We visited the bold figurative works on the walls and then cocktailed at the pool bar. Afterwards, we, unlike everyone else, didn't have a taxi waiting for us so we actually walked down the road. There was a daunting black James Bond-type armoured Hummer outside too. Just as we were about to hail a cab, we noticed that there was music emanating from the National Theatre nearby. We decided to check it out.

The next moment, Ruby was taking photos—she's an ardent Insta woman—of what seemed to be a band on the red carpet. Within seconds, the lanky be-dreaded, be-hatted, be-shaded main man had ushered us onto the red carpet as well and then into what turned out to be The Young Ghanaian Achievers' Awards. Losso Saabele—king of afro-pop and dancehall—was up for Artist of the Year.

Here we were in our casuals amidst Ghanaians dressed up to the nines in sparkly shoes and sequinned dresses. The award ceremony was slightly shambolic—sorry Ghana—nominations were missed. And sin of all sins—our man should have won and he didn't. It's now being re-awarded to him. Talk about La La Land. Anyway, he did invite me for a little dance as part of his performance which of course I rose to the occasion for!! And Ruby recorded!

And then Losso, his crew and the Rs went back to the Kempinsky Hotel for a little after-party. It did it give me great pleasure to witness Losso with his unicorn-like front dread wandering around this ultra-shiny hotel occupied mostly by foreign military-medal-adorned dignitaries.

This was only Day Two. The rest of the trip saw us continuing to have a blast. Ruby turned out to be a perfect travelling companion. I was the guidebook queen—I like actually reading about the places—and she was the savvy tech queen. Which meant we both organised but in different ways. I researched places to go, she was able to book hotels and guide taxi drivers (we wondered how anyone ever got anywhere in Accra because none of them had a clue where we were going). She had a local SIM card, I opted not to.

There was a sense of equality. She is good at snooker, and I am good at table tennis! The snooker was in a nightclub, the tennis at the eco-lodge Meet Me There. Payments were shared easily. Phew. Ruby is more than generous. She lent me 3,000 local cedis (about £350) when I couldn't withdraw enough to travel East.

Meet Me There turned out to be a delightful destination—we had the best rooms (one each still) right on the lagoon. Every detail had been attended to—gorgeous décor, carved wood tables, amazing food, compost loos, ever-friendly staff. And we were actually in the middle of the local Dzita community. Local fishermen/boys were all around. There was a dispute one morning which MMT staff went over to successfully mediate. An older man had accused the younger ones of overfishing the lagoon and he was probably right. And there were deeply expressive church services that went on next door. Don't go to Ghana if you are uncomfortable with noise!

All the profits from MMT go to their Dream Big Ghana Foundation. One morning, the co-manager, Christian, took us to see the magnificent compost toilets—purple paint and tiles with showers too—that they had built in the local school. And they also had created ones in the local villages. There are big public defecation and urinating issues in Ghana. The NGO also does educational workshops about the 'compost' which can be used to fertilise crops and that is the whole circular point. Great activities as well as an educational centre with books and computers for local children. And tree-planting.

Next was the mountains of the Eastern Volta region—the river was dammed in the '60s to make a huge, huge lake which provides most of Ghana's electricity—and here in these much more basic lodgings, we decided to share a room. It was a big dormitory room and it went well. This was the new Ruby and Rose sharing a room period.

We loved the mountains. Cooler and more innocent. On the first afternoon there, in the highest village in Ghana, it was a Friday and there were about five processions going on. They were transporting their dead loved ones—often in ambulances with the sirens blaring out—to their homes for a wake. The atmosphere was celebratory. Everyone ignored us which we were very happy about. And they didn't seem to mind us being there either. The next day, their loved ones would be taken to the cemetery. This was happening all over Ghana.

There were a few difficult moments later on in the trip but we dealt with them well. Ruby—with her tech-savvy—booked us into a dodgy hotel where we actually had to share a bed. That was fine in the end but the hotel was a guest house in the middle of nowhere. And then there was the characterful Rasta in Cape Coast in the West who charged us 60 US dollars for a shared room that turned out to have no water (yes it was a serious local problem but other hotels had paid to have extra water). And he had omitted to tell us. We had to get angry and demand our money back for the other two nights. We managed it and remained united.

We shared a sense of curiosity and desire to learn about Ghana and

Ghanaians. We both like to mix up our experiences. And we both loved travelling around—that on the road feeling.

Our new ways of seeing included appreciating the Ghanaians for their eagerness to connect, their friendliness, their expansiveness, their grace. One of my son's best friends is just like that, but I hadn't realised that it was because his grandma is Ghanaian and she looked after him as he was growing up. She passed on this sense of ease and generosity.

Well, it was a wonderful 18 days. We packed so much in. And I haven't even mentioned how intrepid Ruby is. I found her inspiring. I ended up doing something that I would never do—using a rope to descend some rocks. I only did it because she had already done it.

Rwanda has been mentioned.

How I Found My House in the Magical Spanish Hills

By Becca Leathlen

I started my Spanish adventure in 1997, just as Tony Blair ended 18 years of Conservative rule with the slogan 'Things Can Only Get Better.' I was one of a number of young BBC journalists helping with the count on Election Night, but soon after fled the BBC on a trip to Mojácar in Spain, on the pretext of finding a cheap house to buy. I didn't seriously think I would get one.

Accompanying me was my old friend Mark P, who had ridden to Mojácar on his motorbike a decade before. My friend Lucy's house was empty, so we stayed there. We had instructions to call Jacqueline, the French postwoman for the mountain villages, who put the word out for villagers with houses to sell.

It was a beautiful early-summer day and the road to the mountains twisted and turned up through arid countryside, almond trees and old ruins until arriving in the pretty whitewashed village of Bédar, with a long view back down to the sea.

Jacqueline was waiting in one of a pair of bars facing each other on the road in. Tall and thin with a mahogany tan, long black hair framing strong, handsome features, and wearing lots of silver jewellery—she was unmissable.

Jacqueline drove us down a narrow unpaved road running under the looming peaks. We undulated through tiny settlements and over a *rambla* [dry riverbed] before accelerating up a perilously steep bank on the other side, to end up at a collection of three or four houses strung out along the top. We bumped down a track to one, a wide, two-story house set in an overgrown garden with several olive trees.

I don't remember much about the house, apart from that the kitchen was outside, and the water supply was rationed from the nearby *balsa* [water store] where you took your turn on a rota with the neighbours. There was a ramshackle outhouse, and I remember standing near it while Jacqueline and a neighbour discussed which of the stones on the ground marked the house's boundary. The discussion went round and round, much like the roads that had brought us there. Then, none the wiser, we all piled back into the car for the drive back to Bédar where Jacqueline dropped us at the bar and drove off.

I remember feeling out of my depth, and telling Mark that what I'd really like would be something less remote, perhaps a little house on the edge of a village. We decided to have a quick drink before driving back—and then I realised that the key to our hire car was no longer in my possession. I tried to call Jacqueline but got no reply. There were no buses. We were stranded.

What happened next was, as they say, fate.

A young blonde dressed in black leather came through the door and strode up to the bar. After exchanging a few words with the bartender, she came over and asked where we needed to go. When we said *Mojácar*, she offered to drive us. As we weren't in a position to refuse, we accepted.

Nadja was Swiss, and although quite fluent in English, all her sentences came out back to front. When I told her that we'd been looking at houses, she said that she had one to sell, 'with mains water, electricity, a telephone socket and seven terraces.' It sounded very grand so, to rule it out more than anything, I asked how much. 'Four million pesetas,' she replied (approx. £16,000). It was the same price as the house we'd just looked at.

What's more, Nadja's house was on the edge of a small village—just as I'd wished for.

When we reached the main road, our saviour pulled into a garage and bought three cans of lager from a vending machine in the forecourt. We drove the rest of the way to Mojácar swigging beer and listening to her peculiar jumbled steam-of-consciousness conversation. I concluded she was very sweet but most likely mad.

I didn't think I'd call about the house, but a few days later curiosity got the better of me and we made a date to visit.

To get to Lubrín we had to return to Bédar and carry straight on, up a narrow white asphalt road that twisted its way through a magical landscape of hills studded with olive trees, yellow broom and thyme. At the top we passed the village of El Campico before descending to El

Marchal where the road broadened out and continued another five km to Lubrín.

The strange thing was how at home I felt. While the views were far-reaching and magnificent, the road itself felt cocooned and cosy. We didn't meet another vehicle that day or in the years to come, I rarely did. If it did happen, I often knew the driver, and we'd stop to chat.

Nadja and her English boyfriend Steve were expecting us. Margaritas tumbled over their garden wall, and on the left of the house were the seven terraces Nadja had referred to, planted with almond trees and flowers.

By the end of the week, we'd agreed on a price and employed a *gestor* to manage the sale. We sealed the deal over a breakfast of beer and tapas in Mojácar.

Back then, Lubrín was my freedom. The village seemed not to have changed since the '50s. Set in a valley, whitewashed houses were built up the side of a hill, around an enormous red brick church in the middle.

My house, later christened Casa Becca by a guest, was set off to the right, built into the side of 'El Castillo.' Many Spanish towns have a 'castillo' hill, on top of which the original Moorish watchtower would have stood.

All the roof beams were tree trunks, gnarled and twisted, interspersed with traditional *caña*—cane. Stone stairs led up to a low-ceilinged dining room leading to a big kitchen with an enormous fireplace at the end. There was a windowless 'cave room' with a huge rock from the mountainside protruding within. More rooms led around to a third bedroom opening onto the front of the house at the other end. The bathroom, down by the main front door, was a very basic affair with an old toilet and a plastic shower over a dug-out portion of the stone floor. In its 200 years, the house had barely changed.

Although there was a phone socket, there was no phone line and, back in 1997, no Internet. Apart from the 6:00 a.m. bus to Almeria City, there was no public transport, either. Compounded by the feeling that I'd stepped back in time, Lubrín felt properly remote. Nobody would ever find me. I'd been unhappy at the BBC so it was a huge relief to find myself there, completely cut off from social pressures.

I turned into another person when I was in Lubrín. Scruffy, dusty, carefree. I wore flowery shift dresses and tatty shorts. The only other foreigner in the town was a Dutch guy who I never met. My friends were old men who regaled me with tales about the village and my house's past. I found out that Casa B had been the home of the village *transportista* who took goods and passengers to the coast in his donkey and cart, and that a man had been shot outside during the Civil War.

My main friend was Paco, a portly fellow of about 60. He had small, dainty feet and spoke in a soft, high voice, often reciting poetry or playing with words. Like many men from the village, he'd emigrated during Franco's rule. He'd worked in Switzerland as a carpenter—he said he'd made furniture for David Bowie.

Another frequent visitor was Christobal, a wizened, Steptoe-like man who would exhort, 'Mujer, mujer!' [Woman, woman] in the style of a whiny flamenco singer at the start of every sentence, while encouraging me to buy his house or be his wife.

Paco and I became good friends. Even though he didn't speak any English and I not much Spanish, he was an excellent communicator and we understood each other surprisingly well.

Soon after I bought my house, Paco took me to his land in La Alcarria, a beautiful valley on the other side of the main road. On the land was an old trunk which he ceremoniously opened to take out two fold-up chairs—one for me, one for my friend. He set them out and we sat down—looking north over an infinity of hazy mountain ranges—the ones in the foreground like rows of reclining elephant backs. Paco loved his land and was planning to build a house on it.

When I think of the early days I remember warm friendships and laughter. Paco would accompany my friends and I on excursions in the car, or come round for raucous suppers on the patio, or we'd have mad nights out in what I christened the 'Young Mans' Bar' next to the post office, where the clientele would chorus 'Paco Toro!' when he arrived with two young women on his arm. When I was the only foreigner in town it really was fun.

Slowly but surely, Lubrín caught up with the rest of the world.

A few settlers from England arrived every year. There was Ponytail John, who built his own house out in the campo, and Dave Beach, a lugubrious hippie with great taste in music. There was Sally and Ann, possibly the village's first 'out' lesbian couple, and their neighbour Bill, a gay accountant. There was Mandolin John, always with a beautiful girlfriend. Tourists rarely found their way to the village, but when they did, it felt bizarre. To me, they looked big and out of place. Sitting outside the Plaza Bar, they were like giants on a small stage.

Around 2003 the dear little road from Bédar to El Marchal was widened and tarmacked, and with that more and more foreign settlers came. The tipping point for me was when a young suburban couple arrived. Until then, the foreign residents had had something alternative about them, a touch of the pioneer. But these people had none of that. And with that, it was as if my secret hideaway had been busted and my freedom was gone.

Solo Visits

I started coming to Lubrín on my own around 2002. At first, I was nervous. I'd fly in from Gatwick, drive back in my hire car, make the bed and smoke the emergency cigarette I left on the dining room desk. Then I'd go out for provisions from Antonio and Fina's late-night shop—and see who was around. One time I didn't get home till midnight after being waylaid by Mandolin John and a friend of his. Another time, I woke up at 4:00 a.m. in a panic. It was pitch dark and I had the sensation I was entombed within an endless Spanish mountain range—there were no buildings after mine. In my 40s I would often wake up in the night. For a while, an insomniac bird nesting in the roof would be up around the same time, moving about. I found it comforting.

Paco and I grew apart. Lubrín had won the massive El Niño lottery in January 1998 with a prize of 1400m pesetas (about 8.5m euros). Paco was one of the winners. He didn't spend the money at first, but a few years later he bought a radio-controlled airplane and a souped-up black sports car with red flames blazing on the sides. Where once he had been patient and good-humoured, he became impatient and his gentle high-pitched voice became gruff. He'd tear off to holiday towns like Aguadulce in the sports car and return with torrid tales of his exploits.

They wouldn't let him build a house in La Alcarria (the plot was just one metre too narrow). Bitter, and obstinate to the last, he built a swimming pool instead and put a squalid kitchen and bathroom underneath. He surrounded the pool with weird totems like plastic fans and dolls' heads on sticks.

There was a succession of dogs he didn't know how to look after and on occasion he'd chase English settlers in his car. The gentle, communicative Paco I knew and loved had vanished, and when I asked people how he was, they just shook their heads and said, 'perdido'—lost. He died in 2010.

Middle Years

So far, I'd only visited Lubrín for short holiday breaks but when I started my Spanish rug and tile business it became the base for buying and sourcing expeditions. From 2006 onwards, I'd embark on huge solo road trips around Andalusia several times a year. I visited Valencia, too, to go to the Cevisama tile fair, once driving 400 km cross-country from there to Cordoba to visit our main supplier. I visited Granada and embarked on crazy missions to find new suppliers in a series of remote locations. I particularly loved going to Priego de Cordoba, a baroque gem perched atop a cliff in the Sierra Subbetica Natural Park. I'd stay at Hostal Rafi where the bar was like a Spanish version of the US series *Cheers*. Rafi was even playing Bruce Springsteen the first time I went. My second visit coincided with a noisy religious procession, the virgin being borne through the streets, children dressed up for their *communion* and a major football match blaring out from TVs. Hostal Rafi was in the middle of it all—the centre of the world!

Priego was four hours from Lubrín. Driving there in the autumn you'd see bonfires blazing high on the horizon. There were deserted mountain passes where you could go for hours without meeting a soul. At these times, I'd marvel at how, sometimes just the day before, I'd been caged like a bird in my London shop watching traffic thunder by, and now was soaring free in the mountain air, maybe 100 miles away from anyone else.

Occasionally I ended up in dangerous situations like the time I took the wrong route to the pretty village of Castril, 890 metres above sea level on the edge of the Cazorla National Park. As the track got narrower and narrower, I found myself with no choice but to accelerate up the precipitous bends with an overweight load of wholesale ceramics in the back. Dusk was falling and I remember thinking, 'no-one knows where I am and I might die,' followed by a half-crazed relief when I reached the top to witness a herd of goats galloping home in a cloud of dust. It was a quintessential Spanish moment.

In 2016, Lubrín became my freedom for the third time. Disgusted by the Brexit vote in March 2016, my first thought was to leave the UK.

On the basis of having a Spanish house, I applied for Spanish residency. To my surprise, the application was successful and I moved out in 2018.

Today, Lubrín is firmly rooted in the 21st Century. There are street lamps along the road in, and a small industrial estate just north of my house. There's a world-class olive oil press, a honey factory and modern milking sheds for the goats. The once-silent hills are full of light and noise. There's a small housing estate opposite me, too, mainly occupied by British families who now make up a sizeable proportion of the population.

Stubbornly 'unreformed' for years, Casa B has been updated to make her long-term habitable. The tree trunk roof beams have gone, as has the insomniac bird. The cave room has a window. The dining room and kitchen have been knocked together and the ceilings raised. A proper bathroom has been added.

I study Spanish, teach English and Creative Writing, blog, write and walk the hills. Everyday life is time-consuming—I collect my water from the mountain spring at El Campico and drag it up to my house in a trolley. In the winter I must bring in wood, make fires and clean the stoves. More satisfying, this year I picked my olives for the first time and took them to the press in exchange for some superb Lubrín olive oil.

It's been a little tough, establishing a life here on my own. It can be awkward negotiating social groups as an older single woman. It's taken time to find work, or friends on my wavelength, but I keep on. Perhaps the fourth freedom will come when I really don't care what other people think.

In the absence of family, Casa B has been my continuity. Last March, returning from winter respite on the coast, it was surprisingly nice to be back. Even though I had to hoover the flaky paint off the walls and clean surfaces thick with muddy dust, it was just lovely to hear the birds again, and the goat bells, and the church ringing every quarter-hour. Enduring country sounds. The sounds of home.

Postscript

In June 2021, I went to a dance performance at Kensal Green Cemetery in West London. **Dance Me To Death** was a project started by AofA's Rose Rouse, with all the dancers in their 60s or older. At the after-party, I was on a table with a couple from Clapham. When I asked if they knew the province of Almeria, the woman gave a little start. She said that she'd visited a place called Bédar one Christmas in the '70s. Back then, black-clad village ladies washed their clothes at the communal fountain and collected water in huge water jugs on their heads. Donkeys were the main means of transport, roads were few, and Fi and her boyfriend had walked four miles up to the village from the bus stop. On Christmas Eve, the village ladies taught her to dance Flamenco—she pulled her body up straight to demonstrate. She looked happy as the memories resurfaced, and I thought how great it was that we should meet by chance almost 50 years later, two strangers transcending time and space to share our experiences of a tiny, faraway place that has meant so much to us both.

Perhaps the magic lives on, after all.

My Love Affair with Italy

By Annie Rose

The route to Italy began when my daughter came home for the weekend with a copy of an advertisement that she had found in the *Sunday Times* Lonely Hearts section and I think she wished to divest herself of coming to seek me at weekends so that she could spend more time with the current boyfriend. The advertisement said that the gentleman concerned had a cottage in Wales and a house in Italy and was looking for someone to share his life with and I put it on one side thinking he would have loads of applicants.

One day I was feeling particularly lonely, and I decided to phone him, bearing in mind that I hadn't seen a photograph as this was before the days where you swipe left or right based on physical characteristics. We had a chat on the phone, and I felt quite excited to be asked out on my first date. I dressed very carefully in a red dress and high heels (never usually wear these things). I found my date waiting for me in a high street in a mid-Wales town and we went to a rather seedy pub full of slightly inebriated locals. To say it was 'love at first sight' was simply not the case and in fact, it was very much the opposite. He was a slightly rotund, very well-dressed businessman whose accent belied his private education and his Italian ancestry. We looked slightly out of place I have to say in this rather run-down Welsh pub on a Saturday night.

The conversation though was interesting, and we spoke of many deep things such as the sudden death of his previous partner at a young age and his heartbreak at this. I saw a survivor and someone who was very likeable. I spoke of my yearning to travel to see other countries now that my children had grown up and I had time on my hands not to mention the unfaithful but long-lasting relationship with a younger man (we can go there another time). Richard—yes, that was his name—talked of how he longed to

209

wander the beaches with his dogs on a rope lead and get rid of all connections with money and become a gypsy. I have to say I only found out later than he knew how to sell himself, but I digress from my story.

I got ready to leave and said that I had enjoyed his company, but I didn't think we were especially suited. I also thanked him for arranging to meet and moved to get up and go and I wished him well with finding the right person. He then said: 'Would you like to eat?' and I had to admit to feeling peckish and so we found a local Indian and we ate a good curry. He confided that I was the fourth date of the evening and that there had been 350 applicants so far, but I was the best of them all.

Of course, after the troubles of my previous relationship where I had lost not only my husband but most of our worldly goods which went to buy his new younger model a house and car—this somewhat bolstered my ego. We parted as friends and he said that he would phone me before he left for Italy the next day to complete on his house and I wished him a good trip and drove away thinking that I would never hear from him again. Yet, the next morning I received a text thanking me for a beautiful evening and promising to ring me on his return from Italy.

My thoughts returned to him during the week as I wondered whether he had completed on the house and then on Thursday morning he texted me to say that he had completed upon the house. And I replied that 'I am delighted that you have achieved your dream' as he had been born in Florence and the text came back to say 'you are my dream' and I honestly had to get out of the bath to read it properly because the bath was steaming up the screen of my phone. I had never considered leaving Mid-Wales again let alone taking up with a foreigner who admitted years later that he had sent it over a drunken lunch with his sister.

During the time that Richard was away, there were several gossipy lunches with girlfriends and the consensus was that what had I got to lose? Well, there was the issue that he wasn't my physical type; my style of man was more along the lines of a tortured poet but as my friends pointed out my last attempt at tortured poets had certainly not gone well. A week after Richard's return from Italy he invited me to his farmhouse in South Wales and we sat outside drinking gin and tonics and the first night he cooked me a beautiful meal of roast duck with all the trimmings and the housekeeper had put flowers in the spare room next to my bed.

We spent the days exploring the nearby market town and getting to know each other and, in the evenings, we ate out in Abergavenny. It is true that Italian men have the gift of romance and this one played Maria Callas, and I began to enjoy the ease of his company. Despite the heavy romancing, I continued to sit on the fence but four weeks later the school holidays were drawing close; and Richard made me an offer of two weeks in Italy followed by two weeks in Spain and I was absolutely hooked. I had probably been planning to spend the holidays scrubbing the skirting boards and put that against jetting off to a country that I already loved and of course, I accepted.

Before we left, I was introduced to the Italian mother and she was utterly lovely a gorgeous, lithe lady in her late 80s living in Fulham. She had once been part of the Folie Bergère in Paris where she had met her Italian Count but sadly the Florentine family didn't feel the same. I too was similarly dismissed when I met Richard's children who apparently treated all his girlfriends in the same way and would clearly have preferred him to return to their mother so that they could resume their private education.

I had anticipated a lazy drive down through France to Italy but any hopes of that were dismissed as we navigated the M4 to the ferry. Once Richard joined the motorway down to the South, I began to realise there is no such thing as a lingering road journey to an Italian. It was hot and he drove very fast and in mid-France, I began to dream of flights wondering how much more I could take of this road trip with Puccini blaring from the speakers. I quickly learned that Italians manage their women in a manner that is subtle but designed to get their own way. We arrived at the house 18 hours after we left Dover having navigated the long incline to the house, a truly nail-biting drive and one of the most dangerous in Italy. There are 13 hairpin bends and some of them are the switchback type. Passing places are few and it is a single-track road much beloved by cyclists and people in camper vans seeking a rural idyll after the joys of Florence, Rome, and Sienna. We arrived about 3:00 a.m. in the morning. I was absolutely shattered and planned to catch the first flight home from Pisa as soon as morning light dawned.

I awoke the next morning to warm sunshine flooding the room and threw open the shutters and I was blown away by the view. It was literally love at first sight as my eyes took in the rugged mountains, the breath-taking views and the valleys shimmering in the warm sun below. I would come to love that view and I drank it in every morning and was there until late evening draining the last drop of prosecco from my evening aperitif.

211

You couldn't hear a sound and after the hectic drive and the journey, I felt that I had come home.

Many people experience this when they first come to Italy and indeed, I had felt this on my first trip, but something gripped me on that visit that has never left my soul. I love the bones of Italy and I don't feel the need to do the touristy things that Italy offers to many (although I do them in passing) but it is the experience that grabs me more than anything. It is being alive under the Italian sun as it were and simply being and there is no more pleasurable meditative state.

Every day I fell further in love with Italy and Richard. I would sit and people watch, and few words were exchanged between Richard and me as I immersed myself in people watching and eating dinner late in the evening at different restaurants. I loved to peek into doorways as we paused to gaze at the tranquil gardens where I imagined sitting in the evenings. The Italians, of course, rarely sit in their gardens during the day preferring to shade themselves from the sun. I lit candles in the evening on the terrace and Richard prepared simple food, which we bought from the market vendors during the day.

Richard and I were not lovers before we embarked on the trip but I fell in love with him during this trip. It wasn't my usual passionate kind of encounter but the simple love of a man and woman who meet in mid-life and are appreciative of the time they spend together and are merging in a kind of simplicity that is hard to define. We spent long hours listening to the voice of Maria Callas singing arias from *Madam Butterfly* and indeed the aria was played at Richard's funeral some eight years later. Richard admitted that the trip was one of the happiest that he had ever made to Italy. Just us and the landscape—what a joy!

We returned to Italy every few weeks (flying, of course). Richard didn't change, and many times he dragged me from the sanctity of the house back into the hire car to various sites of interest such as Florence, Siena and Assisi where I was expected to drink in the atmosphere in a few hours.

Richard proposed after a visit to Bologna to see his sister and he bought me the most beautiful diamond ring and I think I was the happiest I have ever been. We married in Florence just before Christmas 18 months later on a beautiful frosty, snowy day in the Palace Vecchio. The wedding ceremony was conducted in Italian by candlelight with beautiful frescoes in the background and centuries of history surrounding us.

The years I experienced with this man were years that I will never forget, and he never made life easy, but he did his absolute utmost to make me happy. When he became ill six years after we married, it didn't slow him down and he didn't involve me in his treatment. He died two years later, but he gave me something that was beyond money. He introduced me to a different way of living and a life that I had never experienced before. In the last two years of his life, I gave up my job and we spent time in Tenerife because he liked the climate and the small mountain house remained closed. I was with him in the final stages of his life and his last words to me were *don't leave me* as he sank into a morphine-induced sleep.

I was heartbroken and it was two years before I was able to return to Italy as I couldn't face returning to the house and life there without him. He left me his share of the small mountain house and I knew it would be hard in practical terms to live there full time and so started to think that selling the house was my only way of keeping afloat. I hadn't realised the extent of the practical problems that living in Italy inevitably brought until I started to engage with bureaucracy. I spoke only a little Italian and even now it is a work in progress, I learned that Richard's way of dealing with taxes was to ignore them. This is not so easy for the person left behind. I came to realise that the man whom I loved so deeply had left me his part of the house but not the income to support it. I returned to my job and picked up the threads of my life and paid off all the taxes that were owed. Healing came more slowly and there were relationships post-Richard, but they were not important.

I yearned to spend more time in my Italian home and popped over for brief visits to pay bills but I couldn't face spending longer without the man I had loved so much by my side. It was the support of a loving therapist that made me see that I could create new memories and that Richard would want me to return and I began to want to give it a try. I cleared the house of memories and had the place revamped and so I started to appreciate once more the peace of the country I had come to see as home. I decided to cash in my pension to give myself some capital and a monthly income, but I also negotiated a few hours of teaching on Zoom and I managed to sustain a level of income that would make living in Italy work. I was faced with loads of practical problems such as driving on the other side of the road in the terrifying mountainous area in which I live, but is something I was able to overcome.

My week is now punctuated with visits to the Wednesday market in the nearest village after navigating the 13 hairpin bends where I buy locally grown fresh vegetables and fruit often for as little as one euro. I also buy a spit roast chicken from the rotisserie in the marketplace, and I eat this with fresh salad or pasta. On Saturday, I get on the local train to visit Lucca and enjoy a cappuccino with a friend and perhaps wander around the market to see what bargains are available. I have picked up designer cashmere sweaters for as little as five euros. Once a month there is the antique market where people gather to buy the beautifully restored, shabby chic furniture and magnificent chandeliers. I often join friends for lunch and revel in the odd purchase I make such as crystal chandelier droplets for my Christmas tree. Trains are cheap in Italy, and I can travel to other places quite easily to experience a different side of Italian life.

I live in the moment in Italy and appreciate the compensations of my life as I get up to greet the dawn on my terrace and gaze down to the valley below watching as the sun clears away the clouds. I can often be found swaddled in a blanket, sipping my morning tea alone on my terrace engulfed by the silence. I am alone but the airport is not far away and I am only half a day's travel away from my children and friends.

Single women are drawn to Italian life and there are always people around who will chat and readily express their envy when they realise you are not a tourist but live there. Friends who visit are drawn to choosing their own place, but when they return home; I return to my life of silent contemplation where I read by my fireside in the evening, or I light a candle and enjoy a glass of frizzante wine alone. I don't often feel lonely because I have found my peace and I have memories from the past and hopes for the future that I am planting as I go. There is no rush even though my memories of Richard remind me that life is brief and that all we have is now. However, I know that I have everything and that is more than enough.

Deep in the soul, below pain, below all the distraction of life, is a silence vast and grand—an infinite ocean of calm, which nothing can disturb. Nature's own exceeding peace, which passes understanding. That which we seek with passionate longing, here and there, upward and outward; we find at last within ourselves.
—Richard Maurice Bucke

On The Road

By Gillian Capper

I have, impulsively, bought a very large Ford Transit campervan conversion called Kingsley. And he's a bit camp! Part of the trend for what is being called *The Gentrification of VanLife* apparently. He's got a white ceramic countertop sink with curved tap, matching rectangular Subway tiles behind the hob, a mirror with a seagrass fringe that looks like a parasol on a tropical beach, and two sets of dinky little spice jar shelves which have been a joy to fill. (Cumin, coriander, chilli flakes and salt? Or plasters, rubber bands and marijuana?)

I had a glorious few days online shopping for everything else a VanGran like myself might need. I bought a beanie hat with an integral head torch (yay!); a 15-metre food-grade hose pipe for the water tank; a lidded salad bowl; a Bivvy Loo (don't ask) and much, much more.

But here's the thing: one month on and I've only dared to take the van out once. I drove it nervously to a garage where I practised filling up, repeating *diesel, diesel, diesel* under my breath like a madwoman so I didn't use unleaded by mistake. And now I feel the need for a long and uninterrupted rest. Indoors. What's happening to me?

It's not as if I'm new to VanStuff. Once, when I was 21, I drove a 10-ton Ryder rental truck from the East coast of the U.S.A to California. For two years in the '70s, I double d-clutched an old hippy-painted ambulance full of inflatables around London and Europe for the community theatre Action Space. I fell in lust with a very hairy Australian Clown who lived in his Mercedes Fuck Truck in the car park of the Oval House Theatre Club. Oh, that van!

And in 2014, aged 62, I finally got a Vroom of My Own, an ancient RomaHome called Marjorie. She looked like a biscuit tin on wheels. With old-fashioned-flesh-toned-underwear coloured paintwork and upholstery. No power steering or other modern gizmos. Every time I climbed aboard, I felt an ecstatic thrill of freedom, hope, and the promise of adventure.

Not this time. I feel as if I've been muffled by a blanket of trepidation. I fret about every detail and threat to equilibrium. I've even caught myself wondering how quickly I can sell it on without losing face. I'm feeling OLD—in a trembly, wavery, weedy way that I cannot stand.

I've never been scared of getting old. When I was young, I knew instinctively I would improve with age and I have. Yes, I am labouring under the delusion that I'm still *going from strength to strength*. But if logic decrees this cannot be possible, then I still aspire to be the kind of old woman who retains the fuck-off fearlessness and *one of the boys* machismo of my younger self.

Well, it's a fact that I can no longer turn the knob of a gas bottle with my arthritic fingers. But I am still capable of squatting in the grass to take a pee and getting up again (I am pathetically proud of this). And I chose to buy the van, too; it wasn't forced upon me by the government. So maybe it is just a question of busting out of the lockdown mindset.

I've also realised that in all my fantasies about VanLife, I'm not exploring picturesque villages and churches or walking miles along the coastal path. I see myself all cosied up under the duvet of my van bed, with a good book, back doors open to the sunshine dappling through the branches of a wildwood, kettle whistling on the hob. I'm really after a form of Outdoor Hygge, in a *second childhood* Wendy House. It's comfort-nesting for the empty-nester.

But it's also a bijou rehab Halfway House; locked safely in a tiny cladded cell, parked parallel but yards apart from other human beings, breathing in your own bubble of fresh air, yet only inches away from the hoots and scrabblings of Nature—simultaneously comforting and threatening, like Real Life. Just what the doctor ordered in fact: the perfect substitute drug for weaning off the opiate of lockdown.

Now it's over (fingers crossed) I can see there's one good thing to be said for lockdown: it was very good practice for being house or bedbound in the future. I feel comforted by the prospect of guilt-free days of the internet, and all the films and podcasts that await me in my dotage. But that is definitely for the future.

Now it's The Now and I'm beginning to feel its power again. I've stopped doing Research (or Armchair Campervanning as my best friend calls it). I've snoozed the addictive Women with Campervans group I joined on Facebook. I've booked two nights at a campsite on the edge of Exmoor.

No, I haven't slept in Kingsley yet. But I'm well on the way to refining my ideal Spotify playlist: 'Baby Driver'; 'Hit the Road, Jack'; 'Baby, You Can Drive My Car'; the entire re-mastered soundtrack of *Easy Rider*... I'm as ready as I'll ever be for The Summer of VanLove. And quite excited.

May we all feel a sense of hope and freedom and the promise of adventure, now that we are *on the road'* again.

Note—Gillian had a couple of years VanAdventuring and then sold it and bought a little house in central Portugal. The next story, we hope.

Shank's Pony—Travels on my own feet

By Nadia Chambers

Some of my earliest memories, growing up as a child in inner-city London, involve walking. Walking everywhere. I recall trotting alongside my mum, her pushing my sister in a pushchair whilst I clung onto the side handle as we marched, always purposefully, along city streets, through parks, over bridges, past shops and offices and through the *back doubles* (one of my mum's favourite phrases) from the council estate where we lived to just about everywhere we needed to go. We walked mostly out of necessity, walking is free and when you don't have much money, it becomes an obvious way to cut costs.

We also walked because my mum, Geordie lass that she was (and still is) was used to walking to get from A to B—whether that was the six-mile round trek in all weathers to get to and from her local school or the I-don't-know-how-many-miles round trip to get my sister and me to nursery before she set off to one of her many part-time jobs. When the young me got tired of walking, I was invited to step onto the footplate of the pushchair and hang onto the crossbar as mum then transported two youngsters across town.

We moved to the south coast of England when I was 11 and the walking continued as, at that time, we didn't have a car and, well, old habits die hard. When I started work as a student nurse in the local hospital, I used to get up before 6:00 a.m. in order to walk to work to start an early shift at 7:00 a.m. When I had children of my own, I would walk everywhere because getting a pushchair on and off the bus was too much of a pain.

Our family prospered and as we became a little more affluent and I was able to have my own car the day-to-day walking turned into going out somewhere for the deliberate purpose of walking: beach, forest, hillside or field—just being outside propelling myself under my own steam, often with kids and picnics in tow.

As an adult, I gave a name to that which I just knew to be true as a child—walking is what we are built to do. It is as necessary to our wellbeing as fresh air and human touch. When we walk, we connect, with our own rhythms and ourselves and with the environment through which we pass. When we walk, we breathe the way we're meant to breathe. We also see the day change in front of us and we are part of that.

I started doing longer distance walks almost by accident when a girlfriend asked me if I'd like to go on a walking holiday in the French Pyrenees—an offer I couldn't refuse. From that point onwards I've been hooked and now a trip without a walking element just feels like a wasted opportunity to really get to know somewhere and to gain a sense of place.

I've enjoyed walking with groups and alone but the best times have been walking with my best friend. In 2018 we completed the 500 plus miles of the Camino Frances, carrying all of our own kit. What an absolute privilege and joy that was.

Earlier that year we had set out on the Great Stones Walk (from Swindon to Salisbury) and, partway we were halted by the snow that accompanied the Beast from the East.

What follows is an account of that walk and the more recent finale.

The Great Stones Walk from Swindon to Salisbury

February. Perhaps not the best month to undertake a long-distance walk (just under 55 miles) but Catriona and I have scuba-dived in the cold dark waters of the Solent, run miles and miles in sub-zero temperatures, body boarded in the icy alpine white waters of the Isere and completed a marathon on a very warm day. Suffice to say that we are women of a certain age and temperament and it takes a lot to put us off when we have decided to do something. The something on this occasion being the Great Stones long-distance route, which runs north to south through the Wiltshire countryside, linking England's great prehistoric sites of Avebury and Stonehenge.

Our mini-adventure started modestly, alighting from the train in Swindon and transferring to a local bus, which would deposit us near the distinctly non-neolithic roundabout where our first night's pub accommodation was located. The cold weather, icy wind and snow were already making itself felt across the country to the north of us and a weather warning had been issued for the part of the world that we now planned to hike across for the next five days. Perfect.

Overnight accommodation in a pub near a roundabout always seems like a great idea when you book it—it's cheap and there is beer readily available. When you actually arrive, especially in inclement weather, it's more often than not a bit of a let down. It's noisy due to the traffic, it's rarely a gastronomic delight, the rooms are usually a bit sad and not in the least bit luxurious and they never offer packed lunches for the following day. So it's cheap plus beer that scores the only points out of five if you were doing a review on Tripadvisor.

However, beer and a meal of deep-fried stuff ensured a good night's sleep and the breakfast the following morning provided enough bread to fashion a couple of marmalade sandwiches and biscuits for a packed lunch and coffee to fill up my flask (an essential bit of kit that goes on every single walk). We set off in a light sleet, wearing multiple layers of thermals and waterproofs, and headed for the start of the route: Coate Water Country Park.

This is a surprisingly lovely part of Swindon where there is a lake, constructed in the 1820s to provide water for the Wiltshire and Berkshire Canal and is now a haven for wildlife as well as an open-air swimming area during the warmer months. From here our route took us across the M4, via the Iron Age fort of Barbury Castle and the steep slope of Barbury Hill onto the Ridgeway National Trail for several miles before looping off to take in Avebury and its remarkable stone circle.

The Ridgeway is often described as Britain's oldest road and it is now a national trail, extending from Wiltshire, along the chalk ridge of the Berkshire Downs, including footpaths and parts of the ancient Ickneild Way from Streatly, through the Chiltern Hills to Ivinghoe Beacon in Buckinghamshire. As we marched along the deep ridges of frozen solid mud, I thought about the 5,000 years of footfall that this route has seen, the ancient people's whose footsteps we were shadowing and how cold they all must have been without a down jacket and alpine grade waterproofs!

Our arrival in Avebury bought us into the village through the fields that were just beginning to grey out in the failing light of the late afternoon, we were both taken aback by the sudden appearance of the great stones, bleak and beautiful with their dusting of snow. Almost the entire village of Avebury is encircled by the stones and the effect is enchanting. I am so glad that we experienced this in mid-winter when the absence of tourists made us feel like the first people to have set eyes upon this prehistoric monument.

Avebury also left me with a warm fuzzy feeling because we stayed in a fantastic B & B where we were treated to tea and cake on arrival, had sherry and chocolate in our room, plus access to a very large bathtub and, as well as a substantial breakfast, plus we were supplied with a great packed lunch.

Day Two of our walk saw us heading towards East Chisenbury via Overton Hill and Casterley Camp. It was bitterly cold and windy with regular blasts of fine, icy snow. Our eagerly anticipated packed lunch was taken in the porchway of All Saints Church at Alton Priors where we discovered that Branston pickle does indeed freeze in a cheese sandwich and that ice crystal in your drinking water bottle can give the illusion of having a cheeky gin and tonic! A short *praise the Lord* for the flask of coffee ensued and we continued on our way, getting blown up the hill towards the edge of Salisbury plain where we spent what seemed like a very long time trekking alongside the huge MOD *Danger—Keep Out* fence, with our heads down to avoid being ice blasted by the now driving snow and listening to the occasional muffled boom of artillery being fired somewhere in the distance. As the snowdrifts started to deepen and the countryside turned white and silent (now that the day's tank shelling practice had ceased) we descended along strangely quiet country lanes, empty—apart from a few abandoned cars that had fallen foul of the snowy roads, to arrive at the Red Lion pub, and its unbelievably gorgeous accommodation at Troutbeck, in East Chisenbury.

To say that I was overjoyed when I discovered that the restaurant at the Red Lion is run by an epic chef whose menu is superb would be a gross understatement. To add that I was deliriously happy when we discovered that we would be snowed in for the next two nights (drifting snow, high winds and a red weather warning from the Met office should not be ignored!) would be a very accurate description of my state of mind that evening.

We spent the following day messing around up on a small hill just outside of the village. This involved an Olympic standard toboggan run using a survival bag and drinking real gin and tonic from our water flasks.

Our husbands had been instructed to stay away for another night (for their own safety of course) before coming to rescue us in a Landrover.

February 2020. February again. This time we had storm Dennis to contend with! Trina's husband dropped us off early on Sunday morning in East Chisenbury. It was raining steadily with no sign of letting up so ponchos were donned over waterproofs, gaiters and thermal layers and we set off for the relatively short (nine miles) walk to Amesbury which is about three miles from Stonehenge. It was actually very pleasant to be walking along English country lanes with high banks and hedges giving shelter from the storm winds.

I could see this day unfolding in an uncomplicated way. Then we rounded a bend to find the road ahead flooded with at least a metre deep water and just very narrow grass banks, backed by blackthorn bushes, on both sides. We hopped onto the right-hand bank and started to gingerly pick our way along. At the halfway point the bank narrowed even further and the choice lay between getting soaked or getting impaled. But I spotted a five-bar fence on our right a couple of feet ahead. We could climb over the fence, into the farmyard and clamber over a large pile of soil to walk along the edge of the farmer's field parallel to the road until we found another exit, beyond the flood back onto the road. Plan thus agreed, we scrabbled along the diminishing bank, launched ourselves onto the fence and clambered over.

Success. Or maybe not. I placed my walking pole onto the earth pile only to watch it sink into several feet of soft and sodden manure. Great. Now we had cow poo Armageddon on one side and blackthorn, hawthorn and a helpful barbed wire fence on the other. We opted for sharp things. Picking our way along a two-inch furrow that seemed to be relatively clear of smelly stuff we were focused on getting to the grass about 20 yards ahead when the wind picked up and we spent the next jolly half hour wrestling our ponchos out of the thorny grip of the hedges. When we finally made it to the muddy but clean (kind of) haven of the grassy field the heavens opened and the rain sluiced down. We were very glad of this hosing as it washed all the cow pats off!!! I can't imagine the reception we would have got, had we turned up at our accommodation later that day in our original state.

When we did get to the Stonehenge Inn (mediocre carvery pub, bleak rooms, no breakfast included—give it a miss) we decided to have a late lunch—(at the aforementioned mediocre carvery) and then hunker down to binge watch TV before an early night. As the springs were actually visible through my mattress I slept on top of the duvet, in my clean clothes ready for the next day, using a bath towel as a blanket!

All in all, it was an excellent walk. We enjoyed, as ever, lots of mini-adventures and lots of laughs. Our friendship has been cemented by many shared experiences but our walks together have enabled a depth of sisterly camaraderie that I don't think would arise from any other activity.

My Beloved River

By Caroline Rosie Dent

I could feel my heart beginning to swell as I approached the brow of the hill, and I freewheeled down, until there she was before me—my beloved river: my place of sanctuary and delight. At that moment, tears started falling.

I had discovered her by accident, one beautiful summer's day, when friends invited me to a small music festival along her banks. Her dancing waters, wild hedgerows, swooping birds and bobbing barges all framed by an open sky, cast a spell over me. A hidden jewel in a grubby city. It was love at first sight. I walked along in wonder—my breath and then my feet gradually slowing down—as if merging into flow with her own gentle rhythm, and a feeling of coming home enveloped me.

Within days, I was back again, this time cycling for miles and miles along her towpath, until I had left the noise and chaos of London far behind me

And so my love affair began. Each day, upon waking, my eyes would turn to examine the light peeping around my blackout blind, and if it was the right kind of brightness—I came to know the quality of light intimately—I would be straight out of bed, on my bike and wending my way towards my lovely Lea.

I would come to know every curve of her sinuous length, her unique sounds, her subtle and intoxicating scent, her changing beauty throughout the seasons.

In the beginning, I would occasionally invite another to join me, to delight in sharing this newly discovered beauty with them, but I soon realised that most people did not see what I saw. They tended to bring the city with them, so after a few failed attempts, I kept her to myself.

It became a reclusive period for me. I encountered few people on these journeys, for which I was grateful, as my tears could then surface unimpeded by self-consciousness. I must have been a strange sight in those days, this weeping woman of the waters.

I was in a period of intense overwhelm. The advent of menopause had brought with it a deluge of tears, which begged for release, and over time, these journeys morphed into grief rituals that felt both cleansing and healing as the river received my tears again and again.

I would cycle for hours on end, my feet barely touching the ground, often until darkness fell, when I would reluctantly go home in a state close to euphoria. A friend who was into martial arts told me the euphoria was due to all the chi I had taken in.

My acupuncturist told me that menopause is a time of too much fire energy (yang) and that I was naturally seeking out its opposite through the element of water (yin), which is receptive and balances the fire so it doesn't consume us. This all made sense, but I chose not to think too much about the whys and wherefores then.

All I knew was I never wanted to return to my house at the end of the day. Being under a roof felt very oppressive at that point, like a heavy lid that could not contain the overwhelm inside me. I have always wanted to live in a place with a roof garden, and on the days I could not get to my beloved river, I would sit at my upstairs window for hours, watching the changing colour and light of the evening sky above the rooftops opposite, like a series of Rothko paintings, until the last band of light surrendered to night. I at least had this.

But the river was where it was at. Something deep within me craved to be in continual flow and the river echoed this back to me. My tears were part of this flow and so I wept as I cycled.

There was something about the rhythm of cycling, the continuous turning of the wheels, no beginning and no ending, that was very much in alignment with the flow of the river itself, and also in alignment with some deep need within myself, too. I often heard myself softly whispering: *Going... going... going.*

I was learning to open to the river within me, allowing my feelings to flow unhindered by thought. There was a sense of comfort in this inner place of aching sadness, this place of acknowledgement, this place of truth.

Emotional honesty was everything, and I made a conscious decision early on, to not question these tears, but to simply allow them to flow.

Swedenborg says that rivers are the spiritual representation of *truth*, and in Russian the word for water means *liberator*; both felt true for me. It was definitely a time of truth and letting go.

I never asked myself why I was weeping. Thoughts were like red lights that would stop the natural and spontaneous flow of feeling so I learnt how to jump the lights. These journeys became meditations.

I have always had a huge propensity for tears. According to my mother, I cried non-stop as a baby and the few photographs of me from that period show a glum-looking child wearing a permanent frown. Like so many of the Dr. Spock generation, I never had a place where my tears were fully received, not as child, nor later as an adult.

My mother was unhappy, tired, depressed and angry for much of the time, when I was growing up, and there wasn't space for extra tears in our house. The allocation had been used up and, as a child, I knew better than to trigger more in her.

'*You* are a survivor,' my mother would say emphatically throughout my life. 'I don't worry about you.'

So I cried alone in a tiny closet in the bedroom I shared with my younger sister, and even now, I can recall the comforting embrace of its walls as I crouched in the dark and wept and raged.

The life partners I chose were all walking wounded themselves, revealing my tendency to seek out hearts that had been closed by pain and fear. I fell into the role of rescuer perfectly.

At the river, all the losses of a lifetime seemed to be presenting themselves for feeling and healing.

So I cycled, feeling deep into this well of sorrow, the most tender of spots. I was a human version of the weeping willow, finding sustenance at the water's edge.

The river became a mirror for my soul, a loving embrace in times of emotional emergency, my place of sanctuary—asking no more from me than that I come unarmed and unquestioning, to seek solace in her watery gaze.

I came to feel that deep connection with nature that leads us to connection with our own nature. Mother Nature, my own nature, my relationship to my own mother, then a learning to be my own mother through this watery journey of aloneness and allowing my own tears to be felt and released.

I began to wonder whether the extreme fear of death that plagued me as a child, stemmed not simply from a fear of annihilation, but also from fear of aloneness, of abandonment, of being forgotten. Nature herself was helping me to make friends with this sense of aloneness.

'All your feelings are welcome here,' she whispered gently to me. I was not alone after all.

I became increasingly aware of a universal sadness that permeates all of life, that is part and parcel of the human condition, and there was a growing awareness of the unexpressed tears of others—all those *others* who, just like me, were also feeling overwhelmed, scared and vulnerable, and a sense of *we're all in this together* arose, which provided great solace. To be alone did not mean to be lonely.

Away from the river, I began volunteering in a sanctuary for suicidal people. The river had been teaching me how to be quiet and to really hear my own cry, and so I started to learn how to be with the river in others. The river was everywhere. In all of us.

During this time, I was listening to a lot of melancholy music and sacred chants on my little iPod shuffle which went everywhere with me, and sometimes I sang or chanted quietly as I cycled. Native American and devotional chants, mainly.

I began singing simple chants to the cows I passed in the fields, and when I discovered a dairy farm close to the river, I began singing to the newly-born calves which were separated into tiny pens. My heart hurt for these animals, these mothers and babies torn apart. I felt I was singing to their sadness, saying: 'I understand and I am sorry.' They would gather in front of me and respond with their mournful eyes. We were in it together.

Later on, when I discovered stables along the route, I would stand with the horses and hum gently to them. In those moments, I was simply resting in the collective sadness of this broken world.

It probably sounds as if those times were just about tears of sadness, but many of my tears, especially later on, were tears of joy at all the beauty I discovered around me. So much beauty everywhere! Rivers full of blue sky one moment, turning into molten streams of golden green the next. Joy and sadness were becoming close friends.

I found a hill where I would often stop and sky-gaze. Nobody could see me there so I felt very free, and I would spend hours lying in the soft grass, watching the clouds drifting through the blue, listening to the sound of the bees being seduced by the blossoms in the hedgerow. Life in all its fullness. I felt such joy in those moments, and then I cried from the sheer beauty of it all, as I realised there is a bittersweet joy that can only be experienced through embracing impermanence, and I found it here, in this sublime display of transient beauty.

As I look back now, some eight years later, I see clearly that a transformation was taking place, almost a rebirth. A new path was forming. My old life as creator of beautiful *things* no longer attracted me in the same way, and my creativity was taking on a more inner form. I was moving away from *things*, and towards *feelings*.

My lifelong enquiry around death and dying was growing. I began volunteering with the terminally ill and I discovered Death Cafes. When I first heard about the new role *death doula* which involved accompanying the dying, I knew immediately that I wanted to be part of this new death movement. I am now a trained *end of life doula* who hosts a Death Cafe. I have left my old life behind, like a worn-out skin.

I can still be found at the river most weeks, but no longer every other day. Over these years, my glorious obsession has expanded to embrace lakes, and I now find myself being increasingly drawn to the wide-open spaces of estuaries, places it is impossible to see where the land ends and the sea and sky begin. No beginning and no end. Everything connected in a shimmering mirage of oneness. Life merging back into itself, boundless and ever changing, reaching into this great mystery we call life.

SECTION EIGHT
LOCKED DOWN

A Guide to Surviving a Pandemic

By Sophie Parkin

To make it through a pandemic—if you are me—You will need:

A telephone, modern mobile pref
Some books, assorted 50-100—fiction, poetry, short stories, history, philosophy, autobiog, art, various dictionaries
A wifi connection + laptop
One projector
Some empty jam jars—about 30
Weekly delivery from Oddbox—fruit and veg
A diary
Coffee and herbal tea
Paint (I use pigments and refined linseed oil but tubes are fine too), canvas, paper, brushes, turps, rags
Chocolate milk, chocolate bars—whatever takes your fancy current fav Tony Chocolonely
A bottle of dark rum—good quality for emergency chocolate milk
Some wine, European, good quality
Regular mail delivery
Postcards, envelopes and stamps
A crush, it is nice to daydream of another time and place
Five empty note/sketchbooks without lines and at least 10 Muji 0.5 ink pens
A garden, seeds, trowel and enthusiasm
A comfortable bed and bedding. I am happiest with French linen sheets and an eiderdown both underneath and on top, but I believe this is my particular
An alarm clock for meditating set to 31 mins

A radio
A sewing basket
A comfortable chair/sofa for reading/ watching films/meditating
A yoga mat
A bicycle—this is now less necessary since it was stolen
Walking shoes
Good neighbours
Friends and family who can use WhatsApp
A surreal sense of humour
A slug of empathy
A barrel of not taking yourself too seriously
A box of good imagination
A sprinkling of willpower
A bucket of curiosity
A pinch of perspective
A carton of top non-judgment, and some apologies
A Spotify account
A lot of deep breathes
A note in the kitchen that reads—Happiness Comes from Within
Ingredients are not necessarily in that order

Most recipes don't have such a large selection of ingredients (unless they are Christmas cake) but surviving a pandemic requires emergency supplies. It's like preparing to make Christmas cakes for royal families everywhere in the world. Except it's just me, by myself now.

This is a luxury. I did have my gorgeous son with me for the first nine months, but we couldn't cope in a one-bedroom flat, and now he lives elsewhere, and I visit twice a week with shopping. Alone with all these ingredients in this second lockdown, I feel less in need of so many jam jars. The jam jars are to distribute all the ginger marmalade, aubergine Sri Lankan chutney, lemon curd and salsa verde that I make. The last lockdown I tried to learn Spanish every day for a month now I can't remember a word. Gracias!

I'm certainly utilising my living room with all the paints, pigments and canvas which has become a studio. It's no longer just a reading room with its large bookshelves, dining room with its table, or cinema with the one bare wall where I project from my laptop countless Preston Sturgis, Powell+Pressburger, Hitchcock, Fellini and De Sica movies. Here I have the separate space that allows me not to leave the flat and not feel that cabin fever will overwhelm me. Some days I run down the four stairs into the kitchen and out into the garden, then back again and every other day or so, I go to the Post Office, then buy milk and bread from the bakers. I was going on bicycle rides as well, but that will have to wait until spring. I hope someone is enjoying my rusty old gold Raleigh.

I wake in the morning, always trying to remember enough of my dreams to write something down. I seem to alternate between Armageddon, last place on earth, or expensive costume dramas in luxury mansions with endless performances. Some days there is total clarity, others a thick fog and then two days later it comes to me. I was in Italy!

I jump out of bed and say as I draw the curtains, 'What Amazing things will happen today?' because you never know. The time can be anything from 8:00-10:00 a.m., and I have no need to be strict about getting up. With no appointments for work or social, does it matter what time I start my meditation? But the one thing I've learnt is that meditation delayed can often mean it never appears. And a day without reflecting is like a day without sunshine, I'd rather have it even if it's for only 15 mins.

Why I have spent so many years not meditating is beyond me. I suppose it's why so many people I know don't practice at all. It's free. It requires no membership contract, studio or equipment, other than you and your dedication; in other words, it's almost too good to be true. So most people don't believe it will benefit them because it requires only willpower. Meditation is the only proved discipline that keeps the brain cells expanding as we get older. It keeps me calm with a sunny disposition; it delights me with unexpected ideas and delivers what I need from the universe. The other day I opened my eyes, knowing that my purpose was to inspire joy. I don't have to win a prize. I have to bring joy, what a relief! So with that in mind, I always wear nice bright clothes, do my hair and makeup plus never forget a hat. Other people have to look at me in the street, so I try not to be an eyesore!

I have breakfast every day, something I used to think below me. Usually some muesli with plain live yoghurt and a homemade fruit compote with ginger. And sometimes some fresh fruit on top too—gild that lily. I have a lurking glut of kiwis, and yet I eat the peach. I make coffee from two different ground coffee types in a cafetiere with milk in a Mottoware jug heated up in the microwave. I drink my coffee out of a handmade @MandeeGage mug.

It's these small rituals in a diary of nothing that gives urgency to the day. Sometimes I will eat breakfast, exercise, shower, meditate, and then have my coffee and sit down to work on my laptop or my phone, topping up social media, reading what's on other peoples' minds, and adding funny thoughts into the Vout-O-Reenee's WhatsApp group. Though my business premises are closed, my business is never closed. There is plenty to keep one person busy looking after members, applying for grants, working out ways to make money whilst my partner is furloughed on the other side of the world. I've had my website re-designed, a shop built, ticketing put in—the whole caboodle but I have to make the caboodle.

I tend to do my reading in the morning, or first thing, my writing. However, my painting is a thing of the night, and there is nothing I like more than listening to philosophical podcasts whilst grinding pigments. I am on a Jungian bent (This Jungian Life, Salome the Red Book) at the moment though I have been obsessed for the last few years with the Stoics. There is no doubt that Stoicism from Epictetus, Marcus Aurelius, Hecate, and Seneca helps keep me sane when the world tells me otherwise. These books are by my bed.

I will paint before as well as after I make dinner. And when I say make dinner, that's one of my great pleasures—lunch will be a piece of toast some cheese and homemade chutney—but for dinner, I will slow roast tomatoes with chipotle, garlic and oregano from Mount Parnassus near Delphi. I will make a tortilla from scratch to have with the tomato sauce and a salad with watercress and oranges. Yes—all that care just for me. And I might even make a rice pudding. And why wouldn't I? If I am not willing to spend time on myself, why would anyone else? I am beginning to understand that what we do in the outside world is responding to the deficit within. That for us to change the world outside our walls, we must change our relationship with ourselves. Jung calls this shadow work.

The things annoying you about the outside world are usually things about yourself you haven't accepted. Like that bossy blustering Boris who never thinks before he speaks, or Priti Patel just trying to wing it with so little substance and so much confidence in deriding others. I see all that in myself sometimes, and it makes me want to gag, but I'm conscious, and I'm not sure how much of the government is, any government in the middle of this crisis.

I like sending postcards and packages to my friends and family. I like waiting in a Post Office queue just watching. I'm lucky enough to live between Stoke Newington and Stamford Hill's Jewish community. I love seeing the families from my window on Friday nights and Saturday dressed in their best-going-to-synagogue wear. The kids are all in matching outfits playing in the streets on their scooters or pushing their younger siblings in prams, the boys and men huddled together in their tailored suits, white stockings and fur hats discussing the Torah. Social distancing seems a million miles away as it does on Church Street where the affluent anoraks parade inside and outside the expensive American health food stores. I want to shout; 'Try the Turkish family store.'

The peacocks are hibernating I expect, sewing fabulous costumes of colour and spectacle. When spring hits us, I anticipate a magnificent carnival display down Dalston! I have been mostly darning, using bright embroidery threads to decorate the holes left by the ravenous moth family that stuffed itself silly over Christmas on my cashmere, Merino and lambswool. Now my jumpers, jackets and scarves look like they've been flicked with paint from a rainbow palette. I hope to start a trend that will stop people from throwing moth-eaten garments away by upcycling them into the height of fashionability so that people in Chelsea will be faking/making holes to 'get that look.'

Darning moth holes allows me to watch old Hollywood movies or Netflix rubbish without feeling I'm squandering time. Because the cost to me is that I will never get this lack of pressure back again, which is silly because I will, I give myself the pressure, so I can damn well take it away. I worry that I will never have enough time to read all the books I want to, write all the books I need to, (slightly less worried about this as there are more than enough books in the world), paint all the paintings I want to, make all the people I love, feel truly loved. As I'm also the bringer of joy, there's no option to be lazy.

Today I talk to my daughter Carson in Ramsgate on WhatsApp video. This is as close as we get to a hug. I'm so proud of her. Tomorrow I'll visit my mum with a box full of homemade food. She likes trifle, so I always make a version of that. It's not as if she can't cook her food and maybe I do it as much for me as for her. Mum and I, we're good. She said; 'If it's this pandemic that takes me then that's what it is, I've had a great life, and I'm 88 almost 89, and maybe I'm not meant to live to 100, I've got to go sometime.' I like that sanguine acceptance. Yes, we do have to go some time, it's just, are you ready to leave the party? Have you done the work you were put on this earth to do?

Have you fulfilled your destiny? I know I haven't, I'm sure my mum has, but I will miss her like hell when she leaves. But I will see that she knows I love her and I know she has loved me. However, I don't think she'll be going anytime soon, she's just had her second vaccination and feels 'full of beans and quite cosy', plus she is starting a new series of collages.

At some point during the day, I will make cups of tea, eat chocolate, make phone calls or send texts to check that those I love are okay. I might make something from all the fruit and veg from my weekly Oddbox delivery. Now, what shall I do with white carrots, pickle them? And all those parsnips? Some nights I have a glass of wine. Most nights not but I like the thought that I can.

Just before bed, I'll do the washing up, make a large cup of chamomile and mint tea, brush my teeth, touch my toes and thank the universe for another day that's rushed by. When I finally tumble into bed at night, it is with a definite sense of abundance, sometimes it's after a warm bath with scented oils, but I have a propensity to fall asleep in baths, so I put the radio on quite loud. I don't intend to drown. I like my bedsheets to be French linen, white, clean and with an eiderdown and quilt and lots of pillows. There are piles of books to peruse whilst I lather unguents into my face and hands like a 1950s sitcom. I listen to the late news either at 10:00 or 12:00 p.m. There are no rules since I got divorced two years ago!

I'm accountable to no one and yet to everyone in a pandemic, for though we must keep apart, we must always remember that especially post Brexit, no man is an Island. That when we come through this, whenever that is, we will continue to give each other a helping hand, as well as all those hugs we've missed and not to stand with harsh judgements over each other's behaviour. The other day I had a surprise phone call from an old friend who rang to see how I was getting on; 'I suppose you're madly creative', he said. 'Painting, writing…' Yes, I answered all that. I felt too guilty to tell him about my moth embroidery, marmalade making, gardening, conversations with the squirrels and birds; it seemed too much like virtue signalling.

As enjoyable as I'm finding this time, life should not be about treading water. I do not wish that we go back to how we were before Covid when there is so much more joy to be created and shared. We can invent a better way to be together. Perhaps we are all being recalibrated so that our pre-pandemic, anxious, rushing, headless chicken within disappears.

Living through Lockdown

By Hanja Kochansky

Eighty-three-year-old writer and actress Hanja Kochansky—Hanja died in 2022—was living alone and on lockdown in London. Everyone over the age of 70 has been asked early in 2020 to self-isolate for 12 weeks. But what does that mean exactly? Advantages of Age asked Hanja to tell us what her days are like. And what resources she has.

The word isolated comes from the Latin *insula*, which means island. And here I am on a desert island in the centre of a densely populated and noiseless city.

As soon as I wake up and turn on my radio, I'm bombarded by terrifying news and a wave of sadness washes over me. Who could have ever imagined that the plague would invade our world? How long will this horror last? Then, I remind myself to take it one day at the time. I tell myself that I am on the retreat I've always wanted to take but never did and now it's been imposed on me.

After a glass of hot water, I go to my computer. Facebook and *The Guardian* keep my interest up for quite a while. I have a coffee and eat a too large amount of my digestive thins before I take a shower.

My daughter WhatsApps me from Long Island. She notices my wet hair and says, 'I see you've had a shower, Mum.'

'Of course. Why wouldn't I?'

'Oh, I don't know. I thought maybe you wouldn't bother, given you're not going out.'

'Of course, I bother. But anyway, I do go out. I'm allowed to do shopping.'

We chat about how awful Trump is, about how we are coping and how is it with the kids at home now. There's going to be no anticipated graduation for my granddaughter. I was going to go for that in June. All plans are on hold.

I do my exercises. Mostly tai chi and chi kung which I follow on YouTube. On Tuesdays and Fridays, I do a proper class with my tai chi teacher on Zoom. Zoom is a marvel.

Given the lovely weather, I go down to my itsy bitsy garden and plant violets and poppies. Poppies remind me of my childhood summers on the Dalmatian coast.

I sing "You Belong to Me" when I wash my hands. *See the pyramids along the Nile, watch the sun-rise on a tropic isle...*

Avocado on toast is a perfect lunch. Amazon has run out of the organic apple juice I normally have, so I make lemonade with the lemons I got with my last order from *Farmdrop*. I can get just about anything from them. Organic food, household goods and what-have-you, but I prefer to take a saunter to my well-stocked Waitrose at the Angel in Islington. After all the rain I need to stretch my legs now on these sunny days. I must walk or my legs will lose muscle. On the way, I walk through a park and hug a tree.

My son skypes from Sienna, where he is housebound with his wife and two small children. 'You must not leave the house at all, Ma.' He warns me. 'I have friends in London and they can bring you anything you need.'

'Thanks, Kas, but I absolutely need to go out.'

'If you get sick, Ma, I won't be able to come and look after you.'

'Don't worry Kas, I don't think, that after all I've gone through in my life, it's in my karma that I should die here, alone like a dog.'

'Oh, I wish you'd stay at home, Ma.' My worried son insists.

A friend once told me how she'd always felt safe when her husband and two children were all at home in the evening, and nothing bad could happen to them. Only, one night her husband had a heart attack and died. So much for feeling safe at home.

An often-repeated platitude is, 'We are all in this together.' No, we are not, mate. Some are on luxury yachts, others on ships, boats, overcrowded ferries and dinghies. And some are wading through treacherous seas.

My large sitting-room bay window overlooks a lawn. I watch squirrels scamper as pigeons and magpies peck for food on the green grass, while at the same time, keeping an eye on the self-confident, stalking cats who belong to some of my neighbours whose much anticipated, twice-weekly Bingo in our communal room, is now prohibited. The fox no longer comes in the evenings. I miss her—she kept me in touch with the foxy me.

How are junkies coping without their fix? How are prostitutes surviving without their tricks? I think about the rough sleepers and the old age homes where older people are dying alone. I think about what will happen to the refugees in overcrowded camps when the assassin virus finds them. How terrifying it must be for them. I'm so sad about Italy, *il Bel Paese*—the beautiful country. Something has shifted. The earth has struck back.

I am, at all times, grateful for my blessed life, with enough money to get by as I reflect on the poverty which will get even worse and financial anxiety will see a flurry of mental illness. As though there isn't enough of it already. Happy to be on my own, my heart goes out to the overcrowded families who have to learn, or not, to put up with each other day and night. I fear there will be a lot of physically abused women in these tough times. And children.

And what about the thousands on cruise-liners not allowed to dock? Or the ones stuck in other countries who are not able to come home? What will happen to them?

The virus is the revolution. More than a million heroic people have signed up to help the NHS! I was gutted when I found out the dolphin in the Venice canal was an Instagram joke, but the sky is now visible in China, rivers and seas are cleaner, there has been a significant drop in pollution, ozone levels are up. The end of knife crime without Pretty Patel's intervention is a blessing. I wonder how she feels about the prisoners that are being released. In their case, just goes to show that it's an ill wind that blows nobody any good. Nazanin Zaghari-Ratcliffe is on temporary leave from prison in Iran, and there is talk of a possible reprieve. She must be living in a balloon of agitation.

In the afternoons, I write. What better for a writer than a retreat?

Possibly, because I don't love washing dishes, I don't feel like cooking much, but I know I have to eat well because healthy food is a must. I make myself a large bowl of fruit and nuts topped with kefir and homemade yoghurt, which I buy from the kind Kurdish shopkeeper near my house on the Caledonian Road. His wife, who makes the yoghurt, has been getting racist abuse, he tells me. 'Oh, I'm so sorry,' I say and feel guilty. For what? For the privilege of my white skin.

Maybe I'll have a glass of wine and eat one of the packets of precooked lentil dahl and spicy beans which only need to be heated. Or maybe I'll make myself a toasted cheese and tomato sandwich, or dine on fruit: pineapple, mango, apples. And a cookie. I have these delicious salted caramel biscuits and must be careful not to binge on them. I have a feeling that by the time this Groundhog Day is over I'll have put on weight.

The endless pings on my smart-phone announce constant messages. There's no time for boredom. There is no shortage of stimulating articles on the computer, and I am addicted to Radio 4. I'm sure to always find something interesting to listen to. Or I can watch a movie on the iPlayer, Amazon, YouTube, Curzon Cinema or BFI. There are myriad choices. This, alas, stops me from reading much of *The Leopard*, the book I'm currently enjoying.

In the evening I try to do some stretching yoga, but I don't always manage it.

With another glass of hot water, I take the supplements which I really should take in the morning. Bs, Ds, Cs and what have you.

By midnight, I'm ready to turn off the computer, do my toiletries and get to bed. Before falling asleep, I thank the universe and my angels for another serene day and send white light to the world.

But this is early days and I'm super curious about how I and the world will be changed when the nightmare is over. Hopefully, we'll have become wiser.

Libido in Lockdown

By Stella Ann Sonnenbaum

The lockdown stopped all of us in our tracks—people are dying, others are fighting for survival… so why do I keep talking about sexuality and pleasure?

Just a week before everything closed down, I realised I wouldn't be able to make it to Canada to see my beloved. I lay in bed, feeling sorry for myself, and longing for sex and touch. In the midst of feeling quite miserable and tearful, I had a sudden flash of insight—my feelings are the result of how I see myself—I was making the situation worse by projecting a 'poor abandoned me' image onto it!

Instead, I imagined myself being held, being sexual—my body memory instantly recognised the situation, and made me feel warm and yummy and expansive—and much happier with the situation.

Our society is not exactly pleasure positive. It takes courage to take our pleasure seriously and to put our love for ourselves and our partners first. It also takes courage to continue to show ourselves as sexual beings when getting older. An emergency situation does not mean that we ourselves need to adopt the pain around us. We can let it in, feel empathy, and breathe it through us.

Figuratively speaking, we need to put our own oxygen masks on, before helping others.

Loving touch and sexuality are great immunity and happiness boosters.

Pleasure is needed, in emergency times. Lovers continue to make love if they can, babies are born, birds are flying free and happy, flowers grow.

Last Saturday I had 100 people—mostly men—booked for our free webinar 'Liberate Your Libido.' How can we liberate our libido in lockdown, and why would we even want to?

There is a life after Covid-19. I don't know about you, but I want to imagine skipping into the sunset, feeling juicy!

Being stopped in our tracks could be exactly the reason we can reconsider what is truly important for us.

Many years ago, I was in a sexless relationship. I have a healthy libido, and I had just never come across a man who deals with his sexuality all by himself, and truly didn't like partner sex. It was like a chore for him, and he tried to avoid it. At some point in his life, he had decided he was 'no good' at it, and had left it at that. 'Surely we can fix that somehow,' I thought. (Never try to fix your partners, please!!). Meanwhile, I was hoping and suffering. By and by, the situation took its toll. I felt unseen, and something very important in me felt unacknowledged. It took a toll on my self-esteem. It was time to do something. I knew about Tantra and dragged him to a Couples Weekend Retreat. And then another one! He must have loved me very much to step out of his comfort zone to such a degree, and I really want to acknowledge that, too.

For me, Tantra was where it all started. I stepped into my femininity and started to own it, instead of hiding it away. I embarked on a beautiful spiritual journey of heart-opening. It also transformed my relationship, brought intimacy and communication, and owning up to vulnerability, even though it didn't bring sex back to a degree that I could truly let go, and enjoy.

Fast forward, I met Joseph Kramer, the founder of Sexological Bodywork, started training with him, certified in Sexological Bodywork and Somatic Sex Education, and founded my company Stella With Love.

I know what a difference it can make to be in a happy sexual relationship and to have satisfying solo play, and my endeavour is to bring this to others, too.

This lockdown is an opportunity for many of us to step into new and better ways, involving more of ourselves, and is a chance of taking close look at how we see ourselves because that might determine our actions.

There is no imperative to be sexual, not with your partner, nor with yourself.

I would just invite you to consider if you have decided at some point in your life that there is only this much pleasure available to you, and then left it at that? There may be another way!

I know very happy and loving sexless marriages, with separate bedrooms, where the higher sexed partner engages in regular extensive and satisfying solo play. Did I mention he is in his 70s?

I also know about men well in their 70s who are VERY sexually active, with one, or multiple, partners.

Our sexual journey is ongoing, and I hope that we will continue engaging with it, and find new pleasure zones and preferences all the time, and particularly as we get older.

I think it makes for happier lives to include our sexuality, and to engage with our sexual pleasure, and age is not really an excuse to refrain from it. On the contrary!

Yes, our libido might vary, however, the rule 'use it, or lose it' is also true. Body memory fades over time, and it's good to remind ourselves of the source of so many delicious pleasures.

A lot of men I see in my private practice would like to find a solution for performance issues, and I decided to compile 80% of my tools in an E-book, which is the handbook for my seven-week online course for men. The course is aimed at making solo play more satisfying and whole-bodied, falling in love again with your own sexuality, taking pleasure to new dimensions, and transforming your lovemaking skills via pleasure, and staying in the moment, rather than working towards a goal.

Particularly, it teaches tools to last longer, because 60% of my male in-person clients would like to learn that, and have more fun in the bedroom.

It's never too late to reinvent ourselves, and find new bliss—whether solo or with our partners—and we can all do with more pleasure in this long lockdown period!

Living in London during Lockdown

By Michele Kirsch

LOCKDOWN: Day something. I forget exactly. The Vicar.

My vicar is bellowing to me from safety across the road. He is trying to put social distancing into a spiritual context, but he has to almost shout for me to hear him, and he's just not a shouty vicar. I get the giggles and drift off into fantasy, even though this is the first conversation I've had in days.

Vicar dream: in my mind's eye I see him preaching to NO ONE at the church behind my block of flats. He does the sermon and then asks the invisible congregation to line up for communion. He realises there is no one there, so he eats all the wafers himself, and guzzles the wine. 'This is my body, this is my blood. WHATEVER!'

Pissed and sated on communion wafers, he recites the scripture that starts, 'My God, my God, why has thou forsaken me?'

But that's just in my cabin fever imagination. I actually have the vicar here on the pavement outside the chip shop. The first human real-life voice, not counting the phone or Zoom meetings, in days. Have I already forgotten how to talk to people, even if the talking is nearly shouting, six feet away?

He says that isolation is not the same as solitude and that solitude can be a good thing, and can put us in conscious contact with God. I'm paraphrasing here. He references the movie *Papillion*, and then we both say, at the same time, 'But he escaped!' And usually, when you say the same thing at the same time, you shout 'SNAP' or 'JINX' but you know, we're in a pandemic and I don't want to jinx the vicar. I need all the help I can get. So far, this has been a high point of lockdown. That and getting four tins of plum tomatoes left outside my door on my birthday. Lockdown has made me SUCH a cheap date.

247

EARLY ON: Day something, when it still felt like a novelty. The study of Torpor.

I think I will take very well to isolation. I was agoraphobic for large, inconvenient chunks of my life, and being alone, in my own space, was a blessed relief from the gut-clenching anxiety prompted by being with other people in public spaces, far away from home. Back then, isolation was called avoidance behaviour, and I was told, repeatedly that avoiding the thing I feared most would feed the fear and make me more screwed up, which it did. It took time and coming through a raging pill and alcohol addiction, to let me undo all the damage I had done by NOT going out, not doing normal life. It's not healthy, but I know how to do it.

So the thought of having to isolate for very legit reasons, the health of myself and other people, seems a cinch. It is JUSTIFIABLE AGORAPHOBIA, and I don't have to let people down, the way I used to. The whole pantomime of 'Sorry, something suddenly came up' is no longer necessary. This is gonna be like pulling one long-ass sickie that's actually for the common good, as well as my own. It reminds me of that *New Yorker* cartoon with the guy at a desk, on the phone, saying, 'No, Tuesday's no good. How about never? Is Never good for you?'

Not only can I stay home from work and meet-ups without the inconvenience of being ill, but I can do great, creative, mind-enhancing, body hardening things. I signed up for a free course at the Open University; Animals at The Extremes: Hibernation and Torpor. I love a course with the word Torpor in it. I am ALL ABOUT the Torpor. But to counter the inner sloth, I do workouts with YouTube, tattooed sensation Betty Rocker. I get over my aversion to Uber, tidy lady Marie Kondo, and tidy and order all my clothes in the Kondo style, even watching shirt folding tutorials to maximise my space in an aesthetically pleasing way. All this frantic productivity lasts until a friend sent me an article saying that you don't have to be frantically productive in lockdown. So that's a relief. I go from hyper-activity to TORPOR, in about a day. Doing nothing, is much easier than doing loads of things. Who knew?

A BIT LATER: Day something. I should probably get some food. And drugs.

The novelty of doing nothing is not exactly starting to wear off, except I do worry that I am getting awfully good, awfully fast, at doing very little. One thing I have not been paying attention to is my medication. I am running low on my blue and brown asthma inhalers, and my thyroid pills. I go down to Boots near Liverpool St. station and the City is desolate, pin-drop quiet. Everybody has GONE. 'Everybody is dead,' I think, melodramatically, and then add 'Or just at home watching telly.'

I am also running low on food. Food is becoming quite central to other people's lockdowns. My Facebook timeline is filled with domestic Gods and Goddesses, all displaying that Sourdough bread, or that beautiful Persian meal, or *Locktails* made of Ben and Jerrys, Crème de Menthe and some holiday liqueur. People are exchanging information about where to get eggs, where to get flour, and other now elusive staples.

I have to go to the shop and queue and socially distance and stand forlornly in front of the now-empty shelf that used to have some ingredient I fancied, like tinned tomatoes, or marrowfat peas, or baked beans. Highly processed, and a bit disgusting. I can't believe I'm a cook. The foods I crave—beans on toast, peanut butter and jam sarnies—are childhood staples. Am I regressing, or is it just a craving for some earlier, innocent time when the kind of thing that's going on now, this pandemic, was something from an episode of *The Twilight Zone*? Dystopia does funny things to the appetite. My friend Nick asks if whacking chilli sauce over sauerkraut counts as kimchee. Of course, it does.

LATER: I actually know this day. 4th April. My birthday. Followed by Easter! Hurrah. Festive fun.

On my birthday I throw myself a surprise party. It's great. I have party bags and Soul Classics on the stereo. I put on my best frock and shout 'Surprise!' to myself. I have no cake, but jazz up some digestive biscuits by sprinkling them with icing sugar. I give myself presents, which include a box of chocolates, and a sexy dress. But the thing is, I don't like chocolate, and the sexy dress is already mine. I know it's the thought that counts, but I don't think a lot of thought went into these presents. While dancing to the Temptations and swigging Ribena undiluted straight from the bottle, I say to my cats, 'This party kind of blows.'

On Easter, I read the Bible, and sing 'Lamb of God you take away, the sins of the world...' in the style of a tone-deaf Mariah Carey, drawing out each syllable until I am totally out of breath. I do all this totally bare arse naked. Because I can. This kills about five minutes of festive fun. Then I make myself an Easter egg hunt, only I don't have any eggs cos there are none at the shops. So I hide a box of Vegan egg replacer from myself. And find it again in two minutes. I am alarmed that it took me that long. I might be losing the plot.

LATER STILL: Day something. Ah, the interweb!

Spending much more time on social media, and little rituals emerge, which give me a sense of belonging. Each morning Nicholas does his interpretive dad dancing, on camera, with his dog in the background, looking at times, terrified and other times, bemused. Then Naureen takes the register, a la school mistress, and asks who is alive. It's like a virtual game of schools, and our 'class' has gone from simple 'Here, Miss!' responses to depraved, *To Sir, With Love* style naughtiness. Virtually we 'throw' things, light cigarettes, swig from whiskey bottles. We have gone from being eager, suck up kiddies to a kind of virtual lockdown Behavioural Unit for maladjusted isolators. My virtual friends have become my lifeline, entertaining me when I feel low and conspiring, with me, to be irreverent, no matter how awful the news is. And the news is totally shit, every day.

People are playing a lot of participatory games on Facebook. Here are all these famous people I met, but one of them is a lie. Here are 10 LPs that changed my life. Please describe me using a word starting with the letter L. Here are 15 jobs I had in my life and guess which one is a lie. These games, some of which I play myself, are like those games you played on long car journeys, vaguely diverting you from the slow build of car sicky queasiness. Thing is, none of us know when this journey is going to end, which EXIT we will take. I am starting to feel a little bit ill, the games and quizzes not quite diverting enough to stop asking; 'Are we there yet, mum?'

FINALLY: Day something, before tomorrow, but after yesterday. It's good to talk.

I have a brilliant idea, which is to ring two people a day, two people that I wouldn't normally speak to because work, life, no time, yadda yadda. Well, I have a TON of time now. I ring _____, holed up in his penthouse over a whorehouse in a red light district far, far away. The prostitutes have scarpered but forgot to take the goldfish. My pal has a new focal point of the day, which is to feed the fish. He's delighted he has found a purpose, a thing to do. And it's all going so well until the caretaker comes back. The caretaker now oversees the fish feeding operation. He's stolen _____'s job. And in fact, he's stolen the joy that I get from asking him how the fish is doing.

Then there is _____ in NY. She lives two blocks from the totally overrun Elmhurst Hospital in Queens, with refrigerated trucks for the dead bodies parked outside. She's trying to figure out a way to get to Costco without passing the trucks, which are scary and depressing.

I am speaking to friends in Moldova and Bangkok. And Hull. People who are stone-broke, and people who will be able to ride this out, financially. People who are doing tons of things, and people who are doing nothing. I am finding that in isolation, I am more connected to other people than I have been in a long time.

Will I use this time productively? I doubt it. I'm certainly not going to write the great Pandemic novel. I'm gonna go grey. I'm gonna run out of savings. I'm probably not going to get fit. I'm gonna watch waaay too much Netflix, and play all my records and dance like no one is looking because NO ONE IS LOOKING. I'm not going to think about what the future has in store for me (or any of us) because I've come to the conclusion that the future is none of my damn business.

Lockdown for a Live-In Carer

By Lili Free

There's being a live-in carer when you can get out and about, visit a friend, see your kids, indulge in a spot of raving from time to time and generally remain connected to the outside world. Then there is being a carer during the lockdown. It's the hardest job I've ever done and I review my situation often, surprised that I ended up here. I'm also grateful when I think about where I might have found myself when the orders were issued globally to 'stay at home.' It could have been anywhere, considering I've been wandering the planet, home-free for the best part of seven years.

I know what's going on in the world right now and am aware that there are millions of people suffering greatly during these 'unprecedented' times so any challenging aspects of the job I write about please know that I'm not complaining, only describing.

I've always been a fundamentally caring person, but when I retired from my last career, I imagined I'd be doing less caring, not more. For nearly 20 years, I had a successful career as a Tantric Sex Goddess—a healer, therapist, relationship coach, masseuse, group facilitator and author. Upon retirement, I changed my name—a kind of magic spell to manifest more freedom in my life and took off to the other side of the world to write the memoirs of my tantric sex years. Falling in love with New Zealand, I returned three times over the next three years. It was a relief to be far away from the responsibilities I'd carried and to finally live the dream—travelling while writing. As is often the case, the book took longer than expected and I wasn't earning much as I flitted about. As exciting as Tantric Goddessing had been, I had no desire to return there but I did need to start thinking about producing some kind of income.

On one of my trips back to England, a friend begged me to go to Kent and look after his 99-year-old mother. It wasn't long after my own mother had died. She had suffered from Alzheimer's for 10 years and spent the final four of those in an upmarket care home. I couldn't look after her myself for too many reasons to go into here but I visited regularly. If truth be told, it was too close, *we* had been too close and I could hardly bear witnessing my beloved mother's slow and inexorable deterioration. Her relatives wanted to be in charge of her care and I was happy to step back, supporting the team with some distance between us. Nevertheless, I couldn't help but feel guilty that I'd not taken on the role of my mother's primary carer. This job with Cynthia was a chance to give something back, make amends perhaps. Human emotions are complicated and I'm not inclined to spend a lot of time trying to make sense of that particular tangle of feelings.

I agreed to test the waters for three months and thought I'd just about tolerate the work. Unexpectedly, I loved it and stayed for six months. Cynthia and I bonded. Perhaps it was because I was hired directly by the family and felt a confidence, I may not have felt had I started my caring career thrust into a random family through an agency. My friend and his siblings were so grateful to find someone they knew and trusted, they were behind me every step of the way. I felt free to 'be myself'—mostly patient, kind and funny and sometimes emotional, impatient and grumpy.

I was Cynthia's first carer and for the first month or so she was resistant to having me there. I won her over but not with charm. I realise now it was by being authentically me. We would laugh together, cry together and watch Zoe Ball on *Strictly Come Dancing* **every single day.** We felt at ease. When you do everything for someone—feed them, wash them, walk them to the toilet—for days and months on end, unless you are an automaton a symbiosis occurs, one becomes emotionally-entangled. Love happens.

My time with Cynthia came to an end (she got a new carer and is still going strong, now a 100 years old) and I flew back to New Zealand for the final furlong of my overseas adventure. My oldest son and his wife were expecting their first child and I knew when I returned to England, it would be to settle for good.

Another friend pleaded with me to look after his mum and dad. There's a lot of need for it out there, it seems. So here I am now in my ninth month of caring for a couple who've been married for over 60 years.

They've become like family. Valerie and Thomas both have dementia to varying degrees, diabetes, a fair few health issues and wear accident-proof pants. They move slowly, with walkers. Valerie, who is 84 is sweet, bright and easy. Thomas, 86, is mainly sweet, bright and easy but can also be infuriating, bullish and can drive me crazy. He went to Cambridge and has an impressive brain on him, which shines through in some of our conversations. I can only imagine what it must feel like to lose control of one's mind and body, basically one's *life,* so of course I have compassion.

But I hope *I* don't live to the point where somebody's telling me when I have to go to bed and how much chocolate I can eat. We've been locked down together in this house for four months now. Thomas has raised his voice a number of times. I've managed to raise mine only twice, a fact of which I'm proud. I've learned to become less emotionally reactive and more stolidly patient. The only exercise they get is shuffling back and forth between the three rooms they're confined to inside the house, with the occasional foray out to the garden. They need me to get them in and out of the door. They need me for most things.

Before COVID, I would drive them out to local restaurants where they were loved by staff, some of whom had known them for years. They had rather a lovely life. The threat of the virus has rendered them house-bound with no visitors. Lockdown was the point at which their carer also became their cleaner, hairdresser, entertainer and full-time chef. We're all aware that they're in a comparatively fortunate situation. I do my best to keep us all from going mad, but it's the Groundhog Dayness of it that gets to us all. Their food preferences are limited, as is their concentration. Toilet accidents are regular occurrences and there is a lot of frustration and apologising on their part, with me saying, 'Don't worry, it's not your fault'. Fortunately, all three of us have a sense of humour and laugh often.

Although the end of lockdown will be welcomed by Thomas, Valerie and I—being a carer is about taking the bad with the good, going with the flow and being responsive in the moment. Of course, I miss certain aspects of my Tantric life but although my days are pretty unsexy right now, caring for the elderly isn't that far from what I understand to be the true meaning of Tantra. The transformation of poison into nectar. Yin and Yang—the light and the dark. Hey ho. Namaste.

Contributors

Rose Rouse is the co-founder and editor of the Advantages of Age website, she is the acquiring editor for the site advantagesofage.com. She also curates the FB group Advantages of Age—Baby Boomers and Beyond. She's a poet, author, journalist and grandmother. She always wears a flower in her hair. https://www.roserouse.co.uk/

Leah Thorn is a spoken word poet, workshop facilitator and speaker. She has made award-winning poetry films screened at feminist, eco and poetry film festivals internationally.
Her latest campaign 'a:dress,' uses message-adorned clothes, poetry, film and Subversive Catwalks to raise awareness about fast fashion's devastating contribution to climate crisis.
    https://www.leahthorn.com/older-women-rock
    https://loveolderwomenrock.wordpress.com/

Suzanne Noble co-founded Advantages of Age, a writer, podcaster and jazz/blues singer. She is passionate about helping people over 50 to manifest the life they desire, whatever that means to them. Together with Mark Elliott, she delivers Startup School for Seniors.

Judy Piatkus founded global publishing company Piatkus Books which became one of the most successful indie publishers of recent years. Judy successfully sold the company in 2007 and is now an independent consultant, mentor, founder of network ConsciousCafe and award-winning author of her own business memoir *Ahead of Her Time*. www.judypiatkus.com www.consciouscafe.org

Caroline Bobby is a psychotherapist and writer. She loves life and looks forward to death. She lives in London with Leonard the Dog (named out of her love and gratitude to Mr, Cohen) and Bebe, the small, three-legged black panther. postcardsfromtheedge.com

Elizabeth Shanley has written since she was a child. She has worked in the public and private sector, as a change leader and is a passionate advocate for the NHS. The daughter of an Irish migrant father and Scottish mother, she lives in North Wales with her two dogs.

Lindsay Hamilton is a psychoanalytic psychotherapist, writer and visual artist based in southern Spain. Lindsay lived and worked in London for 30 years, though Andalucia in Spain has also been her (first and second) home for decades. Information about her online psychotherapy practice can be found at lindsayhamiltonpsychotherapist.co.uk. Her favourite word is petrichor.

Ruth Fox is an older woman living in Sheffield UK. She finds great joy in the beauty of the natural world and in her work helping others to rediscover their own power and freedom. Recently she began to write about some of her experiences.

Asanga Anand is an 80 year-old retired GP who lives in idyllic rural North Wales on 14 acres of land. He paints water colour landscapes and acrylic and ink abstracts as well as having a long-standing passion for mountains. He is still rock climbing despite injuries and heart problems.

Lili Free's previous incarnation was as Kavida Rei, Tantric Sex Goddess. During this period she wrote *Tantric Sex and Ultimate Erotic Massage* for Dorling Kindersley. She has two sons, both of whom she is immensely proud. She now lives in Brighton, within cuddling distance to her two granddaughters.

Philip Pool is a conceptual artist from Brighton working on projects based around photography. Phil turned to photography in their 40s to express their passions for open expression, age positivity and equality of opportunity. Phil has two adult children and the loves of their life are the artist, Titch Anstey and the sea.

Monique Roffey, FRSL, is an award-winning Trinidadian born British writer of novels, essays, literary journalism and a memoir. *The Mermaid of Black Conch* won the Costa Book of the Year Award, 2020, and was nominated for eight other major awards. Her work has been translated into many languages. She is a co-founder of Writers Rebel within Extinction Rebellion. She is a Professor of Contemporary Fiction at Manchester Metropolitan University.

Becca Leathlean is a writer and teacher with a long-term love of roots reggae. She discovered Advantages of Age in 2020. Writing for them, and meeting another member, Debbie Golt, inspired her to return to London to take up opportunities as a vinyl DJ and broadcaster. She's since written about these experiences for *The Guardian*, Vinyl Factory and Sonic Street Technologies. She's also launched a Community Interest Company, Creative Writing in the Community. beccaleathlean.co.uk

Michele Kirsch is a writer, mother, raconteur and crazy cat lady. Her memoir *Clean* (Short Books) won the RSL prize in 2020 for the first book written by someone over 50, which she very much is. She works in a recording studio and gets to hear music all the time. She is obsessed with late '70s NYC and is writing a novel about it.

Eileen Kay is an ex-BBC slave, radio traffic presenter in PJs, failed comedian, retired teacher and travel writer: *Noodle Trails, Volume* 4 is out in late 2023. Born in the USA, now a UK citizen, she moves between Scotland, Budapest and Thailand and that's another whole story. https://www.facebook.com/profile.php?id=100035141327939

Clare Cooper has worked in magazine publishing for over 40 years; 29 of which were spent in the Fiction Department of *Woman's Weekly* magazine. She is currently Associate Editor for *Pen to Print's WriteOn!* Magazine, both editing and writing regularly for them. claredotcooper.wordpress.com

Serena Constance is a UK based writer, storyteller, poet, performer and community campaigner. She is also a Death Doula in training, a psychopomp and a rune reader. As a family historian, she works to heal ancestral storylines that hold past traumas.
Her website is www.runesnroses.com

Nadia Chambers was born in 1960 and has previously enjoyed a successful career in nursing and health care development. She is now a retiree who loves to tour in her motorhome, garden, swim in the sea, hike, spend time with family and friends—especially when it involves making feasts—and to write about her mini adventures and general love of life.

Ivan Pope is a writer of fiction and non-fiction, artist and long distance cyclist. He is an artist who graduated from Goldsmiths College Fine Art BA with the YBA generation. As an entrepreneur he invented the cybercafe and founded the world's first web magazine. He is an Associate of the Centre for Memory, Narrative and History at Brighton University and his current interdisciplinary research examines the landscape as archive. http://ivanpope.com

Peter Marriott is a broadcaster, writer and recently retired academic. Diagnosed with MS in 2016, he now lives in Sheffield, where he happily watches the ducks on the canal from his warehouse apartment, debates with fellow academics about Hegel and Heidegger and plays the trumpet.

Philip Oswald picked up a guitar at 12, has never put it down; seeing Jimi Hendrix on TV was a pivotal, and he continues to study 'world' music, perform live and record. He had a heart attack a couple of years ago, the backwash from a youth of drinking and smoking, but is lot calmer now.

Cheryl Reum is still maintaining her weight at a comfortable 67 kg. However she has gained an entire new life. Living in a beautiful fairy tale home in East London South Africa on a river with her beloved heart partner whom she met 20 months ago. She is a retired gypsy with a life partner project that she is loving, cooking vegetarian meals, gardening, playing Scrabble, writing and reading books. She describes herself as 'happy ever after.'

Ursula Troche, born 1971 'between Berlin Wall and North Sea. Lived in London 1991—2018, worked between (performance) literature and live art. Poems published in Manifold, etc., work exhibited at Palmsest, etc. Since moving to the Solway border-region, she developed the Pick Up the Pieces project—https://ursulatroche.wordpress.com/

Nikki Kenward is an CranioSacral therapist and International Healthcare Educator specialising in gut health especially relating to stress and trauma. Nikki teaches this work internationally and has written a book *Overcoming Chronic Digestive Conditions*. When not doing this Nikki is a Theatre Director specialising in circus and physical theatre.

Dr. Eva Chapman is 76 and a grandmother of seven. She was a teacher, a psychotherapist and businesswoman. She became an author in her 50s after reconciling with her father after a 35-year rift. *Sasha & Olga* was the result. *Sexy at 70* is her fourth book. She and Jake just celebrated their 40th anniversary. Her website is www.evamariachapman.com and her website with Jake Chapman is https://relating-manual.com

Suzanne Portnoy is the author of the best-selling explicit memoir *The Butcher, The Baker, the Candlestick Maker: An Erotic Memoir* (Random House, 2006), *The Not-So-Invisible Woman* (Random House, 2008) and the play *Looser Women*, which was performed in 2011 at the Edinburgh Festival. She has been a publicist for the last 20 years.

Nancy Jainhill, an unapologetic feminist, appreciates the complexity of what "feminism" represents, both in the abstract and personally, embracing the more inclusive perspective of intersectional feminism. Her personal struggles to assume the equality that she espouses has been an impetus for her writing, which most recently has focused on matters of sexual justice. See www.nancyjainchill.com

Lena Semaan spent over two decades in London as a brand strategist and winning awards as a copywriter, ghostwriting several books for Random House and delivering words on demand to a variety of clients. She's currently setting up her own website. www.pensiveandwild.com

Luke Ball is an ex-GP who has spent many years living in India in the spiritual tradition. More recently, he's been writing poetry, particularly poems about the effects of his second wife, Nadja, dying.

Jane Duncan Rogers is an author, speaker and coach who founded Before I Go Solutions in 2016. This unusual social enterprise is dedicated to helping others get their end of life plans completed, with a mission of having end of life plans become as commonplace as birth plans. www.beforeigosolutions.com

Kate Tym and Kate Dyer are the founders of Coffin Club UK and also their own celebrant business—Kate and Kate Celebrants. Through Coffin Club they provide funeral education and celebrant training. They live in the South East and have one husband, one dog and three kids, each. To find out more go to www.coffinclub.co.uk

Dr. Annie Llewellyn spends her time between life in Italy and life in Wales. It involves quite a lot of travelling but this keeps things interesting and she has been a member of Advantages of Age for several years and thought others might enjoy one of her love stories (which we all have inside of us) as this forms the basis of her life in Italy.

Gillian Capper teacher, performer, poet, journalist, mother and grandmother—is happily retired, living solo in Dorset with her dog Hector. She spends half the year in an off grid stone retreat house in the mountains of Portugal trying to embrace the full catastrophe. Still searching, grieving, learning.

Caroline Dent embarked on a lifelong exploration of death and metaphysics from the age of 20, in order to overcome her overwhelming fear of death. This led to her training as an end-of-life doula, and running 'death cafés,' spaces where taboos around death are gently broken down through conversation.

Sophie Parkin is an author and artist. She has written many books and painted a lot of self-portraits. She started an arts club called Vout-o-Reenees and The Stash Gallery. @theStashGallery @sophieparkinwriter. She emphasises that the copyright for the piece in this book is hers.

Hanja Kochansky was a Croatian writer and actress. A refugee to Italy during the Second World War, in 1948 she went to Johannesburg as an emigrant. In 1966, she played one of Elizabeth Taylor's handmaidens in the film *Cleopatra*. In 1972, her book, *Freely Female: Women's Sexual Fantasies*, was published by Ace Books in New York and was on the reading list for women's studies programmes at a number of American universities. She wrote regularly for Advantages of Age about her extraordinary life.

Stella Anna Sonnenbaum is a Somatic Sexologist and Certified Somatic Sex Educator with a busy in-person and online practice in Central London, UK. She helps individuals and couples address and overcome issues about sexuality, and improve communication about touch preferences. Stella also facilitates workshops, and was on ITV's 'My Mum, your Dad' as an Intimacy Coach. **https://stellawithlove.com**

Other Riverdale Avenue Books You Might Enjoy

Miss Pamela's Writing School for Electric Ladies
Edited by Pamela Des Barres

Flashes: Adventures in Dating Through Menopause
By Michelle Churchill

Tornado: A Breast Cancer Log
By Mary Anne Mohanraj

Naked in 30 Days:
A One-Month Guide to Getting Your Body,
Mind and Spirit in Shape
By Theresa Roemer

Printed in Great Britain
by Amazon

40482858R00155